Practice⬛⬛⬛ners®

Arthur E. Jongsma, Jr., Series Editor

Helping therapists help their clients...

Treatment Planners cover all the necessary elements for developing formal treatment plans, including detailed problem definitions, long-term goals, short-term objectives, therapeutic interventions, and DSM-IV™ diagnoses.

- ❑ The Complete Adult Psychotherapy Treatment Planner, Fourth Edition ......978-0-471-76346-8 / $55.00
- ❑ The Child Psychotherapy Treatment Planner, Fourth Edition ....978-0-471-78535-4 / $55.00
- ❑ The Adolescent Psychotherapy Treatment Planner, Fourth Edition..............978-0-471-78539-2 / $55.00
- ❑ The Addiction Treatment Planner, Fourth Edition ....978 0 470 40551 2 / $55.00
- ❑ The Couples Psychotherapy Treatment Planner ....978-0-471-24711-1 / $55.00
- ❑ The Group Therapy Treatment Planner, Second Edition................................978-0-471-66791-9 / $55.00
- ❑ The Family Therapy Treatment Planner ....978-0-471-34768-2 / $55.00
- ❑ The Older Adult Psychotherapy Treatment Planner ....978-0-471-29574-7 / $55.00
- ❑ The Employee Assistance (EAP) Treatment Planner ....978-0-471-24709-8 / $55.00
- ❑ The Gay and Lesbian Psychotherapy Treatment Planner.............................978-0-471-35080-4 / $55.00
- ❑ The Crisis Counseling and Traumatic Events Treatment Planner..............978-0-471-39587-4 / $55.00
- ❑ The Social Work and Human Services Treatment Planner.........................978-0-471-37741-2 / $55.00
- ❑ The Continuum of Care Treatment Planner..978-0-471-19568-9 / $55.00
- ❑ The Behavioral Medicine Treatment Planner ....978-0-471-31923-8 / $55.00
- ❑ The Mental Retardation and Developmental Disability Treatment Planner......978-0-471-38253-9 / $55.00
- ❑ The Special Education Treatment Planner ....978-0-471-38872-2 / $55.00
- ❑ The Severe and Persistent Mental Illness Treatment Planner, Second Edition ...978-0-470-18013-6 / $55.00
- ❑ The Personality Disorders Treatment Planner..978-0-471-39403-7 / $55.00
- ❑ The Rehabilitation Psychology Treatment Planner.......................................978-0-471-35178-8 / $55.00
- ❑ The Pastoral Counseling Treatment Planner..978-0-471-25416-4 / $55.00
- ❑ The Juvenile Justice and Residential Care Treatment Planner..................978-0-471-43320-0 / $55.00
- ❑ The School Counseling and School Social Work Treatment Planner ....978-0-471-08496-9 / $55.00
- ❑ The Psychopharmacology Treatment Planner...978-0-471-43322-4 / $55.00
- ❑ The Probation and Parole Treatment Planner ....978-0-471-20244-8 / $55.00
- ❑ The Suicide and Homicide Risk Assessment
  & Prevention Treatment Planner ....978-0-471-46631-4 / $55.00
- ❑ The Speech-Language Pathology Treatment Planner.................................978-0-471-27504-6 / $55.00
- ❑ The College Student Counseling Treatment Planner..................................978-0-471-46708-3 / $55.00
- ❑ The Parenting Skills Treatment Planner...978-0-471-48183-6 / $55.00
- ❑ The Early Childhood Education Intervention Treatment Planner...............978-0-471-65962-4 / $55.00
- ❑ The Co-Occurring Disorders Treatment Planner ....978-0-471-73081-1 / $55.00
- ❑ The Sexual Abuse Victim and Sexual Offender Treatment Planner...........978-0-471-21979-8 / $55.00
- ❑ The Complete Women's Psychotherapy Treatment Planner ....978-0-470-03983-0 / $55.00
- ❑ The Veterans and Active Duty Military Psychotherapy Treatment Planner..978-0-470-44098-8 / $55.00

The **Complete Treatment and Homework Planners** series of books combines our bestselling *Treatment Planners* and *Homework Planners* into one easy-to-use, all-in-one resource for mental health professionals treating clients suffering from the most commonly diagnosed disorders.

- ❑ The Complete Depression Treatment and Homework Planner ....978-0-471-64515-3 / $48.95
- ❑ The Complete Anxiety Treatment and Homework Planner.......................978-0-471-64548-1 / $48.95

Practice*Planners*®

TheraScribe®

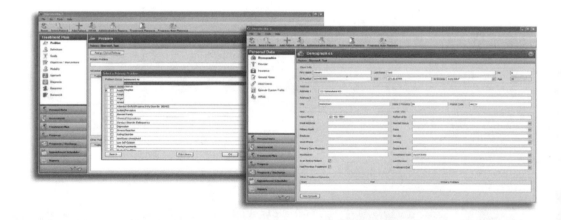

Addiction Treatment
Homework Planner

PracticePlanners® Series

Treatment Planners

The Complete Adult Psychotherapy Treatment Planner, Fourth Edition
The Child Psychotherapy Treatment Planner, Fourth Edition
The Adolescent Psychotherapy Treatment Planner, Fourth Edition
The Addiction Treatment Planner, Fourth Edition
The Continuum of Care Treatment Planner
The Couples Psychotherapy Treatment Planner
The Employee Assistance Treatment Planner
The Pastoral Counseling Treatment Planner
The Older Adult Psychotherapy Treatment Planner
The Behavioral Medicine Treatment Planner
The Group Therapy Treatment Planner
The Gay and Lesbian Psychotherapy Treatment Planner
The Family Therapy Treatment Planner
The Severe and Persistent Mental Illness Treatment Planner, Second Edition
The Mental Retardation and Developmental Disability Treatment Planner
The Social Work and Human Services Treatment Planner
The Crisis Counseling and Traumatic Events Treatment Planner
The Personality Disorders Treatment Planner
The Rehabilitation Psychology Treatment Planner
The Special Education Treatment Planner
The Juvenile Justice and Residential Care Treatment Planner
The School Counseling and School Social Work Treatment Planner
The Sexual Abuse Victim and Sexual Offender Treatment Planner
The Probation and Parole Treatment Planner
The Psychopharmacology Treatment Planner
The Speech-Language Pathology Treatment Planner
The Suicide and Homicide Treatment Planner
The College Student Counseling Treatment Planner
The Parenting Skills Treatment Planner
The Early Childhood Intervention Treatment Planner
The Co-Occurring Disorders Treatment Planner
The Complete Women's Psychotherapy Treatment Planner
The Veterans and Active Duty Military Psychotherapy Treatment Planner

Progress Notes Planners

The Child Psychotherapy Progress Notes Planner, Third Edition
The Adolescent Psychotherapy Progress Notes Planner, Third Edition
The Adult Psychotherapy Progress Notes Planner, Third Edition
The Addiction Progress Notes Planner, Third Edition
The Severe and Persistent Mental Illness Progress Notes Planner, Second Edition
The Couples Psychotherapy Progress Notes Planner
The Family Therapy Progress Notes Planner
The Veterans and Active Duty Military Psychotherapy Progress Notes Planner

Homework Planners

Brief Couples Therapy Homework Planner
Brief Family Therapy Homework Planner
Grief Counseling Homework Planner
Group Therapy Homework Planner
Divorce Counseling Homework Planner
School Counseling and School Social Work Homework Planner
Child Therapy Activity and Homework Planner
Addiction Treatment Homework Planner, Fourth Edition
Adolescent Psychotherapy Homework Planner II
Adolescent Psychotherapy Homework Planner, Second Edition
Adult Psychotherapy Homework Planner, Second Edition
Child Psychotherapy Homework Planner, Second Edition
Parenting Skills Homework Planner

Client Education Handout Planners

Adult Client Education Handout Planner
Child and Adolescent Client Education Handout Planner
Couples and Family Client Education Handout Planner

Complete Planners

The Complete Depression Treatment and Homework Planner
The Complete Anxiety Treatment and Homework Planner

Practice*Planners*®

Addiction Treatment
Homework Planner

Fourth Edition

James R. Finley

Brenda S. Lenz

WILEY

John Wiley & Sons, Inc.

This book is printed on acid-free paper. ⊗

Published by John Wiley & Sons, Inc., Hoboken, New Jersey.

Published simultaneously in Canada.

Limit of Liability/Disclaimer of Warranty: While the publisher and author have used their best efforts in preparing this book, they make no representations or warranties with respect to the accuracy or completeness of the contents of this book and specifically disclaim any implied warranties of merchantability or fitness for a particular purpose. No warranty may be created or extended by sales representatives or written sales materials. The advice and strategies contained herein may not be suitable for your situation. You should consult with a professional where appropriate. Neither the publisher nor author shall be liable for any loss of profit or any other commercial damages, including but not limited to special, incidental, consequential, or other damages.

This publication is designed to provide accurate and authoritative information in regard to the subject matter covered. It is sold with the understanding that the publisher is not engaged in rendering professional services. If legal, accounting, medical, psychological, or any other expert assistance is required, the services of a competent professional person should be sought.

Designations used by companies to distinguish their products are often claimed as trademarks. In all instances where John Wiley & Sons, Inc. is aware of a claim, the product names appear in initial capital or all capital letters. Readers, however, should contact the appropriate companies for more complete information regarding trademarks and registration.

For general information on our other products and services please contact our Customer Care Department within the U.S. at (800) 762-2974, outside the United States at (317) 572-3993 or fax (317) 572-4002.

Wiley also publishes its books in a variety of electronic formats. Some content that appears in print may not be available in electronic books. For more information about Wiley products, visit our website at www.wiley.com.

Library of Congress Cataloging-in-Publication Data:
Finley, James R., 1948-
  Addiction treatment homework planner / James R. Finley, Brenda S. Lenz.—4th ed.
    p. cm. — (Practice planners series)
  Includes bibliographical references.
  ISBN 978-0-470-40274-0 (paper/CD-Rom)
  1. Substance abuse—Treatment—Handbooks, manuals, etc. 2. Substance abuse—Treatment—Planning.
I. Lenz, Brenda S. II. Title.
  RC564.15.F555 2009
  616.89—dc22
                                                                                    2009000842

Printed in the United States of America

10 9 8 7 6 5 4 3 2 1

This book is dedicated to our loved ones, who've given us so much encouragement and been so unselfish in the face of our work's demands, and to all the clients and colleagues who've taught us and inspired us over the years. Without you all this would be impossible. Thank you.

CONTENTS

PRACTICE*PLANNERS*® SERIES PREFACE

Accountability is an important dimension of the practice of psychotherapy. Treatment programs, public agencies, clinics, and practitioners must justify and document their treatment plans to outside review entities in order to be reimbursed for services. The books and software in the Practice*Planners*® series are designed to help practitioners fulfill these documentation requirements efficiently and professionally.

The Practice*Planners*® series includes a wide array of treatment-planning books, including not only the original *Complete Adult Psychotherapy Treatment Planner, Child Psychotherapy Treatment Planner,* and *Adolescent Psychotherapy Treatment Planner,* all now in their fourth editions, but also *Treatment Planners* targeted to a wide range of specialty areas of practice, including:

- Addictions
- Behavioral medicine
- College students
- Co-occurring disorders
- Couples therapy
- Crisis counseling
- Early childhood education
- Employee assistance
- Family therapy
- Gays and lesbians
- Group therapy
- Juvenile justice and residential care
- Mental retardation and developmental disability
- Neuropsychology
- Older adults
- Parenting skills
- Pastoral counseling
- Personality disorders
- Probation and parole
- Psychopharmacology
- School counseling
- Severe and persistent mental illness
- Sexual abuse victims and offenders
- Special education
- Suicide and homicide risk assessment

- Veterans and active duty military
- Women's issues

In addition, there are three branches of companion books that can be used in conjunction with the *Treatment Planners,* or on their own:

- ***Progress Notes Planners*** provide a menu of progress statements that elaborate on the client's symptom presentation and the provider's therapeutic intervention. Each *Progress Notes Planner* statement is directly integrated with the behavioral definitions and therapeutic interventions from its companion *Treatment Planner.*

- ***Homework Planners*** include homework assignments designed around each presenting problem (e.g., anxiety, depression, chemical dependence, anger management, eating disorders, or panic disorder) that is the focus of a chapter in its corresponding *Treatment Planner.*

- ***Client Education Handout Planners*** provide brochures and handouts to help educate and inform clients on presenting problems and mental health issues, as well as life skills techniques. The handouts are included on CD-ROMs for easy printing from your computer and are ideal for use in waiting rooms, at presentations, as newsletters, or as information for clients struggling with mental illness issues. The topics covered by these handouts correspond to the presenting problems in the *Treatment Planners.*

The series also includes:

- Thera*Scribe*®, the best-selling treatment-planning and clinical record-keeping software system for mental health professionals. Thera*Scribe*® allows the user to import the data from any of the *Treatment Planner, Progress Notes Planner,* or *Homework Planner* books into the software's expandable database to simply point and click to create a detailed, organized, individualized, and customized treatment plan along with optional integrated progress notes and homework assignments.

Adjunctive books, such as *The Psychotherapy Documentation Primer* and *The Clinical Documentation Sourcebook* contain forms and resources to aid the clinician in mental health practice management.

The goal of our series is to provide practitioners with the resources they need in order to provide high-quality care in the era of accountability. To put it simply: We seek to help you spend more time on patients and less time on paperwork.

ARTHUR E. JONGSMA JR.
Grand Rapids, Michigan

PREFACE

CHANGES IN THIS EDITION OF THE HOMEWORK PLANNER

The field of psychotherapy in general, and addiction treatment in particular, continues to evolve. Since completing the third edition we have seen ongoing movement from fixed, program-driven interventions toward more flexible, individualized, assessment-based, clinically driven treatment. Providers and consumers seek approaches recognizing the impact of client readiness and motivation in the treatment process. People enter treatment at all stages of readiness, and clinicians need to help some increase motivation for change and others move from one stage of readiness to the next. We have revised assignments with stages of readiness and change in mind and added appendices to help select exercises based on American Society of Addiction Medicine (ASAM) criteria. At the same time, there is more demand for treatment strategies and interventions to be evidence-based, and we have sought to reflect this trend.

While we have updated and retained the 88 exercises in 42 problem areas in the third edition, in response to feedback from colleagues and clients we have condensed some content. We have reduced the overviews to one page or less apiece. Most exercises are one or two pages in length, and none are longer than three pages. Our hope is that these changes will make this book even more useful than the previous edition. We believe it is more important than ever to include therapeutic homework in treatment for several reasons:

- The process of working on these exercises between therapy sessions helps clients integrate their treatment into their daily life and all the environments in which they live.

- When newly recovering people encounter problems and challenges, it seldom happens in session—in a way, these homework assignments enable us to extend the reach of the process from individual or group sessions into the client's home, work, and social life.

- As we noted in the preface to the third edition, homework makes effective use of the time between sessions, empowers the client and leads him/her into a more active role in treatment, gives the therapist documentation of progress and a vehicle for giving the client feedback, and provides the client a reference to keep and use long after treatment ends.

USING THIS BOOK

This revision is a companion to the fourth edition of the *Addiction Treatment Planner*. It is compatible with the fourth edition of the *Therascribe*® treatment-planning software. As before, you can look assignments up by issue or assignment title in the table of contents; use the appendices to cross-reference assignments with treatment issues; and use the enclosed CD-ROM to install the assignments on your computer as Micro-Soft Word documents and print them as they are or customize them by rewording items, adding a logo or other art, or however else you choose. For further instructions please see "About the CD-ROM" at the back of this book.

You may also use the companion CD-ROM add-on module with the *TheraScribe*® treatment-planning software to import goals and exercises directly into treatment plans.

As always, if you have suggestions, or want to tell us which features you find especially useful, please contact us via John Wiley & Sons, Inc. We are always grateful for feedback and have found it helpful in bringing you the best resource we can. Thanks for making the world a better place.

UNDERSTANDING CODEPENDENT BEHAVIORS

GOALS OF THE EXERCISE

1. Implement a plan for recovery from addiction that reduces the impact of adult-child-of-an-alcoholic (ACOA) traits on sobriety.
2. Decrease dependence on relationships while beginning to meet one's own needs.
3. Reduce the frequency of behaviors that are exclusively designed to please others.
4. Choose partners and friends who are responsible, respectful, and reliable.
5. Overcome fears of abandonment, loss, and neglect.
6. Understand the feelings that resulted from being raised in an addictive environment and reduce feelings of alienation by seeing similarities to others raised in nonaddictive homes.

ADDITIONAL PROBLEMS FOR WHICH THIS EXERCISE MAY BE USEFUL

- Borderline Traits
- Dependent Traits
- Partner Relationship Conflict
- Sexual Promiscuity

SUGGESTIONS FOR PROCESSING THIS EXERCISE WITH THE CLIENT

The "Understanding Codependent Behaviors" activity is for clients with patterns of co-dependent relationships, enmeshment, and boundary issues. It teaches clients about addictive relationship dynamics, then heightens motivation by focusing on the threat this poses to recovery, ending by directing clients to further exploration of issues of co-dependency. Follow-up may include discussing the issue with the therapist, group, and sponsor; support group referrals; bibliotherapy; and videotherapy (e.g., *Rent Two Films and Let's Talk in the Morning* by John W. Hesley and Jan G. Hesley, also published by John Wiley & Sons).

UNDERSTANDING CODEPENDENT BEHAVIORS

Codependency is addiction to a relationship. A codependent tries so hard to "fix" or "save" someone else that his/her own life is left in turmoil. No one can control anyone else—other people's troubles are mostly due to patterns only they can change, so trying to change them leads to one painful disappointment after another.

1. There are reasons we're drawn to relationships in which we try harder to solve our partners' problems than they do. These patterns are often related to having grown up with parents or other adults who suffered from alcoholism, other drug addiction, or other addictive disorders, and may echo our childhood relationships with those adults. Have you been in painful relationships for any of these reasons?

    _____ You felt needed.

    _____ It was intense and exciting from the start.

    _____ You felt intensely and "magnetically" drawn to them.

    _____ They made you feel strong, smart, and capable.

    _____ The sex was incredible.

    _____ You identified with the hardships they'd suffered—your heart ached for them.

    _____ You felt that you could help them and change their lives.

2. Here are signs of codependent relationships. Again, please check off any you've experienced:

    _____ Manipulation and mind games take up a lot of time and energy.

    _____ You're often worried that the relationship will fall apart, so you walk on eggshells.

    _____ You keep your partner away from your other friends and family because they don't get along, or you don't think they would.

    _____ One of you spends a lot of time rescuing the other from problems, again and again.

    _____ You try hard to impress your partner and keep secrets; you fear your partner would reject you if he/she knew about parts of your life or past.

    _____ You get in heated arguments that don't make sense to either of you.

_____ The relationship became very intense very fast when you first got together.

_____ One or both of you feel a lot of jealousy and insecurity about the relationship.

_____ The relationship is never boring, but it's usually stressful.

_____ You go back and forth between feeling abandoned and feeling smothered.

3. There's a strong connection between stress and relapse. Looking at the items you checked for question 2, how could a stressful relationship lead you to relapse and how do you feel about that risk?

    _____

    _____

4. Most people who get into codependent relationships don't just do so once. Each of us has a type we're most likely to be drawn to. What unhealthy patterns do you see in the people you find attractive?

    _____

    _____

    _____

    _____

Be sure to bring this handout back to your next session with your therapist, and be prepared to talk about your thoughts and feelings about the exercise.

UNDERSTANDING FAMILY HISTORY

GOALS OF THE EXERCISE

1. Implement a plan for recovery from addiction that reduces the impact of adult-child-of-an-alcoholic (ACOA) traits on sobriety.
2. Decrease dependence on relationships while beginning to meet one's own needs.
3. Reduce the frequency of behaviors that are exclusively designed to please others.
4. Eliminate behaviors that are dangerous to self or others.
5. Eliminate self-defeating interpersonal patterns in occupational and social settings.
6. Choose partners and friends who are responsible, respectful, and reliable.
7. Overcome fears of abandonment, loss, and neglect.
8. Understand the feelings that resulted from being raised in an addictive environment and reduce feelings of alienation by seeing similarities to others raised in nonaddictive homes.
9. Learn new ways to interact with the family in adult life.
10. Obtain emotional support for recovery from family members.

ADDITIONAL PROBLEMS FOR WHICH THIS EXERCISE MAY BE USEFUL

- Childhood Trauma
- Family Conflicts
- Parent-Child Relational Problem

SUGGESTIONS FOR PROCESSING THIS EXERCISE WITH THE CLIENT

The "Understanding Family History" activity may be used effectively with clients experiencing shame, confusion, or anxiety as a result of seeing themselves repeat negative behaviors seen in childhood caretakers. It may be useful in couples therapy, since many ACOA individuals form relationships with partners with similar backgrounds. For clients struggling with acceptance and forgiveness of their parents or of themselves, this activity may help in understanding the roles of addiction and powerlessness in distorting values and behaviors. It may also be useful for clients who have parenting issues in recovery to understand the roots of their children's behaviors.

UNDERSTANDING FAMILY HISTORY

It's important to understand the role of family history in addictions, not to assess blame but for your own recovery and your family's future. This exercise looks at how family history affects us.

1. As a child, what did you learn about drinking, drug use, or other addictions in your family?

   _____

   _____

   _____

   _____

2. What problems, if any, did your family have because of these behaviors (e.g., violence, divorce, financial problems, dangerous or illegal activities, or other worries)?

   _____

   _____

3. Please describe the typical atmosphere in your family when someone was drinking, using drugs, or engaging in other addictive patterns, and its effects on you then and now.

   _____

   _____

   _____

   _____

4. Here are some common patterns in families struggling with addictions, related to the unspoken rule "Don't talk, don't trust, don't feel" that develops as other family members, especially children, try to avoid confrontations or disappointment due to the inability of addicted adults to be nurturing and dependable, or to cope with the emotional pain that is the result of that inability. For each pattern, give an example from your childhood and an example of how you can make healthy changes now.

   a. Dishonesty/denial

      (1) Childhood example: _____

      _____

(2) Working for healthy change: _____

_____

b. Breaking promises
    (1) Childhood example: _____

    _____

    (2) Working for healthy change: _____

    _____

c. Isolating/withdrawing
    (1) Childhood example: _____

    _____

    (2) Working for healthy change: _____

    _____

d. Emotional/physical/sexual abuse and neglect
    (1) Childhood example: _____

    _____

    (2) Working for healthy change: _____

    _____

e. Influencing others to act in self-destructive ways
    (1) Childhood example: _____

    _____

    (2) Working for healthy change: _____

    _____

f. Confused roles and responsibilities (e.g., children taking caring of adults, people blaming others for their own actions, etc.)
    (1) Childhood example: _____

    _____

    (2) Working for healthy change: _____

    _____

5. What good relationship patterns from your childhood do you want to continue and pass on?

_____

_____

_____

_____

Be sure to bring this handout back to your next session with your therapist, and be prepared to talk about your thoughts and feelings about the exercise.

IS MY ANGER DUE TO FEELING THREATENED?

GOALS OF THE EXERCISE

1. Develop a program of recovery that is free from substance abuse and dangerous/lethal behaviors.
2. Terminate all behaviors that are dangerous to self or others.
3. Decrease the frequency of occurrence of angry thoughts, feelings, and behaviors.
4. Verbalize core conflicts that lead to dangerous/lethal behaviors.
5. Recognize the first signs of anger and use behavioral techniques to control it.
6. Think positively and realistically in anger-producing situations.
7. Come to see that anger is a secondary emotion responding to fear or anxiety in response to a perceived threat.
8. Learn to self-monitor and shift into an introspective and cognitive problem-solving mode rather than an emotional reactive mode when anger is triggered.
9. Shift from a self-image as a helpless or passive victim of angry impulses to one of mastery and ability to choose responses to feelings.

ADDITIONAL PROBLEMS FOR WHICH THIS EXERCISE MAY BE USEFUL

- Dangerousness/Lethality
- Oppositional Defiant Behavior
- Posttraumatic Stress Disorder (PTSD)

SUGGESTIONS FOR PROCESSING THIS EXERCISE WITH CLIENT

The "Is My Anger Due to Feeling Threatened?" activity is suited for clients who are capable of introspection and who desire to change reactive patterns of anger. It may be useful when clients describe perceptions of being unable to control their anger, have patterns of impulsive anger disproportionate to the triggering event or situation, or express regrets over their actions when angry. Follow-up can include keeping a journal documenting angry impulses and the client's use of this process to manage his/her reactions.

IS MY ANGER DUE TO FEELING THREATENED?

A wise person once said that every problem starts as a solution to another problem. When anger becomes a problem it is often this kind of failing solution to another problem. Once we see this, it's easier to let go of the anger and find another solution that works better.

What kind of problem makes anger look like a solution? When is anger useful? It's good for one thing: energizing and preparing us to fight. It's the "fight" part of the "fight or flight" instinct that is any creature's response to perceived (whether real or not) danger. When we feel angry, chances are that we feel threatened.

This instinct developed in prehistoric people over thousands of generations. Nearly all the threats they faced were physical (e.g., wild animals or hostile strangers). In those situations anger served them well.

Some dangers are still physical, but more often we face threats we can't fight physically, like bills we can't pay. There are threats to our self-images and our beliefs about the world, which can feel just as dangerous as threats to our careers or health.

In this exercise, you'll think about a situation that has triggered your anger and identify both the threat that the anger wants to fight and another solution that will work better.

1. First, it's important to recognize anger as soon as it starts to develop. To do this, you need to watch for the early warning signs of anger, physical and mental.

    a. Here are some common physical effects of anger. Please check any you experience.

_____	Muscle tension or shaking	_____	Rapid heartbeat
_____	Rapid, shallow breathing	_____	"Butterflies in the stomach"
_____	Reddening of the face	_____	Agitation and restlessness

    b. Our thinking changes with anger, often in these ways. Again, check any you experience.

_____	Impulsiveness and impatience	_____	Feelings of power and certainty
_____	"All or nothing" thinking	_____	Taking things personally
_____	Inability to see others' perspectives	_____	A sense of having been wronged

2. Now think of a situation that has been an anger trigger for you—one that comes up over and over or has led to serious consequences because of your angry actions. Briefly describe the situation.

    _____

    _____

3. Study the situation, and identify the threat that triggered your anger. What was threatening to happen? Were you at risk of not getting something you wanted, or of losing something you already had and valued? The item under threat could be physical well-being, a relationship, a career or life goal, your self-image, or even your values and beliefs about the way the world works. Explain how this situation threatens you.

    _____

    _____

4. Think of a solution that will give you better results and cause fewer problems than acting in anger. Describe the solution and how you'd put it into action.

    _____

    _____

    _____

    _____

5. After you've thought about triggers and solutions, what are your thoughts and feelings about the situation? Do you feel more in control?

    _____

    _____

6. When you feel your anger building, pause to ask yourself, "Where's the threat, and what else can I do about it?" This way, you can take control of your feelings and actions. This is hard at first, but if you keep doing it, the pause and the question become automatic, just as the flash into rage was automatic. When you pause automatically and think this way, you control your anger, rather than it controlling you. At first, reminders help; think of someone you trust to help you with this. Explain what you're doing, and ask him/her to watch your mood and if you start looking angry, remind you to pause and find the threat. Who is that person, and when will you talk with him/her about this?

    _____

    _____

Be sure to bring this handout back to your next therapy session, and be prepared to talk about your thoughts and feelings about the exercise.

IS MY ANGER DUE TO UNMET EXPECTATIONS?

GOALS OF THE EXERCISE

1. Develop a program of recovery that is free from substance abuse and dangerous/lethal behaviors.
2. Terminate all behaviors that are dangerous to self or others.
3. Decrease the frequency of occurrence of angry thoughts, feelings, and behaviors.
4. Verbalize the core conflicts that lead to dangerous/lethal behaviors.
5. Recognize the first signs of anger and use behavioral techniques to control it.
6. Think positively and realistically in anger-producing situations.
7. Learn and implement stress-management skills to reduce the level of stress and the irritability that accompanies it.
8. Learn to self-monitor and shift into a thinking and problem-solving mode rather than a reactive mode when anger is triggered.
9. Increase self-esteem, purpose for living, and learn how to help others in recovery.

ADDITIONAL PROBLEMS FOR WHICH THIS EXERCISE MAY BE USEFUL

*   Dangerousness/Lethality
*   Family Conflicts
*   Oppositional Defiant Behavior
*   Parent-Child Relational Problems
*   Partner Relational Conflict

SUGGESTIONS FOR PROCESSING THIS EXERCISE WITH CLIENT

The "Is My Anger Due to Unmet Expectations?" activity is suited for clients who are capable of introspection and who desire to change reactive patterns of anger. It may be useful when clients report feeling unable to control their anger, have patterns of impulsive anger disproportionate to triggering events or situations, or express regrets over their actions when angry. Follow-up can include keeping a journal documenting angry impulses and use of this process to identify trigger expectations and manage his/her reactions.

IS MY ANGER DUE TO UNMET EXPECTATIONS?

People in treatment and recovery programs often say that anger always boils down to fear—fear that we will lose something we want to keep, or that we won't get something we want. Usually, though, the things that we think we will lose or won't get aren't life-and-death matters, and we often react as if they were. A good example is the road rage we've all seen or felt. People have killed each other over who was going to get to the next traffic light three seconds sooner. This seems to make no sense.

When we look more closely at what's going on, though, we'll usually find that when possible losses or disappointments trigger intense anger in us, it's because we expected something different and are disappointed. Sometimes our expectations are based on what we feel is right and fair. These are what some people call the "shoulda-woulda-couldas" (e.g., that the person in the next lane should let us merge instead of speeding up to crowd us out, or that people should be honest and considerate with us). Also, sometimes we expect something just because we want it badly and convince ourselves it should happen the way we want it to.

However, our expectations are often not realistic. That's what leads many old-timers in Alcoholics Anonymous and other recovery programs to say, "An expectation is nothing but a premeditated resentment." By that they mean that when we form expectations, we are often setting ourselves up for disappointment and the anger that follows.

Do you want to avoid getting angry unnecessarily? It's a good idea to do so; anger interferes with a person's judgment, making him/her more likely to act impulsively and do things that damage relationships; undermines recovery; and even weakens the immune system and leaves him/her more vulnerable to cancer, heart disease, stroke, and other life-threatening illnesses.

This exercise will help you get into the habit of avoiding unrealistic expectations, and thereby becoming able to be calm and at peace more of the time and angry less often.

1. Please think back to the most recent time you got angry. What happened?

_____

_____

2. Was the event that triggered your anger something you felt should not have happened the way it did—if so, what was your expectation, and why did you have that expectation?

    _____

    _____

    _____

    _____

3. Often we expect things that experience tells us are unlikely (e.g., expecting someone who is usually late to show up on time, expecting people to be polite in rush-hour traffic, expecting that police officer not to pull us over even though we were speeding). If experience told you that what you expected was unlikely, what would have been a more reasonable expectation?

    _____

    _____

4. As you may be seeing, our expectations are often just plain mistakes in our thinking. If we learn not to make that kind of mistake, we won't be unpleasantly surprised. Acceptance is more comfortable than resentment. Remember, to accept something doesn't mean that we like it, or that we believe it's right—acceptance just means admitting that things are the way they are, and deciding to deal with reality rather than with our fantasies. If you find yourself facing the same situation again, and base your expectations on reality—on what experience tells you is likely to happen—rather than on what you hope for or what you feel should happen, what will your reaction be if events match that different expectation?

    _____

    _____

5. Here are some of the basic mistaken expectations we form and then get angry over. Please give an example of each from your own experience.

    a. Expecting someone to behave differently than the way he/she usually behaves (e.g., expecting love and warmth from a person who is normally cold and sarcastic, expecting consideration from someone who is usually thoughtless and selfish).

        Example: _____

        _____

    b. Taking things personally (e.g., expecting others to be thinking about us rather than about themselves) or expecting to be the center of someone else's world.

        Example: _____

        _____

c.   Perfectionism (e.g., expecting ourselves or others to do something perfectly the first time, or the twentieth time, rather than recognizing that we are human and make mistakes).

Example: _____

_____

d.   Over-optimism (e.g., expecting everything to go the way we want, though it seldom does).

Example: _____

_____

6.   Some other emotions that arise when we form expectations and they aren't met are self-pity, anxiety, and discouragement. In your experience, how have anger, resentment, self-pity, anxiety, and/or discouragement been triggers for your past addictive behaviors?

_____

_____

7.   Because these emotions can be relapse triggers, success in recovery depends on managing them as much as possible. The best way to do this is to avoid setting yourself up for them. The fewer expectations you have, especially unrealistic ones, the less often you'll find yourself feeling miserable, and the easier it will be to stay in recovery and avoid relapse. Please briefly describe a plan to monitor your thinking and emotions, avoid unreasonable expectations or detect and correct them as soon as possible if they come up, and regain your serenity.

_____

_____

_____

_____

Be sure to bring this handout back to your next therapy session, and be prepared to talk about your thoughts and feelings about the exercise.

ALTERNATIVES TO ADDICTIVE BEHAVIOR

GOALS OF THE EXERCISE

1. Develop a program of recovery that is free of addiction and the negative influences of antisocial behavior.
2. Learn how antisocial behavior and addiction are self-defeating.
3. Learn to participate in enjoyable activities as constructive and healthy alternatives to addictive behaviors.

ADDITIONAL PROBLEMS FOR WHICH THIS EXERCISE MAY BE USEFUL

- Chronic Pain
- Eating Disorders
- Gambling
- Substance Abuse/Dependence

SUGGESTIONS FOR PROCESSING THIS EXERCISE WITH CLIENT

The "Alternatives to Addictive Behavior" activity is useful for clients with a generalized pattern of self-medicating uncomfortable feelings with activities that offer instant gratification or mood alteration, who are at risk for switching from one addictive behavior to another and may benefit from insight into their self-medication and awareness of more benign options. The exercise includes a cost/benefit analysis of addictive behavior, examination of underlying needs, and brainstorming other ways to meet those needs. Follow-up may include assignments to investigate groups dedicated to alternative activities (e.g., a hiking club) and a report to the therapist and/or a treatment group on positive experiences.

ALTERNATIVES TO ADDICTIVE BEHAVIOR

For many addicted people, most things they do for fun or relaxation involve drinking, using other drugs, or other addictive behaviors, with destructive consequences. Fun is a vital and necessary part of life. Learning to have a good time and get your needs met in nonaddictive ways is a key part of recovery and is largely a matter of re-education. This exercise will help you identify positive ways to get your personal needs met and find enjoyment.

1. List the major benefits which you got from drinking, other drug use, or other addictive behaviors.

    Physical   **Social**   **Mental or Emotional**

    _____   _____   _____

    _____   _____   _____

    _____   _____   _____

    _____   _____   _____

    _____   _____   _____

    _____   _____   _____

    _____   _____   _____

2. Now list the main drawbacks connected with these behaviors.

    Physical   **Social**   **Mental or Emotional**

    _____   _____   _____

    _____   _____   _____

    _____   _____   _____

    _____   _____   _____

    _____   _____   _____

    _____   _____   _____

_____   _____   _____
_____   _____   _____

3. List the benefits you can think of connected with abstinence from addictive behaviors.

Physical   **Social**   **Mental or Emotional**

_____   _____   _____
_____   _____   _____
_____   _____   _____
_____   _____   _____
_____   _____   _____
_____   _____   _____
_____   _____   _____

4. List the drawbacks you see connected with abstinence from these behavior patterns.

Physical   **Social**   **Mental or Emotional**

_____   _____   _____
_____   _____   _____
_____   _____   _____
_____   _____   _____
_____   _____   _____
_____   _____   _____
_____   _____   _____

5. List as many alternative ways as you can think of to get the benefits you listed for drinking, other drug use, or other addictive behaviors, but without such negative consequences.

Physical   **Social**   **Mental or Emotional**

_____   _____   _____
_____   _____   _____
_____   _____   _____
_____   _____   _____
_____   _____   _____

_____   _____   _____

_____   _____   _____

_____   _____   _____

6. How will you respond to yearnings for the thrill or rush that you got from substance use or other addictive behaviors?

_____

_____

_____

_____

_____

_____

_____

_____

7. List three activities that:

   a. You enjoy: _____

   _____

   b. You think you would enjoy, but haven't tried: _____

   _____

   c. You've heard others talk about and are interested in: _____

   _____

   d. You could enjoy doing alone: _____

   _____

   e. You could enjoy doing with others: _____

   _____

8. Describe a plan to take action within the next week to start practicing an alternative activity.

   _____

   _____

   _____

   _____

   _____

   _____

   _____

   _____

Be sure to bring this handout back to your next session with your therapist, and be prepared to talk about your thoughts and feelings about the exercise.

TAKING DAILY INVENTORY

GOALS OF THE EXERCISE

1. Develop a program of recovery that is free of addiction and antisocial behavior.
2. Take responsibility for one's own behavior.
3. Identify patterns of thought, emotion, and behavior that pose a threat to sobriety and develop a plan of action for improvement.
4. Clarify the importance of taking inventory as part of preventing relapse.
5. Provide a method for taking inventory to continue using in the future.

ADDITIONAL PROBLEMS FOR WHICH THIS EXERCISE MAY BE USEFUL

- Relapse Proneness
- Substance Abuse/Dependence
- Treatment Resistance

SUGGESTIONS FOR PROCESSING THIS EXERCISE WITH THE CLIENT

The "Taking Daily Inventory" activity is designed for clients who are not inclined to introspection and need prompting to self-monitor for addictive patterns of thought, emotions, and behaviors. It highlights any drift toward addictive patterns before actual relapse occurs, and is a good sequel to "Early Warning Signs of Relapse." Follow-up can include reporting to the therapist or treatment group trends that were noted by the client in daily inventories, feedback from the therapist or group about discrepancies between what the client reports and what they observe, and journaling assignments on any consistent challenges identified.

TAKING DAILY INVENTORY

Your daily emotions, attitudes, and actions move you either further into recovery or back toward addictive behavior. Checking your progress frequently is an important part of staying sober.

1. Using a scale in which 1 = low and 5 = high, score yourself daily on these items:

    Moving Further into Recovery: *Moving toward Relapse:*

    Honest with self _____   Dishonest _____

    Honest with others _____   Resentful _____

    Living for today _____   Depressed _____

    Hopeful _____   Self-pitying _____

    Active _____   Critical of self/others _____

    Prompt _____   Procrastinating _____

    Relaxed _____   Impatient _____

    Responsible _____   Angry _____

    Confident _____   Indifferent _____

    Realistic _____   Guilty _____

    Reasonable _____   Anxious _____

    Forgiving _____   Ashamed _____

    Trusting of others _____   Fearful _____

    Content with self _____   Withdrawn _____

    Helpful to others _____   Demanding _____

2. How did you improve today?

    _____

    _____

3.   What roadblock(s) to recovery/progress can you identify today?

_____

_____

4.   What, if anything, do you wish you had done differently today?

_____

_____

5.   On a scale of 1 to 5, what is your level of commitment to recovery today?

_____

_____

6.   What did you learn about yourself today that you can use to assist continued progress?

_____

_____

7.   If you began working on any new change today, what was that change?

_____

_____

8.   Please look at your Moving toward Relapse scores from question 1 and describe one concrete strategy to decrease your risk of relapse and increase your chances of staying in recovery.

_____

_____

Be sure to bring this handout back to your next session with your therapist, and be prepared to talk about your thoughts and feelings about the exercise.

COPING WITH STRESS

GOALS OF THE EXERCISE

1. Maintain a program of recovery free from addiction and excessive anxiety.
2. End the use of addictive behavior as a way of escaping anxiety and practice constructive coping behaviors.
3. Decrease anxious thoughts and increase positive self-enhancing self-talk.
4. Learn to relax and think accurately and logically about events.
5. Identify effective stress-management methods that are already working.
6. Incorporate stress management as part of a lifestyle change and identify areas in which to begin modifying stress responses.

ADDITIONAL PROBLEMS FOR WHICH THIS EXERCISE MAY BE USEFUL

- Medical Issues
- Relapse Proneness

SUGGESTIONS FOR PROCESSING THIS EXERCISE WITH CLIENT

The "Coping with Stress" activity examines the client's existing stressors and habitual responses with the aim of increasing insight and helping him/her reduce stress and improve coping skills. It includes an imagination exercise aimed at motivating the client to work for improvement and bolstering his/her confidence in doing so. Follow-up can include homework assignments to practice new stress-management methods; seeking feedback from family, friends, and others on perceived changes in the client's degree of tension; and reporting back on outcomes.

COPING WITH STRESS

Relapses in recovery from addictions are often triggered by stressful situations, because we have used addictive behaviors as our main tools for handling stress. To stay sober we must find healthy ways to cope with stressors. This exercise will guide you in learning about your stress-management style, your sources of stress, and how you can handle it more effectively.

1. Please list three situations that most commonly trigger great stress for you.

    _____

    _____

2. Please describe a situation in which you used alcohol, another drug, or another addictive behavior to cope with stress.

    _____

    _____

3. How can you tell when you are experiencing stress in your life? Please list your reactions to stress, both physical and emotional.

    _____

    _____

4. What are your usual ways of handling stress? Include both positive and negative strategies.

    _____

    _____

5. Please talk with some people who know you well and whom you feel have good judgement, people you trust to give you straight answers. Ask them to describe what they have seen as your usual reactions to stress in a phrase or short sentence. Describe their answers here.

    _____

    _____

6. Many times, we walk straight into stressful situations we could have bypassed, or we fail to use effective ways to cope that we know we could use. List causes of stress you can control in the first column, and things you can do to avoid or cope with them in the second column.

_____	_____
_____	_____
_____	_____
_____	_____

7. At other times, a situation may be unavoidable, but we increase the stress we experience because of the ways we think about that situation (e.g., predicting terrible outcomes to ourselves and worrying about things we can't change). List causes of stress you cannot control in the first column, and ways you can change your thinking about them in the second column.

Example: Conflicts with spouse and children

Example: Work on communication skills

_____	_____
_____	_____
_____	_____
_____	_____

8. Please describe a stressful situation you handled well and how you did it.

Example: Overloaded at work—Talked with supervisor and asked him/her to prioritize tasks.

_____

_____

9. You can reduce stress by avoiding overdoing things in any area of your life. This will allow you to more effectively handle the stress that is unavoidable. Please list at least one thing you can do today to create more balance in each area listed here.

   a. Relationships with family or friends: _____

   _____

   b. Leisure time/activities: _____

   _____

   c. Work/school: _____

   _____

   d. Community involvement: _____

   _____

   e. Spiritual activities: _____

   _____

f. Proper nutrition: _____

_____

g. Exercise: _____

_____

h. Emotions: _____

_____

10. Picture yourself handling a stressful situation using more effective methods than you would have used when you were practicing an addictive lifestyle. How would this improve the results you get and your quality of life?

_____

_____

_____

_____

What are you already doing differently, and what can you start doing now, to move from your present situation toward the one you imagined?

_____

_____

While you picture this future for yourself, pay attention to how it makes you feel. Talk about this with other members of the treatment group or in your next treatment session.

Be sure to bring this handout back to your next session with your therapist, and be prepared to talk about your thoughts and feelings about the exercise.

MY ANXIETY PROFILE

GOALS OF THE EXERCISE

1. Maintain a program of recovery free of addiction and excessive anxiety.
2. Understand the relationship between anxiety and addictive behaviors.
3. Increase insight and awareness related to feelings and processes associated with anxiety.
4. Decrease anxious thoughts, overall stress, and muscle tension, and increase positive self-talk.
5. Strengthen belief in the capacity to self-manage anxiety without returning to addictive behavior.

ADDITIONAL PROBLEMS FOR WHICH THIS EXERCISE MAY BE USEFUL

- Posttraumatic Stress Disorder (PTSD)
- Social Anxiety

SUGGESTIONS FOR PROCESSING THIS EXERCISE WITH CLIENT

The "My Anxiety Profile" activity is for clients who experience anxiety but feel helpless to change it. First the exercise asks the client to identify how he/she experiences anxiety physically, behaviorally, cognitively, and emotionally. Second, it asks him/her to develop a hierarchy of least to most anxiety-producing experiences. Finally, it asks the client to develop a plan for coping with anxiety. Some clients find it useful to externalize problems, give them personalities and/or name them, and learn to view themselves as active opponents to those problems. This can allow the client to feel empowered and feel that he/she is the solution, not the problem. Follow-up can consist of teaching relaxation and imagery techniques to deal with all levels of anxiety.

MY ANXIETY PROFILE

Everyone experiences anxiety. It is often associated with fears and phobias, nervousness, and panic attacks. Some people are very aware of their anxiety, and others don't become aware of it until it is overwhelming. Some of us experience anxiety mainly over specific situations, and others report more general feelings of anxiety. We worry about the outcomes of events. We're nervous when we do things for the first time, such as going on a date, speaking to a group, or starting a new job. For some, anxiety is short-lived and does not interfere in their lives other than causing mild discomfort. For others, anxiety can cause panicky feelings, prevent them from enjoying many activities, or interfere with their daily living. Anxiety is also related to addictive behavior in two ways: (1) we often feel anxiety when we practice new nonaddictive behaviors, and (2) we temporarily reduce anxiety by engaging in addictive behavior.

This exercise will help you learn about your anxiety so that you can develop strategies to cope with it and avoid returning to addictive behaviors to lessen it.

Anxiety has three components that interact with one another: (1) physical sensations, such as heart-pounding, sweating, and dizziness; (2) thoughts, such as expecting something terrible to happen; and (3) behavioral responses such as leaving situations or avoiding places.

1. Please list the physical sensations that you experience when you feel anxiety. Sometimes our physical cues change as anxiety increases or decreases. Think about the most recent time you felt anxious, or the time you felt the worst anxiety. What were your physical sensations?

    _____

    _____

2. How have you coped in the past to reduce anxiety or avoid anxiety-producing situations?

    _____

    _____

3. What do you think about when you feel anxious? Imagine your anxiety as having a mind and will of its own. What would it say to you so that your anxiety level would

GETTING OF

GOALS OF THE EXERCISE

1. Maintain a program of recovery free 1 Attention Deficit Disorder (ADD).
2. Demonstrate sustained attention and c of time.
3. Understand the negative influence of A
4. Structure a recovery program sufficie negative effects of ADD on learning and
5. Develop positive self-talk when faced w
6. Learn to tune in to physical signs that
7. Identify coping strategies that have wo
8. Develop new skills to cope with inatten

ADDITIONAL PROBLEMS FOR WHICH

- Attention Deficit/Hyperactivity Disord
- Psychosis

SUGGESTIONS FOR PROCESSING THI

The "Getting Organized" activity is for cli ity, or difficulty completing tasks. It can l assistance getting organized. Follow-up ca log of distractions or instances of inat through use of newly learned skills. It is ate and sustain therapeutic momentum a be useful for parents coping with ADD-li clients who struggle with symptoms of AI

rise? Often, our anxious thoughts will overestimate danger, underestimate help that is available to us or our ability to cope, and feed our existing insecurities. Please describe those thoughts and beliefs.

_____

_____

_____

_____

4. When we feel anxious, the emotional and physical parts of our brains override the thinking parts. The result is often that we'll do anything that quickly relieves our discomfort. The problem is that this quick fix becomes a habit. Here's a solution to use in your journal: Following the example provided, list a physical symptom in the left-hand column, the thought connected with it in the center, and a reasonable and positive response in the column on the right.

Physical Sensation	Anxious Thought	Positive Response
I feel warm.	*I'm going to pass out.*	*I'll sit, relax, and cool down.*

5. Another way to get to know your anxiety is to create an intensity scale ranging from very low to extremely high levels of anxiety. Please identify at least one situation or experience for each level and the physical sensations that are associated with each.

Level of Anxiety	Situation/Experience	Physical Sensations
Very low		
Low		
Moderate		
High		
Very High		

6. In looking back over the information you've collected above about your anxiety, what is a word or phrase you would use to describe or name it?

_____

With your therapist or group, please make a plan to work against (your word or phrase) _____ and describe your plan here.

_____

_____

_____
_____
_____
_____
_____
_____

Be sure to bring this handout back to y[...]
prepared to talk about your thoughts and fe[...]

9. Ask someone close to you for feedback about how well you pay attention and follow through in your relationship with him/her. Write this feedback below and describe how you'll address any issues this person points out.

_____
_____
_____
_____

Be sure to bring this handout back to your next session with your therapist, and be prepared to talk about your thoughts and feelings about the exercise.

FROM RECKLESSNESS TO CALCULATED RISKS

GOALS OF THE EXERCISE

1. Maintain a program of recovery from addiction and reduce the negative effects of Attention Deficit/Hyperactivity Disorder (ADHD) on learning, social interaction, and self-esteem.
2. Decrease impulsivity by learning how to stop, think, and plan before acting.
3. Learn the benefits of taking calculated risks rather than acting impulsively.
4. Gain insight into patterns and consequences of reckless behavior and decision making.
5. Learn a method of decision making that leads to more positive outcomes.

ADDITIONAL PROBLEMS FOR WHICH THIS EXERCISE MAY BE USEFUL

*   Attention Deficit Disorder, Inattentive Type (ADD)
*   Impulsivity
*   Mania/Hypomania

SUGGESTIONS FOR PROCESSING THIS EXERCISE WITH CLIENT

The "From Reckless to Calculated Risks" activity is for clients with a history of impulsivity. The exercise asks the client to review past impulsive decisions and consequences and then guides him/her through a technique that encourages more calculated/thought-out responses. Follow-up can include having a client describe a series of self-instructions in situations in which he/she has acted out impulsively. Repetition of this process reinforces the internal problem-solving dialogue necessary for taking calculated risks. If the client is unable to generate personal examples, use scenarios and direct him/her to develop self-instructions for the person in the scenarios.

FROM RECKLESSNESS TO CALCULATED RISKS

All of us assume risks in everything we do. However, the risks we take in a given situation can be reckless, not thinking through the consequences, or calculated. Taking calculated risks involves a number of things. First, it means avoiding acting too quickly on impulses. Next, it involves thinking a situation through to its conclusion and anticipating the consequences. Finally, it calls for making concrete plans before acting. Addictive behavior and ADHD share traits related to recklessness: wanting instant gratification, acting impulsively, and not thinking situations through to their potential outcomes.

If we take calculated risks versus reckless risks, we have the best chance of getting the outcomes we want and avoiding preventable problems. In this exercise you'll review your risk-taking patterns and consider changes to give you more control over your life.

1. List some reckless behaviors you have engaged in, the situations in which you did so, and the consequences.

Behavior	Situation	Consequence(s)

2. For one of the behaviors you listed in question 1, choose a situation with which you continue to struggle. Complete the following formula to learn how to take more calculated risks.

   a. The situation is:

   _____

   _____

   b. What outcome do you want to achieve?

   _____

   _____

c. What are some things you can say to yourself in this situation to avoid an impulsive response, such as "slow down," "don't take it personally," or "relax and think for a minute"?

_____

_____

d. Write out concrete instructions to yourself in the format below.

  • What is the problem?

_____

_____

  • What am I expected to do?

_____

_____

  • What are my options—what other things can I do?

_____

_____

  • What do I want to have happen?

_____

_____

  • The approach that will give me the best chance of the result I want and will minimize difficulty will be...

_____

_____

  • What can I say to myself to help me cope?

_____

_____

  • To avoid this problem in the future, I need to focus on ...

_____

_____

Be sure to bring this handout back to your next session with your therapist, and be prepared to talk about your thoughts and feelings about the exercise.

LEARNING TO SELF-SOOTHE

GOALS OF THE EXERCISE

1. Maintain a program of recovery from addiction and reduce the negative effects of Attention Deficit/Hyperactivity Disorder (ADHD) on learning, social interaction, and self-esteem.
2. Develop the skills necessary to bring ADHD symptoms under control so that normal learning can take place.
3. Learn and demonstrate safe stress-reduction techniques as alternatives to addictive or risky behaviors including substance abuse, gambling, overspending, and sexual acting out.
4. Reduce the impact of medical and other problems on recovery and relapse potential.
5. Reduce feelings of alienation by learning about similarities to others.

ADDITIONAL PROBLEMS FOR WHICH THIS EXERCISE MAY BE USEFUL

- Anxiety
- Borderline Traits
- Chronic Pain
- Eating Disorders
- Grief/Loss Unresolved
- Medical Issues
- Posttraumatic Stress Disorder (PTSD)
- Social Anxiety
- Suicidal Ideation

SUGGESTIONS FOR PROCESSING THIS EXERCISE WITH CLIENT

The "Learning to Self-Soothe" activity is useful to help clients learn to recognize signs that their agitation is escalating and improve their skill at calming themselves. This exercise can be used as a check-in and review at the initiation and/or conclusion of every individual or group therapy session.

LEARNING TO SELF-SOOTHE

For people coping with issues of attention and/or impulsive decision making, learning to calm themselves can help them avoid negative outcomes in many situations. It can improve learning, relationships, and self-esteem. It can replace self-destructive behaviors they may have used to cope with restlessness, boredom, irritability, frustration, and negative reaction from others, as well as reducing impulsivity, distractibility, and other problems related to ADHD. There are many healthy ways to calm down. You may already have some that work—if so, keep using them! This exercise will give you more tactics you can practice and use in your day-to-day activities.

1. Briefly describe any healthy tactics you have found useful in calming yourself when you're agitated (continue to use these as you learn additional methods).

    _____

    _____

2. List some activities you have a difficult time completing, and what self-destructive coping mechanisms get in the way.

    _____

    _____

3. Are there times during the day when it's particularly difficult for you to concentrate, complete activities, get necessary tasks done, or stay calm? If so, when are they?

    _____

    _____

4. Below is a list of calming-down strategies. Choose three from the list and practice each for five minutes at different times, at least three times each day for a week. Keep a record of how calm you feel before and after. Use the following rating scale: 1. very calm; 2. calm; 3. no change; 4. less calm than when you started; 5. much more upset than when you started. Practice them at different times of the day and note whether they work better at some times than at others.

    a. Concentrate on breathing slowly and deeply.

    b. Relax in a quiet place.

    c. Use an external cue for focus (e.g., wrap yourself in a blanket, hold a recovery token, gaze at a candle flame, play soft music, etc.)

d.   Develop a calming mantra or message to repeat over and over again to yourself.

e.   Imagine a peaceful scene full of relaxing details.

f.   Take a walk.

g.   Concentrate on breathing slowly and deeply.

Remember that repetition is the key—the more you practice any of these, the better they will work. Sometimes other people can help us calm down, but we need to have skills in doing this for ourselves in case those people aren't available.

5.   What worked best for you? For items that were not useful, briefly describe what you believe kept them from working for you.

_____
_____
_____
_____

6.   Ask some people you trust what they do to calm themselves. Practice their methods yourself and write the results here.

_____
_____
_____
_____

7.   Write the specific steps you will incorporate into a self-soothing ritual. Which tactics will you use first, second, third ... and so on?

_____
_____
_____
_____

8.   What body cues will indicate to you that you are calm and can stop the self-soothing ritual for the time being?

_____
_____

9.   What physical signs will tell you that you are getting agitated and need to calm yourself again?

_____
_____

Be sure to bring this handout back to your next session with your therapist, and be prepared to talk about your thoughts and feelings about the exercise.

FORMING STABLE RELATIONSHIPS

GOALS OF THE EXERCISE

1. Develop a recovery program that reduces the impact of borderline behavior traits on abstinence.
2. Understand connections between addictive thinking patterns and unhealthy relationships.
3. Learn strategies to form stable and healthy relationships that promote recovery.

ADDITIONAL PROBLEMS FOR WHICH THIS EXERCISE MAY BE USEFUL

- Adult-Child-of-an-Alcoholic (ACOA) Traits
- Dependent Traits
- Partner Relational Conflicts
- Sexual Promiscuity
- Social Anxiety

SUGGESTIONS FOR PROCESSING THIS EXERCISE WITH CLIENT

The "Forming Stable Relationships" activity is for clients whose recovery is compromised by dysfunctional relationships. It guides clients in exploring similarities between addictions and the dynamics of unhealthy relationships, then studying the qualities of healthy relationships. The exercise concludes by offering actions to help clients form healthier relationships and prompting them to identify steps to take during the following month. The exercise is suited for individual or group use, in session or as homework. Follow-up can include reporting on outcomes and bibliotherapy using literature on this topic or videotherapy (see *Rent Two Films and Let's Talk in the Morning* by John W. Hesley and Jan G. Hesley, also published by John Wiley & Sons).

FORMING STABLE RELATIONSHIPS

The ways of thinking that form healthy relationships promote healthy living in general. The stress of a troubled relationship is a common relapse trigger, but a good relationship supports recovery under other kinds of stress. Forming stable relationships is a valuable life skill.

1. Our closest relationships can be the most challenging. We may find ourselves in unhappy situations over and over, knowing something's wrong but not how to get it right. The stress of those problems may lead people into addiction and other self-destructive actions. What would you say are key qualities of healthy and unhealthy relationships?

    Healthy Relationships   **Unhealthy Relationships**

    _____   _____

    _____   _____

2. Unhappy relationships are often like addictions to drugs or such behaviors as gambling, overwork, overspending, and so on. Here are some traits of addictive relationships—for each, please give an example of any experiences you've had that fit that pattern:

    a. *Rapid high-intensity involvement*: We may call it "love at first sight," but it's usually "lust at first sight." As with drugs, we seek instant gratification from intense experiences.

        Example:

        _____

        _____

    b. *Dishonesty, distrust, manipulation, and controlling behavior:* We may try to control the moods, thoughts, and behaviors of others and at the same time blame them for our own feelings and behavior, saying "you made me do/feel/think . . ." We hide things and don't talk about some subjects. We do a lot of "mind-reading," assuming, and hinting instead of being open and direct.

        Example:

        _____

        _____

c. *Desire for total union and social/emotional isolation:* The fear that we'll lose our partners if we let them out of reach, or the feeling that we're incomplete when apart, can lead us to cling to people and smother them. We tend not to have other close relationships, and often not much social activity. We're jealous and want other people all to ourselves, and we often fear what friends and family would say about these relationships (another parallel to addiction).

Example:

_____

_____

d. *Desire to "fix" the other/solve his/her problems:* We may see ourselves as rescuers, drawn to people with many problems and painful lives. This distracts us from our problems and lets us feel generous, feel superior, and feel safe from abandonment because they need us.

Example:

_____

_____

3. A healthy relationship has the opposite qualities. Here is the "other side of the coin," the traits of a stable and positive relationship. Again, please give examples from your own life:

a. *Gradual, step-by-step development:* It's wise to be cautious and not get too vulnerable, physically or emotionally, until we know it's safe.

Example:

_____

_____

b. *Honesty, trust, respect, and acceptance:* In healthy relationships people don't try to control each other. We can put ourselves in other's shoes and accept their right to disagree and make other choices. We can ask directly for what we want instead of hinting or manipulating.

Example:

_____

_____

c. *Acceptance of separateness, independence, and a full social life:* Healthy partners know that they're different people with different interests, histories, and so on. They maintain their other human connections, knowing no one person can meet all their needs. They know they can get along on their own, so they're together by choice, not because they feel they need to be.

Example:

_____

_____

d. *Expectation that each will solve his/her own problems:* No rescuing! Healthy partners know they can't fix each other. We can be supportive without taking on others' responsibilities.

Example:

_____

_____

4. Here are some ways to develop healthy relationships. How can you act on each one?

a. *Work on yourself first:* We attract, and are attracted to, people who are about as healthy and stable as we are—they're our mirrors. To attract healthy people, you have to be one.

What I can do: _____

_____

b. *Look in reasonable places:* Don't look for bread at the hardware store—you won't find healthy people in unhealthy places, or get healthy love from anyone who doesn't have it to give.

What I can do: _____

_____

c. *Be yourself*: To find a partner who accepts you as you are, you must let others see the real you. If you put on an act, no one has a chance to know and accept you.

What I can do: _____

_____

d. *Be picky:* You have the right to be treated well—don't settle for less, or give less in return. Never get involved with someone out of pity or a sense of obligation.

What I can do: _____

_____

e. *Don't try to change people:* People don't change unless they choose to do so. You can't have a relationship with someone's potential, only with the person that exists now.

What I can do: _____

_____

f. *Take your time*: Go step by step. Be cautious and check the other person out as you go. Increase your vulnerability and depth of involvement bit by bit as you see that each step is safe.

What I can do: _____

_____

g. *Get feedback:* Seek out someone you see has good relationship skills and whose wisdom you trust, and get his/her reactions to what's going on in your relationship.

What I can do: _____

_____

h. *Listen to your gut:* Think about past relationship choices that went badly; think back to your inner voice or gut feelings at the time. Pay attention to any uneasy feelings.

What I can do: _____

_____

Be sure to bring this handout back to your next session with your therapist, and be prepared to talk about your thoughts and feelings about the exercise.

SEEING THAT WE'RE ALL JUST HUMAN

GOALS OF THE EXERCISE

1. Develop a program of recovery from addiction that reduces the impact of borderline thinking patterns on abstinence.
2. Terminate dichotomous thinking, unmanaged anger, and fear of abandonment.
3. Learn that fear, anxiety, and self-doubt are normal and universal human emotions.
4. Increase identification with both strengths and weaknesses of other people.
5. Correct distortions in self-perception.

ADDITIONAL PROBLEMS FOR WHICH THIS EXERCISE MAY BE USEFUL

*   Narcissistic Traits
*   Social Anxiety

SUGGESTIONS FOR PROCESSING THIS EXERCISE WITH CLIENTS

The "Seeing That We're All Just Human" activity is aimed at clients whose exaggerated perceptions of differences between themselves and others, devaluing themselves and idealizing others, or vice versa interfere with empathy, relationships, and a healthy self-image. It addresses either/or, good/bad thinking and judgment of self and others by guiding the client to see both others and himself/herself as a mixture of strengths and weaknesses, and to identify ways in which relationships offer complementary strengths and mutual learning. This exercise is suitable for individual or group use, in session or as homework. Follow-up can include keeping a journal on this topic and reporting to the therapist and group on insights and outcomes.

SEEING THAT WE'RE ALL JUST HUMAN

Many people working to overcome addictions struggle with feeling uniquely flawed, with weaknesses and problems no one else could understand. On the other hand, we may feel that we are special in ways that others aren't—smarter, stronger, more sensitive, and more talented. Either way, these beliefs about differences between us and other people can interfere with our recovery and get in the way of forming healthy friendships that will help us heal and grow.

1. If you sometimes feel that you are too different from others for them to accept and understand you, or for you to be comfortable becoming close to them, what do you feel are the differences between you and other people?

    _____

    _____

2. In Alcoholics Anonymous and other 12-Step programs, you may hear cautions against "comparing your insides with other people's outsides." What does this phrase mean to you?

    _____

    _____

3. The way most people use that phrase, it means thinking we're crazy, sick, or weak because other people appear to have it all together, to be calm and confident, while we feel confused, anxious, scared, or overwhelmed. If you've felt this way, please describe the situation briefly.

    _____

    _____

4. Actually, those feelings—confusion, anxiety, fear, and feeling overwhelmed—are normal emotions that every sane person feels at times. Please briefly describe a situation where you felt these feelings but stayed composed on the outside, so that others couldn't tell what you were thinking and feeling.

    _____

    _____

5. Now think about the person you most respect and admire. Do you know of a time when this person felt those same feelings in his/her life? What was happening?

_____

_____

6. Do you respect this person less because he/she was confused, fearful, or over-whelmed in that situation? _____ How did he/she cope with these feelings, and could you use the same coping methods?

_____

_____

7. Now we'll look at strengths. What strengths or personal qualities do you value most highly? Please list the five qualities that are most important to you.

_____

_____

_____

_____

8. For the five qualities you listed, please give an example of a time you've shown each in something you've done.

_____

_____

_____

_____

_____

_____

_____

9. Now list five people you see every day—they may be friends, family members, co-workers, or people you see in therapy group sessions or recovery program meet-ings.

_____

_____

10. Please list one example for these five people of a way you'd like to be more like them.

_____

_____

_____

_____

11. Now list one way for each of these five people in which you feel you could teach them something—an area where you have a strength or quality of which they could use more.

_____

_____

_____

_____

12. Finally, for each of the five, list something important you have in common with them.

_____

_____

_____

_____

13. Take a few minutes, read back over this handout, and think about it. Have your feelings about question 1 changed—do you feel that you are too different from others for them to accept and understand you or for you to be comfortable becoming close to them? Please describe your thoughts.

_____

_____

Be sure to bring this handout back to your next session with your therapist, and be prepared to talk about your thoughts and feelings about the exercise.

CORRESPONDING WITH MY CHILDHOOD SELF

GOALS OF THE EXERCISE

1. Learn how childhood trauma can result in interpersonal problems and addiction.
2. Reduce fear, anger, depression, and increase self-esteem and confidence.
3. Overcome denial, minimization, and intellectualization of the effects of childhood trauma.
4. Reduce anxiety by reframing childhood perceptions of childhood situations using adult insights.
5. Overcome feelings of emotional isolation by providing a corrective experience.

ADDITIONAL PROBLEMS FOR WHICH THIS EXERCISE MAY BE USEFUL

- Adult-Child-of-an-Alcoholic (ACOA) Traits
- Parent-Child Relational Problem
- Posttraumatic Stress Disorder (PTSD)

SUGGESTIONS FOR PROCESSING THIS EXERCISE WITH CLIENT

The "Corresponding with My Childhood Self" activity is for clients stuck in modes of reaction formed in response to childhood trauma (e.g., denial, minimization, or intellectualization used to block painful feelings). It may be useful after incidents in which clients respond inappropriately to situations in ways related to childhood trauma. This may be used with videotherapy (see *Rent Two Films And Let's Talk in the Morning* by John W. Hesley and Jan G. Hesley, also published by John Wiley & Sons). Follow-up may include other therapeutic techniques for addressing unresolved trauma and/or learning and using healthy coping mechanisms.

CORRESPONDING WITH MY CHILDHOOD SELF

If you sometimes feel like a child pretending to be an adult, with a grown-up body but a child's feelings and reactions, it's important to know that most people feel this way at times.

If memories of hurtful things that happened in your childhood sometimes feel as fresh and painful as if they had just happened, you need to know that this is a common experience too. People traumatized as children often feel "stuck," unable to get over long-ago events.

This exercise will help you get "unstuck" by understanding and resolving painful experiences that may still haunt you, and help you use adult strengths to heal the pain of the child within you.

1. Think of a childhood experience that still bothers you, one you'd like to put to rest. If no one event stands out to you, you can think about a period of time, perhaps a difficult year.

2. Try to find a picture of yourself at the time of this event or period, or one taken within a year or so before or after. If you don't have a photo you can do the exercise, but the picture will help you focus.

3. Set aside at least an hour for this exercise, without distractions, in a place where you have privacy and feel safe. You'll need some paper, a pen or pencil, and the picture you chose.

4. Draw a line down the center of a page to make two columns. Over the column on the left, write the first name your friends call you now. Over the right-hand column, write the name you went by as a child. If it's the same name, add your ages now and then for both columns.

5. Focus on the photo. Think about what is going on in this child's world at the time of your life you're remembering. What is he/she thinking and feeling? In the left-hand column, write the first thing you would say to this child if you had that time machine and had the chance to talk with him/her. Stop after a sentence or two.

6. Now switch your pen or pencil to your opposite or weak hand—your left hand if you're right-handed or vice versa. Look at the photo; recall what it felt like to be that child. Imagine having the adult you are now talking with you then, saying the things you wrote in the first column. As that child, what would your answer be? With your weak hand, write a reply in the right-hand column.

7. Switch back to the left-hand column and your strong hand; write your adult's answer to what your child just said. Keep writing back and forth with your strong hand for your adult self and your weak hand for your child. Don't worry about what words or feelings come out. Just write whatever comes to mind. This may feel awkward; that's normal too. Being a child often feels awkward—using your opposite hand helps to get in touch with how it felt and may still feel at times.

8. Stop after half an hour. You may want to plan a time to continue the conversation. Now read through both columns and think about what you wrote. What would it have been like as a child to have an adult with whom you could have talked this way? When you were writing for your child, how did it feel to have someone paying attention?

_____

_____

_____

_____

_____

_____

_____

_____

   Be sure to bring this handout back to your next session with your therapist, and be prepared to talk about your thoughts and feelings about the exercise.

SETTING AND MAINTAINING BOUNDARIES

GOALS OF THE EXERCISE

1. Learn how childhood trauma may have resulted in interpersonal problems and addictive behavior patterns.
2. Resolve past childhood/family issues leading to less fear, anger, and depression and greater self-esteem and confidence.
3. Gain an understanding of personal power to set boundaries for oneself and the right to protect oneself emotionally and physically.
4. Learn to find balance and flexibility regarding roles or boundaries in relationships.

ADDITIONAL PROBLEMS FOR WHICH THIS EXERCISE MAY BE USEFUL

- Adult-Child-of-an-Alcoholic (ACOA) Traits
- Borderline Traits
- Dangerousness/Lethality
- Dependent Traits
- Family Conflicts
- Parent-Child Relational Problems
- Partner Relational Conflict
- Peer Group Negativity
- Sexual Promiscuity
- Social Anxiety

SUGGESTIONS FOR PROCESSING THIS EXERCISE WITH CLIENT

The "Setting and Maintaining Boundaries" activity should be preceded by a discussion to ensure the client understands the concept of boundaries in relationships and to probe what he/she considers healthy, keeping cultural considerations in mind when examining norms and mores with the client. When a client has a clear, functional goal, this exercise is useful in conducting a relationship inventory and identifying areas for growth. Follow-up can include planning strategies for difficult situations described in work on this activity and sharing those plans with the therapist, treatment group, and program sponsor.

SETTING AND MAINTAINING BOUNDARIES

When we have healthy personal boundaries, we can accept positive people and actions in our lives, but protect ourselves from those that are harmful. In trying to protect ourselves, we may have learned not to trust anyone or allow anyone to get close emotionally. On the other hand, in our search for love and acceptance we may have made ourselves too vulnerable and let others hurt us too easily. Healthy boundaries let us choose whom to trust, how far to trust them, and what actions to accept from them. We also learn to respect the boundaries of others in what we do or say to them.

1. List some people with whom you have difficulty setting or maintaining healthy boundaries, along with situations where you have trouble with them, and what the results have been.

Person	Situation	What Happens	How You Are Affected
_____	_____	_____	_____
_____	_____	_____	_____
_____	_____	_____	_____
_____	_____	_____	_____

2. If there are people, situations, or actions about which you are able to set and maintain healthy boundaries, please list them here.

Person	Situation	Action or Behavior
_____	_____	_____
_____	_____	_____
_____	_____	_____

3. Why do you think you are able to set and maintain boundaries with the people, situations, or actions on the second list, but not with those on the first list?

_____

_____

4. How can you use the same methods that work with the second list for the people, situations, or actions on the first list, or use other methods to get the same healthy results?

    _____

    _____

5. What changes would you like to make in your boundaries to help you live a healthy life?

    _____

    _____

    _____

    _____

6. What do you need to do to make these changes?

    _____

    _____

    _____

    _____

7. What will you do if others resist accepting your boundaries?

    _____

    _____

    _____

    _____

Be sure to bring this handout back to your next session with your therapist, and be prepared to talk about your thoughts and feelings about the exercise.

ALTERNATIVE METHODS FOR MANAGING PAIN

GOALS OF THE EXERCISE

1. Practice a recovery program, including 12-Step participation and pain management skills.
2. Regulate pain without addictive medications.
3. Develop healthy options to cope with chronic pain.
4. Reduce daily suffering from pain and substance abuse.

ADDITIONAL PROBLEMS FOR WHICH THIS EXERCISE MAY BE USEFUL

- Medical Issues
- Opioid Dependence
- Substance Abuse/Dependence
- Substance-Induced Disorders
- Substance Intoxication/Withdrawal

SUGGESTIONS FOR PROCESSING THIS EXERCISE WITH CLIENT

The "Alternative Methods for Managing Pain" activity is intended for clients suffering from severe and/or chronic pain who cannot use potentially addictive pain medications. The exercise offers several alternative approaches to managing pain and restoring quality of life without running the risk of relapse which may accompany either use of traditional pain medications or trying to "gut it out" and cope with pain through willpower, risking relapse via self-medication. Follow-up may include assignments to investigate local service providers or support groups, as well as investigation of online resources including the support groups identified in the handout.

ALTERNATIVE METHODS FOR MANAGING PAIN

If you suffer from severe or chronic pain and need to find ways to manage it other than through the use of traditional pain medications, this exercise will help you find those ways, which you can use instead of, or in addition to, potentially addictive pain medications.

1. How does the chronic pain you experience affect your daily life?

   _____
   _____
   _____
   _____

2. Please identify any professionals with whom you're working to manage your pain.

   _____
   _____

   Do those professionals know about your problems with addiction? _____ Are they experienced and qualified in working with people who suffer from addictions? _____

3. What methods of pain management other than medications have you tried?

   _____
   _____
   _____

   If any of those methods have worked for you, which are they?

   _____
   _____
   _____

4. Here are some nonaddictive ways of managing pain. Please talk with your doctor and your therapist about each of these approaches, investigate whatever opportunities your community offers you to try them, and briefly write about what you find.

a. *Over-the-counter (OTC) pain medications.* These are relatively mild pain-relieving drugs with no mind-altering effects. People using these medications need to be careful not to exceed safe dosages. In excessive amounts they can damage the stomach lining, damage the liver and/or kidneys, and in extreme cases cause death. Other pain-relieving medications can relieve the chronic pain of acid reflux and heartburn.

b. *Other non-mind-altering medications.* This category includes medications for joint pain called *Glucosamine chondroitin* and *MSM.* They help the body's natural healing processes rebuild damaged cartilage and connective tissues.

c. *Topical (external) medications.* These are usually ointments that can provide relief for pain from musculoskeletal problems including arthritis and joint injuries. They include pain-relieving ingredients, and some also have anti-inflammatory ingredients which reduce swelling and soreness. Some contain steroid compounds. You should consult with your doctor about using these medications.

d. *Diet modifications.* Sometimes pain is caused by unhealthy elements or deficiencies in a person's diet. Other problems may be due to food allergies—these can cause heartburn, headaches, rashes, and other problems. As part of a medical workup, you should get an allergy screening. You may choose to work with a registered dietician or nutritionist.

e. *Acupuncture.* Acupuncture has been proven to give fast and effective relief of pain in many cases. If you use acupuncture, be sure you're working with a qualified professional.

f. *Therapeutic massage.* This is another technique that, provided by trained professionals, can give quick and lasting relief for many cases of chronic musculoskeletal pain.

g. *Hypnosis.* This is very effective for many people—as with other types of treatment, be sure to work with a professional with the right training, credentials, and experience.

h. *Meditation.* Many pain sufferers find that meditation, especially using guided imagery, can help them detach from their pain. Soothing music can increase the effectiveness of meditation; people undergoing surgery respond better to anesthesia and recover more quickly afterward if they listen to soothing music before, during, and after surgery.

i. *Stretching and progressive muscle relaxation.* The key in using these methods is to avoid pushing the stretch itself to a degree that causes pain or injury. This approach is particularly helpful with back and neck pain, as well as headaches.

j. *Moderate cardiovascular exercise.* If you can exercise, 20 to 30 minutes of moderate cardio workout (enough to make you sweat, but not to cause shortness of breath) will relieve your pain by increasing the brain's levels of neurotransmitters that act as natural pain relievers. Before you start an exercise program, talk with your doctor to make sure it's safe and to ask how to get the most benefit from your workouts.

k. *Laughter.* Hearty or prolonged laughter boosts levels of the same neurotransmitters as cardiovascular exercise, and affects physical pain and emotional distress the same way. Regular laughter strengthens your immune system, improving your resistance to illness.

l. *Pet therapy.* Spending time with an affectionate animal also provides some relief from physical and emotional distress. Hospitals often include pet therapy in treatment.

m. *Spiritual and/or religious activity.* Many find comfort in prayer and the company of others who share their spiritual beliefs. This can reduce the isolation that often comes with intense pain and help people make sense of an experience that seems senseless.

n. *Participation in pain management support groups.* You may find practical advice and support from groups for chronic pain sufferers. You may be able to find them through newspapers or magazines. Local hospitals often have groups, and you may be able to find one by checking with them. There are also several pain management groups you can contact online. To get current info, use an Internet search engine such as Google.com. Some groups with active web sites at the time of this writing are:

1) American Chronic Pain Association: www.theacpa.org

2) Back Pain Support Group: www.backpainsupportgroup.com

3) Chronic Pain Support Group: www.chronicpainsupport.org.

4) National Chronic Pain Outreach Association, Inc.: www.chronicpain.org

5. Please use this space to briefly describe your plan for coping with your chronic pain using nonaddictive methods.

_____

_____

_____

_____

_____

_____

_____

_____

Be sure to bring this handout back to your next therapy session, and be prepared to talk about your thoughts and feelings about the exercise.

COPING WITH ADDICTION AND CHRONIC PAIN

GOALS OF THE EXERCISE

1. Practice a program of recovery, including 12-Step program participation and use of pain management skills.
2. Develop healthy options to cope with chronic pain.
3. Reduce daily suffering from pain and substance abuse.

ADDITIONAL PROBLEMS FOR WHICH THIS EXERCISE MAY BE USEFUL

*   Medical Issues
*   Opioid Dependence
*   Substance Abuse/Dependence

SUGGESTIONS FOR PROCESSING THIS EXERCISE WITH CLIENT

The "Coping with Addiction and Chronic Pain" activity is designed for clients who, as the title indicates, suffer from both addictions and severe and persistent pain. It addresses the perceived dilemma many clients face of reconciling participation in 12-Step recovery programs with the need to use prescribed medications that have a high potential for addiction, as well as noting other sources of emotional and practical support. Follow-up can include referral to appropriate medical professionals and to one or more of the chronic pain support groups cited in the exercise. It is helpful for the psychotherapist to coordinate work on this issue with any other health care providers from whom the client is receiving services, after ensuring that you and the other providers have each received the client's consent to share treatment information.

COPING WITH ADDICTION AND CHRONIC PAIN

Some people suffer from both substance abuse problems and severe or chronic pain. This puts them in a dilemma—the usual treatments for pain are narcotics or other strong medications with potential for abuse and addiction. Often, the pain led these people to begin using addictive drugs. On the other hand, many professionals are reluctant to prescribe strong pain medications, for fear of their patients getting addicted. So if you're in this situation, how can you achieve and maintain a life free of both addiction and ongoing pain? Fortunately, there are solutions. This exercise will help you understand the problem more completely and find some of those solutions.

1. How does chronic pain impact your daily life? Describe the relationship between your addiction and pain management.

    _____

    _____

    _____

    _____

2. Do your medical providers have specialized knowledge in pain management and addictions? If not, can the doctor or other professional with whom you're working give you a referral to a pain management specialist? As part of this exercise, please check on this and let your therapist know. Also, have you talked with them about your addiction history? If not, what keeps you from sharing that information?

    _____

    _____

    _____

3. In recent years the medical profession has found that even drugs that are otherwise highly addictive do not result in physical addiction for pain patients if they are taken in appropriate amounts (i.e., no more than is needed), and for no longer than needed, to control the pain. If you and your doctor plan to manage your pain

this way, what is your plan to avoid taking more than you need and to stop taking the medications (probably by switching to something safer and not so strong) as soon as appropriate, to avoid getting hooked?

_____

_____

_____

_____

4. Another discovery that is changing how pain medications are used: When the medication is taken before pain gets severe, it takes less to block the pain and keep the patient comfortable. This is why hospitals sometimes put people on a regular schedule for their pain medications and give them the medications even when they aren't too uncomfortable. Have you and your doctor talked about this, and if so, what's your plan and how do you feel about it?

_____

_____

_____

_____

5. A danger to watch out for: Many alcoholics and other addicts have found that when they used narcotics or equivalent drugs, although they didn't get addicted to those drugs, their judgment and inhibitions were affected and they relapsed into drinking or using other drugs, because they forgot why it was important to stay clean and sober. How will you avoid this trap?

_____

_____

6. Medical professionals have a central part in pain treatment, but other people also have key roles to play in helping you manage this situation (e.g., your sponsor if you're in a recovery program, family, and friends). How can they help you avoid falling into addictive thinking and behaviors when you're using potentially habit-forming drugs to manage your pain?

_____

_____

7. If you are participating in a 12-Step program, do you know your program's philosophy about the use of prescribed medications? _____ The position of Alcoholics Anonymous is that if your doctor knows your history and is experienced working with people with addictions, and you're taking the medications as prescribed, you're doing what you need to do to stay sober. Other programs have similar views. If others in your group challenge this, they don't know their program well enough. If you have questions, check the official literature.

8. Do you know others in 12-Step programs that have had to take powerful prescribed medications? How have they avoided falling into the trap of substance abuse?

_____

_____

_____

_____

9. In addition to 12-Step or other recovery programs focusing on addictions, you may find help from support groups specifically for chronic pain sufferers. These groups include local organizations, which you may be able to find through your local media (many newspapers publish lists of support groups of all kinds). You may also want to investigate the following online groups, which you can reach through their web sites (please keep in mind that as time passes, these sites may disappear and others appear—to get current info, we recommend using an Internet search engine such as Google.com).

   a. American Chronic Pain Association: www.theacpa.org

   b. Back Pain Support Group: www.backpainsupportgroup.com

   c. Chronic Pain Support Group: www.chronicpainsupport.org

   d. National Chronic Pain Outreach Association, Inc.: www.chronicpain.org

   e. Out of Pain: www.outofpain.com

10. Have you had any contact with any of these groups, either local or online? If so, please identify the groups and briefly write about your experiences with them. If not, please explore the web sites listed and talk with your therapist about what you learn.

_____

_____

_____

_____

11. Please describe the tools, methods, and resources you will use to cope with the combined challenges of addiction and chronic pain.

_____

_____

_____

_____

_____

_____

_____

Be sure to bring this handout back to your next session with your therapist, and be prepared to talk about your thoughts and feelings about the exercise.

ANGER AS A DRUG

GOALS OF THE EXERCISE

1. Maintain a program of recovery that is free of addiction and violent behavior.
2. Decrease the frequency of occurrence of angry thoughts, feelings, and behaviors.
3. Think positively in anger-producing situations.
4. Learn and implement stress-management skills to reduce stress and irritability.
5. Learn to self-monitor and shift to a thinking and problem-solving mode rather than a reactive mode when anger is triggered.
6. Shift from viewing anger as something beyond control to a view of anger, particularly rage, as a chosen way of coping that can be changed.

ADDITIONAL PROBLEMS FOR WHICH THIS EXERCISE MAY BE USEFUL

- Anger
- Oppositional Defiant Behavior

SUGGESTIONS FOR PROCESSING THIS EXERCISE WITH CLIENT

The "Anger as a Drug" activity may be especially useful with angry clients who have also engaged in non-substance-abusing addictive behaviors. It is suggested for use with clients who have some insight into their own feelings or are willing to be introspective. Follow-up can include videotherapy (see the book *Rent Two Films and Let's Talk in the Morning* by John W. Hesley and Jan G. Hesley, also published by John Wiley & Sons) or journaling about experiences using alternative behaviors to cope with feelings that trigger anger.

ANGER AS A DRUG

Does it seem strange to call anger a drug? We usually think of drugs as chemicals, like alcohol, cannabis, cocaine, and heroin. We talk about being addicted to a drug if we keep using it when the consequences are more bad than good and find it hard to quit. People also behave addictively with activities like gambling, sex, eating, spending, and work, and with some emotions. Addictive activities and emotions can cause as much trouble as any substance.

What do these things have in common? They can change the way we feel, quickly, on demand. Physically and emotionally, we can use them to block pain or to feel great. We can become addicted to anything that makes us feel good quickly and easily.

Anger can feel good. If we're anxious or depressed, we may feel weak, uneasy, and ashamed. When we get angry, we feel strong and sure of ourselves. Anger also makes us feel more alert, awake, and energetic. So we may use anger to cope with uncomfortable feelings. Fear, anxiety, or shame can trigger anger so fast we may not realize the first feeling was there.

Like other drugs, anger has negative consequences. It leads to destructive actions. It damages the immune system and raises the risk of cancer or heart disease. In this exercise, you'll look at your anger to see if you've used it as a drug and to find better ways to handle painful feelings.

1. When you've been very angry, in a rage, have you felt weak or strong? Uneasy or sure of yourself? How does anger feel to you?

   _____

   _____

2. Next think about a time when you got very angry. What happened just before that feeling?

   _____

   _____

3. When you think about what was going on before the anger, how did it make you feel? If your anger came up so fast that you didn't have time to be aware of other feelings, what painful emotions such as anxiety, fear, hurt, or shame would be natural in that situation?

_____

_____

_____

_____

4. Another characteristic of many drugs is a rebound effect when they wear off. You may have found that when the anger wore off painful emotions returned. What rebound effects have followed your anger?

_____

_____

_____

_____

5. Some powerful natural mood-lifting and pain-relieving chemicals are produced in the brain by cardiovascular exercise, by meditation, and by laughing hard. Please list some ways you'll try to feel happy and energetic or to cope with emotional pain without using anger or another drug.

_____

_____

_____

_____

6. The next time painful emotions start to trigger your rage, how can you redirect that reaction to something else that gives you better results? If other people can help, what can they do? List two people who can help and describe when and how you'll ask them to help you.

_____

_____

_____

_____

_____

_____

_____

Be sure to bring this handout back to your next session with your therapist, and be prepared to talk about your thoughts and feelings about the exercise.

RESPECT OR FEAR?

GOALS OF THE EXERCISE

1. Develop a program of recovery free of addictive patterns and dangerous/lethal behaviors.
2. Understand the difference between respect and fear.
3. Increase insight into the core motivations that lead to dangerous/lethal behaviors.
4. Recognize early signs of anger and use cognitive/behavioral techniques to control behavior.
5. Increase self-esteem and self-respect.

ADDITIONAL PROBLEMS FOR WHICH THIS EXERCISE MAY BE USEFUL

- Anger
- Antisocial Behavior
- Oppositional Defiant Behavior
- Partner Relational Conflicts

SUGGESTIONS FOR PROCESSING THIS EXERCISE WITH CLIENT

The "Respect or Fear?" activity is designed for the client who has exhibited dangerous behavior that appears to have the aim or effect of intimidating others as a frequent or primary way of relating to those others. Follow-up can include processing the exercise with the therapist or group, guided experimentation with behavioral changes suggested by the content of the exercise, and the assignments titled "Anger as a Drug" and "Is My Anger Due to Feeling Threatened?"

RESPECT OR FEAR?

Unless you're unusual you want people to respect you. The respect of others, especially those most important to us, means so much that people may risk their lives for it (e.g., a soldier who charges a machine gun rather than let his friends down). Seeking respect, many of us have done things that led to serious trouble, danger, or suffering. Wanting respect is healthy—how do we earn it without hurting ourselves or others? We'll start with a close look at the way we think about this issue.

1. First, please describe what the word *respect* means to you. Write down the first thoughts that come to mind about what it means to you, and how you feel about being respected by others.

   _____

   _____

2. Now do the same thing, except that we'd like you to think about what it means for you to respect others. Do you feel good about respecting others, and how would you describe it?

   _____

   _____

3. If you have different views of what it means to be respected and to give respect, you may be thinking of another feeling. What other emotions might fit your answers to questions 1 and 2?

   _____

   _____

4. You may be dealing with a common source of confusion, the fact that many of us have *respect* confused with *fear*. To begin, how would you describe the difference between respect and fear?

   _____

   _____

5. Respect can be described as follows. Please name some examples among people you know.

   a. When people respect someone, they trust that person, feel safe with him/her, and count on him/her to be dependable and treat people appropriately; they like being around him/her.

Names of examples: _____

_____

b. When we respect people, we approve of and admire their actions.

Names of examples: _____

_____

c. We look up to someone we respect and may see him/her as a role model.

Names of examples: _____

_____

6. When people respect someone, how do they behave toward him/her?

_____

_____

_____

_____

7. Now let's analyze what it means to fear other people. Note how this differs from respect. Again, please name some examples of the qualities described.

a. When people fear someone, they feel tense and unsafe around him/her; they are cautious and don't relax around that person, and may try to avoid being around him/her.

Names of examples: _____

_____

b. When a person is feared, others don't trust him/her to treat them appropriately or feel that he/she respects or cares about them.

Names of examples: _____

_____

c. If we fear a person, we may try to keep our children or others away from that person.

Names of examples: _____

_____

8. This leads to a question like the one we asked about respect. When people fear someone, how do they behave toward him/her?

_____

_____

_____

_____

9. If you would rather be respected than feared, you must consistently practice behaviors that earn respect and not fear. Please think of a way you can do each of these in your daily life.

   a. Being honest and dependable.

   How I can do this daily: _____

   _____

   b. Being kind, generous, and considerate.

   How I can do this daily: _____

   _____

   c. Thinking about other people's feelings and dignity and treating them with care.

   How I can do this daily: _____

   _____

   d. Controlling my words and actions even when I'm angry.

   How I can do this daily: _____

   _____

10. If you'd rather *not* be feared, here are things *not* to do—please list examples of actions you'll avoid. If you've been doing these things, these changes will greatly benefit your relationships.

    a. Being unpredictable, undependable, and possibly dangerous to rely on.

    Behavior to avoid: _____

    _____

    b. Being mean, selfish, thoughtless, or inconsiderate.

    Behavior to avoid: _____

    _____

    c. Not caring about other people's feelings.

    Behavior to avoid: _____

    _____

    d. Not controlling my feelings and actions when I'm angry.

    Behavior to avoid: _____

    _____

11. You may still be unsure whether you want to work for respect rather than fear. You may find yourself around dangerous people and think you need to be feared to be safe; you may not have grown up with relationships that weren't based on fear. Some points to consider:

    a. People who are feared are lonely. Your loved ones, friends, and others will be more willing to maintain close and supportive relationships if they respect you rather than fear you.

b. If your loved ones need help with a problem, they're much more likely to let you know if they trust you and aren't afraid of you.

c. Your children will probably follow your example in how they deal with people. They will have much happier lives if you teach them to be the kind of people others respect.

This exercise has guided you in thinking about differences between respect and fear and which you want. Don't be discouraged if you slip back into old patterns under stress. Make amends to anyone you've hurt, learn what lessons you can, and keep working on it. If you're active in a 12-Step program, use the Steps on this—they work. The programs of Adult Children of Alcoholics and Emotions Anonymous may be especially useful. Good luck!

BUILDING MY SUPPORT NETWORK

GOALS OF THE EXERCISE

1. Demonstrate increased interdependence and self-confidence through autonomous decision making, honest expression of feelings and ideas, and reduced fear of rejection.
2. Demonstrate healthy communication that is honest, open, and self-disclosing.
3. Identify and get help from supportive others at home, work, and in other settings.
4. Reduce feelings of alienation by learning about similarities to others.

ADDITIONAL PROBLEMS FOR WHICH THIS EXERCISE MAY BE USEFUL

*   Adult-Child-of-an-Alcoholic (ACOA) Traits
*   Chronic Pain
*   Depression
*   Grief/Loss Unresolved
*   Living Environment Deficiencies
*   Medical Issues
*   Opioid Dependence
*   Peer Group Negativity
*   Posttraumatic Stress Disorder (PTSD)
*   Relapse Proneness
*   Self-Care Deficits—Primary
*   Self-Care Deficits—Secondary
*   Social Anxiety
*   Substance Abuse/Dependence
*   Suicidal Ideation

SUGGESTIONS FOR PROCESSING THIS EXERCISE WITH CLIENT

The "Building My Support Network" activity is intended for clients who are socially and emotionally isolated, or who have formed unhealthy dependent relationships with other people. It works by guiding the client to see interdependence as normal and desirable and to reflect on the positive effects for both helper and "helpee." The exercise goes on to lead the client to make concrete plans to break out of isolation and seek help and support from a network of others in a healthy way.

BUILDING MY SUPPORT NETWORK

When people are actively abusing alcohol, other drugs, or addictive behaviors, they often isolate themselves. Reversing that trait is an important part of recovery. Most people who succeed in achieving long-term abstinence do so with the help of others, not alone.

1. When people come into a treatment program or therapy for an addiction, they may have great difficulty asking anyone for information or help. If this is true for you, why do you think this is difficult?

    _____

    _____

2. If you meet others who are new to a task in which you have knowledge and experience, how do you respond if they ask you for help or advice?

    _____

    _____

3. Do you see others in treatment or recovery getting help and support from other people in recovery, and do you think less of them when they admit they don't know something or ask someone for help? Why or why not?

    _____

    _____

4. What are some areas where you could use information, support, and feedback? Please list three areas that are difficult for you.

    _____

    _____

    _____

    _____

5. Who knows a lot about those areas? List some people you think might be helpful to you by name in each of the following categories.

Names	Categories
_____	Family members
_____	Friends
_____	Coworkers
_____	Support group members
_____	Mental health professionals
_____	Clergy members
_____	Medical professionals

6. Think about how you might ask each of these people for help and support in your recovery. You will probably want to communicate these things:

   a. What you are trying to accomplish to stay clean and sober and change your life.

   b. What goals you have set. These can be things like staying sober for a year, working the 12 Steps, finding six new activities to replace drinking and using, and so on.

   c. What problems you are having difficulty with right now.

   d. How you feel these people can help you achieve your goals and solve your problems (don't ask them to do it all for you, unless it's a special problem and that's their job).

   e. Why you chose them to ask for help.

7. When you have identified people who will help you work on your recovery, the next step is to establish a routine with each of them, because most of us are so busy that we fail to get around to things unless they are scheduled. For example, you might meet with a therapist at a set time each week; have family dinners on certain nights; call a friend at about the same time each weekend; go to a particular meeting daily or weekly; or have lunch with a sponsor regularly. For each of the people you named earlier, when will you meet or talk with them?

Name	When/Where/How I Will Meet or Talk with This Person
_____	_____
_____	_____
_____	_____
_____	_____
_____	_____
_____	_____

_____   _____
_____   _____
_____   _____

8. It can also be an important part of your recovery work to help others yourself, in whatever way you can. For example, you might volunteer a few hours a week to do some sort of service work as a volunteer. If you belong to a 12-Step group, you can volunteer for chores such as making coffee, setting up furniture, cleaning up after meetings, and so on. What service work will you include in your recovery program, and when and where will you do it?

Service Task	For Whom	Time	Place

Be sure to bring this handout back to your next session with your therapist, and be prepared to talk about your thoughts and feelings about the exercise.

HOW INDEPENDENT AM I?

GOALS OF THE EXERCISE

1. Demonstrate increased independence and self-confidence through autonomous decision making, honest expression of feelings and ideas, and reduced fear of rejection.
2. Gain understanding of what is a healthy and realistic degree of independence.
3. Analyze the client's own real areas of independence, potential independence, and need to depend on others to get his/her needs met.
4. Decrease the client's dependence on relationships while beginning to meet his/her own needs, build confidence, and practice assertiveness.

ADDITIONAL PROBLEMS FOR WHICH THIS EXERCISE MAY BE USEFUL

*   Living Environment Deficiency
*   Self-Care Deficits—Primary
*   Self-Care Deficits—Secondary

SUGGESTIONS FOR PROCESSING THIS EXERCISE WITH CLIENT

The "How Independent Am I?" activity is for clients with boundary issues and a pattern of being overly dependent on others. It guides clients in examining what an appropriate degree of independence looks like, and then in making an inventory of things that they do independently, things that could be done independently, and things for which they must go on depending on others. It concludes by guiding the client in the creation of a plan to increase autonomy. Follow-up can include keeping a journal and sharing outcomes with the therapist and treatment group.

HOW INDEPENDENT AM I?

What does independence mean to you, and how independent should you be? American culture tends to teach us unrealistic and unhealthy things about this subject. Men may have been taught that they should be able to handle any problem without help or emotional support. Women may have been taught that it is not feminine to be strong and they should depend on others to take care of them. Neither attitude makes sense. Human beings are interdependent—we all need to be somewhat able to solve our own problems, but also able to get help when something is too big for us, like overcoming an addiction. This exercise will help you figure out your own balance between independence and relying on others.

1. Do you feel you are: _____ too dependent on others   _____ too independent
    _____ about right?

2. List the first five things you can think of that you routinely do for yourself without anyone's help (e.g., paying bills, transportation, cooking, keeping appointments).

    _____

    _____

    _____

    _____

3. Now list the significant things you rely on others to help you with or to do for you.

    _____

    _____

    _____

    _____

4. Of the items you listed for question 3, which do you feel you will always need others to help you with?

    _____

    _____

5. If you did not list anything for either question 2 or question 3, what do you believe is at the root of this (e.g., a belief that you can't do anything, or must do everything, on your own; a lack of knowledge or resources; not trusting anyone; etc.)?

   _____

   _____

6. What things from question 3 do you feel you could and should do for yourself?

   _____

   _____

7. For the items you listed for question 6, what would it take for you to start doing these things for yourself?

   _____

   _____

8. Briefly describe a plan to start doing for yourself one item on your list from question 5.

   _____

   _____

   _____

   _____

9. After answering these questions and making the plan for question 7, has your answer to question 1 changed? _____ If so, how?

   _____

   _____

Be sure to bring this handout back to your next session with your therapist, and be prepared to talk about your thoughts and feelings about the exercise.

CORRECTING DISTORTED THINKING

GOALS OF THE EXERCISE

1. Decrease distorted thinking and increase positive self-talk.
2. Learn how addictive patterns are related to distorted perceptions and thinking.
3. Identify personal patterns of distorted perceptions that are related to addictive patterns.
4. Learn and use tools to identify and correct distorted thoughts and see situations more accurately.

ADDITIONAL PROBLEMS FOR WHICH THIS EXERCISE MAY BE USEFUL

*   Adult-Child-of-an-Alcoholic (ACOA) Traits
*   Anger
*   Antisocial Behavior
*   Anxiety
*   Borderline Traits
*   Dangerousness
*   Dependent Traits
*   Narcissistic Traits
*   Psychosis
*   Social Anxiety
*   Suicidal Ideation

SUGGESTIONS FOR PROCESSING THIS EXERCISE WITH CLIENT

The "Correcting Distorted Perceptions" activity is intended primarily for depressed clients, to address Beck's depressive triad of cognitive distortions (self, situation, and future), and others. It teaches the client about several common forms of cognitive distortion and guides him/her in seeking examples in his/her own life. It follows by offering strategies for overcoming these distortions and asks the client to test them and report the results. This exercise is suitable for individual or group use, in session or as homework. Follow-up could include an assignment to use the corrective strategies at least once a day, write about the results, and report outcomes back to the therapist or treatment group.

CORRECTING DISTORTED THINKING

Distorted thinking is a basic problem in depression, and in any addiction. We experience denial, in which we can't see or understand things that are obvious to other people. We minimize or exaggerate our problems or achievements. We misinterpret other people's words and actions, and we see ourselves as better or worse than we really are. To solve a problem, the first step must be to see it clearly. Even if we know where we want to go and have a map, we can't get started until we know where we are, and distorted perceptions make that impossible. This exercise will help you see how addictive problems distort our perceptions of ourselves, other people, and our situations, and give you strategies to overcome these distortions.

1. *Denial/minimization.* You don't see or remember your destructive behavior and its negative results, or you don't admit to yourself how serious they are. You think you may have missed work three or four times in the last two months when it's really 12 times. You blame arguments with your spouse or partner on him/her and don't take your share of the responsibility. You don't admit that medical, financial, or relationship problems may be linked to your drinking, drug use, gambling, or other compulsive behavior.

   Ways I see this in my life:

   _____

   _____

2. *All or nothing thinking.* You see things as completely good or bad, perfect or awful. Events are wonderful or disastrous; you feel like a genius or an idiot; nothing is just okay or average.

   Ways I see this in my life:

   _____

   _____

3. *Overgeneralization.* If one thing goes wrong, you feel it's a terrible day; if you make one mistake, you feel you *are* a mistake; you use the words "always" or "never" often.

   Ways I see this in my life:

   _____

   _____

4. *Negative focus*. You exaggerate the negative and overlook the good, seeing the thorns but not the roses. This feeds self-pity, which is an excuse to act out.

Ways I see this in my life:

_____

_____

5. *Predicting without facts*. You leap to conclusions about the future, usually negative. You put definite interpretations on events or actions that don't have clear meanings, such as thinking people are mad at you when they don't act happy, and you don't check to see whether your interpretations are right before you believe them.

Ways I see this in my life:

_____

_____

6. *Emotional reasoning*. You assume that your emotions or suspicions reflect the way things really are: "If I feel it, it must be true."

Ways I see this in my life:

_____

_____

7. *"Should" statements*. You guide your actions by what you think you should or shouldn't do, and beat yourself up with guilt and shame when you fail to meet those standards. You may do this to other people, getting angry and judgmental when they don't do what you think they should, even if you never told them what your expectations were.

Ways I see this in my life:

_____

_____

8. *Judgment and labeling*. You judge yourself and others instead of judging your actions or their actions. If you lose at something, you call yourself a loser. If others fail, you call them failures.

Ways I see this in my life:

_____

_____

9. *Taking things personally*. You see other people's actions as being aimed at you, and you feel responsible for things you don't control.

Ways I see this in my life:

_____

_____

10. Here's a strategy to correct distorted thinking: check it out with someone you trust. When you're upset about a situation, talk with your sponsor or someone else you trust who isn't emotionally involved. Tell them what happened. Tell only what you actually saw and heard, not what you believe others were thinking or feeling. Ask your sponsor or friend what he/she thinks, and share your thoughts and feelings. Ask him/her whether it seems you're making one of the mistakes above. Try this and describe what happens.

    _____

    _____

    _____

    _____

11. Here's another strategy. When you feel upset, take a piece of paper and draw five columns. In the first column, describe the situation or event. Use the next column to list your emotions (e.g., anger, fear, despair, worry, confusion, embarrassment, shame). Rate the strength of each emotion on a 10-point scale with 10 being the most intense. In column three, write down what you think about the situation. Now review the distortions described earlier. In the fourth column, write a non-distorted, reasonable replacement thought that is probably true for each distorted thought in column two. Think about this thought briefly. Then, in the last column, list your emotions after filling out column four, just as you did in column two. Have your emotions changed? How will you handle the situation differently than you would have based on the emotions and thoughts with which you started?

    _____

    _____

    _____

    _____

Be sure to bring this handout back to your next session with your therapist, and be prepared to talk about your thoughts and feelings about the exercise.

WHAT'S HAPPENING IN MY EARLY RECOVERY?

GOALS OF THE EXERCISE

1. Develop a program of recovery that includes healthy exercise, relaxation, and eating and sleeping habits.
2. Improve social skills and attend recovery groups regularly.
3. Normalize common stresses and changes newly recovering people experience.
4. Assess current experiences and learn more about feelings, thoughts, and events that may come up during the recovery process.
5. Identify benefits of continuing recovery.

ADDITIONAL PROBLEMS FOR WHICH THIS EXERCISE MAY BE USEFUL

*   Adult-Child-of-an-Alcoholic (ACOA) Traits
*   Borderline Traits

SUGGESTIONS FOR PROCESSING THIS EXERCISE WITH CLIENT

The purpose of the "What's Happening in My Early Recovery?" activity is to normalize the physically and emotionally uncomfortable changes many people experience in early recovery, to relieve anxiety, and to give the client confidence that things will get better if he/she perseveres. The exercise presents a list of common feelings, thoughts, and experiences in early recovery and asks the client to write about his/her experiences with each. This may be given as an individual or group assignment, to be followed by a discussion with the therapist or group, and to establish a baseline from which to track further change in the future.

WHAT'S HAPPENING IN MY EARLY RECOVERY?

Newly clean and sober people often experience some common patterns of events, thoughts, and feelings as they change to a healthier lifestyle. This exercise will help you see where you are in this process and understand that others are feeling the same things that you are.

1. Below is a list of common events people experience in early recovery. For each of the following, please write about whether this is happening or has happened to you. If it has, give an example.

    a. Feeling physical changes in my body:

    _____

    _____

    b. Feelings of hope and exhilaration:

    _____

    _____

    c. Feelings of letdown and fear:

    _____

    _____

    d. Frustration:

    _____

    _____

    e. Feeling more connected to other people:

    _____

    _____

    f. Loneliness:

    _____

    _____

    g. Feeling strange or out of place:

    _____

    _____

h. Cravings, urges, or thoughts or dreams of using/drinking:

_____

_____

i. Feeling doubtful or questioning myself, my spirituality, values, or abilities:

_____

_____

j. Mood swings:

_____

_____

2. The reason I decided to get clean and sober now is:

_____

_____

3. Which items from question 1 do you want to change or modify?

_____

_____

_____

_____

4. Now, an exercise in imagination: Picture yourself in the future, living free of any drug or harmful behavior. What alternative ways are you using in this future to cope with difficult situations and emotions? How does it feel to picture yourself living this way?

_____

_____

_____

_____

_____

_____

_____

_____

_____

_____

_____

Be sure to bring this handout back to your next session with your therapist, and be prepared to talk about your thoughts and feelings about the exercise.

CREATING A PRELIMINARY HEALTH PLAN

GOALS OF THE EXERCISE

1. Extinguish overeating, purging, use of laxatives, and/or excessive exercise or other compensatory behaviors.
2. Learn and demonstrate constructive strategies to cope with dysphoric moods.
3. Use support from others and decrease interpersonal isolation.
4. Determine what people and services will be involved in the treatment process.
5. Take greater responsibility for practicing positive health-related behaviors.

ADDITIONAL PROBLEMS FOR WHICH THIS EXERCISE MAY BE USEFUL

• None

SUGGESTIONS FOR PROCESSING THIS EXERCISE WITH THE CLIENT

The "Creating a Preliminary Health Plan" activity is suited for clients who could benefit from making changes to their current eating patterns or health maintenance behaviors. Also, it can be used with people whose eating-disordered behaviors are no longer providing the anesthetic effect or relief they once did and who are looking for ways to begin getting healthier. It may be useful to have the client create a time frame for completing the assignment's tasks (e.g., physicals, nutritionist/dietician consults) to allow him/her to have more awareness of control over important aspects of recovery. Depending on his/her financial situation and available resources, the client may need more assistance in accessing community-based resources.

CREATING A PRELIMINARY HEALTH PLAN

Recovery from eating disorders spells self-control, freedom from obsession with food and weight, and gaining the energy and ability to deal with people and situations without the distractions of weight and self-hate blocking the way. Ending the secrecy usually associated with eating disorders and building new relationships with food, oneself, and others are important steps in the recovery process. Successful recovery includes giving up eating-disordered and compensatory behavior, addressing other problems (e.g., mood disorders, addictive and/or compulsive behaviors, other psychiatric illnesses, suicidal or self-injurious behaviors), using positive coping techniques (e.g., good nutrition, exercise, support, management of relapse triggers), knowing what triggers eating-disordered behavior, correcting distorted thinking, and planning to deal with relapses.

This exercise will help you identify key issues for planning recovery and setting an initial plan that is both comprehensive and concrete. As you work in recovery, you will be able to use the same format to address new issues that come up in middle and later recovery stages.

1. People seek help for disordered eating for a variety of reasons—shame, disruption to their lives, the urgings of others, illness, etc. Why are you seeking help for this issue now?

   _____

   _____

2. Now that you've decided to get help, let's look at exactly what you're trying to change. How do you act out your eating disorder (e.g., vomiting, eating alone, skipping meals, binge eating, excessive exercise)? Include all behaviors related to your eating disorder.

   _____

   _____

   _____

   _____

3. What emotions do you feel before, during, or after these behaviors (e.g., guilt, fear, anger, shame, depression, anxiety)?

   _____

   _____

4. What thoughts support or help maintain your disordered eating patterns (e.g., "I'm too fat," "I need to be thinner," etc.)?

_____

_____

_____

_____

5. What situations or events trigger or cue you to engage in disordered eating (i.e., stress, conflict, social situations, holidays)?

_____

_____

_____

6. What medical issues do you need to address, either due to past eating patterns or to decrease your risk of returning to using eating or avoidance of eating to cope? If you don't know, when would you be willing to get a physical to check for problems?

_____

_____

_____

7. What are the other related issues you'll need to address (e.g., alcohol/other drug abuse, depression, anxiety, suicidal ideation/behavior) as part of your recovery?

_____

_____

_____

Let's begin putting it all together!

8. Which people can you rely on for support? These can include doctors, family, friends, counselors, spiritual advisors, etc.

_____

_____

_____

_____

9. What support groups are available in your community?

_____

_____

_____

_____

10. Please place your answers for questions 2 through 5 in the column labeled "Disordered Responses." Next, in the column labeled "Recovery Responses," list alternatives. Many people need assistance with the recovery boxes. If you do, ask for that help.

	Disordered Responses	Recovery Responses
Behaviors (Question 2)		
Emotions (Question 3)		
Thoughts (Question 4)		
Triggers (Question 5)		

Finally, please remember that recovery involves continually learning more ways to manage triggers and lapses. Keep thinking of options for dealing with feelings of being overwhelmed, uncomfortable, or stressed by relationships and/or social situations involving food, drink, and challenges to body image. You wrote down some ideas under question 5 in the table above. Keep adding to the list. Here are some strategies you may find useful.

- Attend events that you *want* to attend, not those that you feel you *should* attend.
- Use affirmations (e.g., *I see myself handling this situation positively*).
- Set aside quiet time during stressful periods (e.g., weddings, holidays).
- Plan and practice verbal responses to comments about your weight or eating.
- Hide your scale during high anxiety times or get rid of it all together.
- Rehearse comfortable ways to change the subject or exit an uncomfortable situation.
- Others:

_____

_____

Be sure to bring this handout back to your next session with your therapist, and be prepared to talk about your thoughts and feelings about the exercise.

EATING PATTERNS SELF-ASSESSMENT

GOALS OF THE EXERCISE

1. Increase awareness of disordered eating patterns and motivation to begin a recovery program.
2. Identify the relationship between eating-disordered behavior and addictive behavior.
3. Develop nutritious eating habits and healthy, realistic attitudes about body image and weight.
4. Replace negative, self-defeating thinking about food and body image with more realistic, self-enhancing self-talk.

ADDITIONAL PROBLEMS FOR WHICH THIS EXERCISE MAY BE USEFUL

- None

SUGGESTIONS FOR PROCESSING THIS EXERCISE WITH CLIENT

The "Eating Patterns Self-Assessment" activity is suited for clients who express frustration with others' view that their eating is problematic, who say everything is "under control," or who know their behavior is problematic but feel intense shame and guilt and may deny problems in an effort to maintain secrecy. Getting someone with an eating disorder into treatment can be difficult because they believe they need their eating-disordered behaviors either to cope with emotional distress or to maintain personal control. This exercise is appropriate at the outset of assessment or treatment to paint a concrete picture of what is problematic regarding eating patterns, thought processes, relationships with food, and coping styles and mechanisms. It can be used as a baseline to revisit later in treatment to assess progress. It is not an all-inclusive list of symptoms or behavioral characteristics, but a sampling of many observed in eating-disordered patients.

EATING PATTERNS SELF-ASSESSMENT

Often, people living addictive lifestyles have neglected their health in many ways. One of those ways may have been simple lack of attention to their diets. For others, the relationships they have had with food (e.g., how and what they have eaten, how and why they have focused on their weight) have affected their health for the worse. Eating disorders such as bulimia, anorexia, and binge eating are not simply about diet, food, and weight. They are more complex. Like other addictive behaviors, people use eating and the pursuit of perfect body shape as ways to handle stress, anxiety, and other difficult emotions. Like other addictive behaviors, these patterns become compulsive. This compulsiveness may lead to unusual eating rituals or rules which eventually take over their lives. Also, as with other addictive behaviors, people trying to overcome eating disorders must learn healthy ways to get their needs met, cope with difficult feelings, and develop new relationships with their obsessions in order to succeed.

As with anything, knowing that there is a problem and what the problem is comes before taking action to solve it. We need to know exactly what we're working against, and toward. This exercise will help you start the process of recovery.

1. Below is a list of behaviors associated with eating disorders. Please circle those that are parts of your experience. Completing this exercise may be difficult, particularly listing items that you may not have shared with anyone else. You will need to reflect on the items you selected and talk them over with your therapist and doctor. Remember that recovery is the goal, and any fear or shame you may feel about sharing this information is just part of the problem you are working to overcome.

    •   Dieting, restricting, fasting, or skipping meals

    •   Binge eating (episodes of rapidly eating large amounts of food coupled with fear that you will not be able to stop eating during each episode)

    •   Purging (use of self-induced vomiting, laxatives, diet pills, diuretics, and/or compulsive over-exercise to lose weight, maintain weight, or compensate for perceived overeating)

    •   Obsessively counting calories and/or fat grams

    •   Rituals around food such as cutting it into small pieces, arranging food in a particular way on the plate, or refusal to eat certain items

    •   Discomfort when eating around others

    •   Eating in secret or hoarding food

- Fear of inability to stop eating
- Constant preoccupation with food, appearance, weight, body shape, and/or body size
- Wearing layered or loose-fitting clothing to hide your body
- Chemical abuse or dependence
- Excessive activity, insomnia, and/or restlessness
- Fatigue
- Using fad diets and/or obsessing about "good" and "bad" food groups
- Isolation
- Suicidal feelings or suicide attempts
- Poor impulse control
- Self-injurious behavior
- Intense fear of becoming fat
- Perceiving yourself as overweight or feeling fat when thin
- Perfectionistic or overachieving behaviors
- Guilt after eating
- Irregular or absent menstruation
- Medical complications
- Avoiding eating when hungry/restricting food intake
- Feeling that others want you to eat more
- Low frustration tolerance
- Difficulty handling stress/anxiety
- Difficulty concentrating
- Irritability
- Problems with intimacy
- Difficulty identifying and expressing feelings
- Difficulty asking for help
- People-pleasing behaviors
- All-or-nothing thinking

2. Please review the list above and the items you've circled. What thoughts come to mind when you look at the items you've listed as fitting your experience? In assessing yourself with this information, what conclusions would you draw?

_____

_____

_____

_____

3. How have the items that you've marked led to negative consequences for you (e.g., medically, others' comments, negative feelings)?

    _____

    _____

    _____

    _____

4. What questions does completing this exercise bring to mind?

    _____

    _____

    _____

    _____

Be sure to bring this handout back to your next session with your therapist, and be prepared to talk about your thoughts and feelings about the exercise.

CREATING A FAMILY RITUAL

GOALS OF THE EXERCISE

1. Learn and demonstrate healthy communication and conflict management skills leading to greater harmony within the family and cessation of addictive behavior.
2. Forgive family members' past actions and begin a life of harmony with each family member.
3. Learn and use positive coping tactics and enjoyable/pleasurable activities with family members.
4. Reframe family conflict as an ordinary problem that has a solution.
5. Increase the number of positive interactions within the family.

ADDITIONAL PROBLEMS FOR WHICH THIS EXERCISE MAY BE USEFUL

• Parent-Child Relational Problems
• Partner Relational Conflicts

SUGGESTIONS FOR PROCESSING THIS EXERCISE WITH CLIENT

The "Creating a Family Ritual" activity is designed for clients who experience frequent negative interactions with family members or remain isolated/distant from their families and who want to have closer and more positive interactions. Processing of this assignment may include identifying ways that addictive behaviors have contributed to conflicts or emotional distance. It may be useful to have the client facilitate a family meeting to complete this assignment and practice other important recovery skills (e.g., negotiation, problem solving, communication, stress management, and accountability for behavior).

CREATING A FAMILY RITUAL

Many people in recovery have missed important events in their families' lives due to their addictive behaviors or the negative consequences of addictive lifestyles. When families are enmeshed or disconnected, conflict and misunderstanding occur more often, and resolution of either is difficult. When family members get busy, they sometimes forget how important they are to each other, so family time needs to be scheduled like other important events (e.g., sports practices, support group meetings, and medical appointments). The benefits of scheduling family events are continuity, predictability, meaningfulness, and more closeness and warmth.

The purpose of this exercise is to focus on healthy ways for family members to enjoy being together, to increase stability, to communicate better, and to solve problems together. The more positive interactions that a family has, the more supported its members feel. For you, the person in recovery, this helps you stay clean and sober.

1. Review all family members' schedules for mandatory commitments. Identify possible days and times when everyone is available. Write them here.

    _____

    _____

    _____

    _____

2. Together, make a list of activities that you could share. If you pick activities that everyone likes to do, it will probably be easier to get the whole family to participate. Write them here.

    _____

    _____

    _____

    _____

    _____

    _____

    _____

    _____

    _____

3. Decide whether you will develop a ritual for the whole family (e.g., eating dinner together, going to church together) or one ritual for you and the children and another for you and your significant other. Write your thoughts here.

    _____

    _____

    _____

    _____

4. Make a final decision about what the ritual will be, schedule when you will start the ritual, who will be involved, and how often.

    Activity: _____   Start Date: _____

    Participants: _____   Frequency: _____

    Remember: Make this activity a priority and commit to it. If you don't, other family members will follow your lead. Also, if you have never done this, your family will need time to adjust. You may want to start with a monthly or weekly ritual. As positive experiences increase, your family will become more enthusiastic.

5. How will you and the other members of your family handle arguments, complaints, or criticism in beginning this ritual?

    _____

    _____

    _____

    _____

6. What length of time will you practice your ritual and then check its success? (For a weekly ritual, you may want to give it more than a month before you evaluate. For less frequent family activities, you will need to allow more time.)

    _____

    _____

7. At evaluation time, what adjustments, if any, need to be made?

    _____

    _____

    _____

    _____

    Be sure to bring this handout with you to your next session with your therapist, and be prepared to discuss your thoughts and feelings about this exercise.

IDENTIFYING CONFLICT THEMES

GOALS OF THIS EXERCISE

1. Learn and demonstrate healthy communication and conflict management skills leading to increased harmony within the family and cessation of addictive behavior.
2. Implement healthy coping behaviors to deal with conflicts within the family.
3. Take responsibility for one's own part in conflict initiation and resolution.
4. Learn to identify conflict as healthy or unhealthy, and make decisions about how to resolve it.
5. Learn about conflict triggers to avoid unhealthy conflicts when possible.

ADDITIONAL PROBLEMS FOR WHICH THIS EXERCISE MAY BE USEFUL

- Anger
- Dangerousness/Lethality
- Occupational Problems
- Parent-Child Relational Problems
- Partner Relational Conflicts

SUGGESTIONS FOR PROCESSING THIS EXERCISE WITH THE CLIENT

The "Identifying Conflict Themes" activity is used to help the client assess patterns in conflicts (e.g., topics of conflict, times conflicts are likely to happen, and with whom). It guides the client in looking at initiation or maintenance of a conflict as something in which he/she has an active part, assisting him/her in taking active steps to resolve conflict in healthy ways. This exercise can be used in groups to role-play conflict situations the client has difficulty handling in positive ways.

IDENTIFYING CONFLICT THEMES

Conflict in families is inevitable. On one hand, resolving conflict in negative ways (e.g., ignoring, being physically or emotionally abusive, refusing to admit wrongs, blaming others, leaving) creates more problems and further isolates each person involved from the other(s). On the other hand, resolving conflict in positive ways helps family relationships grow stronger and more supportive. Positive conflict management requires us to ask ourselves what responsibility we have in initiating, maintaining, and resolving any conflict. This exercise asks you to start keeping a conflict journal to gather information about what conflict looks like in your family. Follow this format, and record the conflict in your home for two weeks.

- Date and time.
- Intensity of the conflict (1=very low to 10=very high).
- Situation.
- Who was present?
- My behavior during the conflict.
- What did I want to have happen?
- What was the outcome?

Review your conflict journal after two weeks and reflect on the following questions.

1. What did you notice about the conflicts in your family? Look for themes or patterns.

    _____

    _____

    _____

    _____

2. What times of the day were conflicts or arguments most likely to occur (e.g., upon waking, bedtime, after work/school)?

    _____

    _____

3. List any conflict situations that came up more than once.

    _____

    _____

4. What role(s) do you play in conflicts (e.g., instigator, victim, peacemaker, rescuer, defender, etc.)?

_____

_____

5. Write about any conflict with a positive outcome, including what was different about the situation (e.g., intensity low, got my way, everyone got to express themselves, no name calling, a compromise, etc.).

_____

_____

_____

_____

6. Do you tend to see arguments as right/wrong, win/lose? How do you think this affects conflict?

_____

_____

7. What difficulties did you notice as patterns in resolving conflicts?

_____

_____

_____

_____

8. What do you feel needs to change to reduce negative conflict in your family?

_____

_____

_____

_____

9. Do you tend to get into conflicts with some members of your family more often than others? If so, why do you think this is?

_____

_____

10. Discuss with a counselor or trusted support person ways they deal with conflict in their families and get positive results. Write about what you learned.

_____

_____

_____

_____

11. Write down one thing you can begin to work on in the next week to approach conflict in your family differently.

_____

_____

Be sure to bring this handout with you to your next therapy session, and be prepared to talk about your thoughts and feelings about this exercise.

UNDERSTANDING NONCHEMICAL ADDICTIONS

GOALS OF THE EXERCISE

1. Accept powerlessness over gambling and participate in a recovery program for compulsive behavior other than substance use.
2. Acquire the necessary skills to maintain long-term abstinence from compulsive behavior.
3. Gain an understanding of compulsive behaviors not involving use of alcohol or other drugs.
4. Reduce the risk of relapse by applying techniques that work for substance dependence to other addictive behaviors.
5. Avoid switching addictions to nonchemical behaviors that do not involve alcohol or other drugs but may be equally disruptive to daily life and relationships.

ADDITIONAL PROBLEMS FOR WHICH THIS EXERCISE MAY BE USEFUL

*   Relapse Proneness
*   Substance Abuse/Dependence
*   Treatment Resistance

SUGGESTIONS FOR PROCESSING THIS EXERCISE WITH CLIENT

The "Understanding Nonchemical Addictions" activity is designed for clients whose primary addiction is nonchemical (e.g., gambling, high-risk sex, workaholism, spending, etc.). It is also meant for recovering addicts and alcoholics at risk for switching addictions. Follow-up may include participation in appropriate 12-Step programs, keeping a journal to self-monitor for signs of nonchemical addictive behavior, and reporting back on insights and progress.

UNDERSTANDING NONCHEMICAL ADDICTIONS

Some people suffer from addictions that don't involve using alcohol or any other mind-altering drug. People in this situation can be just as addicted, just as unable to control their behavior, as any alcoholic or addict is unable to stop drinking or using. They can lose most of the same things—jobs, self-respect, money, relationships, and so on. Yet these people might never have taken a drug stronger than children's aspirin and never drunk anything stronger than root beer. Newly recovering alcoholics and addicts are at especially high risk for becoming addicted to other behaviors without realizing that it's happening. The goal of this assignment is to increase your awareness of this danger and suggest some tools you can use to avoid or overcome it.

1. What is the connection between substance abuse and nonchemical addictions? Nonchemical additions are also called compulsive behaviors. People do these things for the same reasons they use alcohol or other drugs—to make them feel better, to help them cope with a situation or solve a problem, or to impress others and gain social status. Can you think of a time when you started doing something to feel good, accomplish a task, or make an impression, and got so carried away you lost control and weren't able to stop when you had planned to? If so, please give an example.

    _____

    _____

2. What kinds of activities came to mind for you when this subject was introduced? Many people think first of compulsive gambling, and if you did, start your answer with that, then add whatever other activities you thought of.

    _____

    _____

3. If you know someone who has succeeded in recovering from a nonchemical addiction, do you understand how they did it? Did they use any of the same methods you may be using with alcohol or other drugs? If so, what are they?

    _____

    _____

4. If they are doing things that you aren't, how could you use some of their techniques either for the same problem they are working on or for other problems in your own life? What are they?

    _____

    _____

    _____

    _____

5. Some of the same methods we can use to overcome chemical dependence (e.g., participating in support groups, learning new coping skills, and finding replacement methods and activities for things we can't safely do any more) can also help us deal with compulsive behaviors outside the realm of drinking and drugging. This isn't a new idea. After all, as those who are involved with Alcoholics Anonymous or another 12-Step program soon learn, the idea is "to practice these principles in all our affairs." What drug and alcohol recovery tools might help you deal with your own nonchemical problems, and how would they help?

    _____

    _____

    _____

    _____

6. Have you also talked about this with people working with you on your substance issues? If so, what did they tell you?

    _____

    _____

    _____

    _____

7. If you are participating in a 12-Step recovery program, are you aware of the policies such programs have developed about addressing other issues in meetings? Some groups are much more open and accepting of a variety of topics than others. What do you believe your group's policy is about this?

    _____

    _____

8. Please describe methods and sources of support you'll use to cope with any addictive problem not involving alcohol or other drugs that you might have now or in the future.

    _____

    _____

    _____

Be sure to bring this handout back to your next session with your therapist, and be prepared to talk about your thoughts and feelings about the exercise.

WHAT PRICE AM I WILLING TO PAY?

GOALS OF THE EXERCISE

1. Lead the client to accept the fact that compulsive behavior is a problem and participate in a recovery program.
2. Lead the client to compare his/her stated values with the actions and experiences of an addictive lifestyle.
3. Challenge the client to establish his/her own measure for consequences that would convince him/her addictive behaviors have become an unacceptable problem.

ADDITIONAL PROBLEMS FOR WHICH THIS EXERCISE MAY BE USEFUL

- Antisocial Behavior
- Opioid Dependence
- Relapse Proneness
- Sexual Promiscuity
- Substance Abuse/Dependence
- Treatment Resistance

SUGGESTIONS FOR PROCESSING THIS EXERCISE WITH CLIENT

The "What Price Am I Willing to Pay?" activity is designed for clients who minimize the impact of addictive behavior. It challenges the client to decide what hitting bottom would mean to him/her and to consider what negative consequences he/she is willing to go through rather than quit. Follow-up can consist of discussing answers with the therapist or group, self-monitoring for ongoing negative consequences of addictive behaviors and discussion of their significance, and the activity titled "What Does Addiction Mean to Me?"

WHAT PRICE AM I WILLING TO PAY?

This assignment will help you clarify your own beliefs about which effects of addictive behaviors such as substance abuse, gambling, compulsive spending, or compulsive high-risk sexual behavior would be so unacceptable that you would have to avoid those effects at any cost, even if that meant permanently giving up those behaviors.

1. You may have heard someone say that for an alcoholic or addict to give up an addictive behavior, he/she has to hit bottom. What does hitting bottom mean to you?

   _____

   _____

2. While some people think hitting bottom means something as drastic as dying, being homeless, or going to prison, it may not mean that for others. The phrase means that some experience is unacceptable—we can't let it happen, or let it happen again, no matter what. Hitting bottom is different for each of us. Think about what it means to you and answer the following questions.

   a. Have you seen someone else experience a consequence of addictive behaviors that you could not tolerate in your own life, and if so, what was it?

      _____

      _____

   b. Have you ever promised yourself that you would give up a certain behavior if a certain thing happened because of it? If you have, what was the experience you told yourself you couldn't tolerate?

      _____

      _____

3. What negative consequences have you experienced in connection with your compulsive behavior? Check any of these that have happened to you, and circle any that you have experienced more than once and write the number of times.

   ☐ Spent more time or money than you meant to on the compulsive behavior

   ☐ Spent money on this behavior that you needed for something else

   ☐ Avoided an activity because it interfered with the behavior

   ☐ Compromised your values over the compulsive behavior

☐ Embarrassed or hurt your family

☐ Been asked to quit by loved ones

☐ Lied about the compulsive behavior

☐ Hidden it from family/friends

☐ Hoarded food/pornography/other things related to the behavior

☐ Been alienated from family/friends

☐ Been unfaithful to your partner because of it

☐ Been divorced/broke up because of it

☐ Lost time from work because of it

☐ Lost a job because of it

☐ Sold or traded possessions to get money for it

☐ Committed a crime while practicing the compulsive behavior

☐ Committed a crime to get money for compulsive behavior

☐ Been arrested, in jail, or in prison because of the compulsive behavior

☐ Traded sex for money for the compulsive behavior

☐ Considered/attempted suicide while practicing the compulsive behavior or due to its consequences

☐ Accidentally killed someone while practicing the compulsive behavior

☐ Intentionally killed someone while practicing the compulsive behavior

4. Now look back over question 3, which you just finished. Have you experienced any of the negative consequences you once said would be unacceptable to you (see question 2b)? If so, which ones? If there are others for you, please list them as well.

_____

_____

_____

_____

5. Picture yourself talking with a close friend, or perhaps a brother or sister, and having him/her tell you about experiencing the consequences you listed for question 5. Picture this person asking your advice about his/her addictive behavior. Would you be worried about this person—would you feel that this was such a serious problem that it would be best for the person to quit completely? If so, what advice would you give him/her?

_____

_____

_____

_____

6. Are there consequences listed in question 3 that you may have experienced once, but that would mean your behavior was out of control if they happened again? Which ones?

_____

_____

_____

_____

7. Are there consequences listed in question 3 which you have never experienced, which would signal to you that you had hit bottom and needed to quit permanently, and if so which ones?

_____

_____

_____

_____

8. Now go back to question 3, and list here any of these consequences you have experienced which you do not consider unpleasant or serious enough to lead you to quit.

_____

_____

_____

_____

9. Review the items you just listed for question 8. By saying that you have experienced these but do not feel they are bad enough to make you quit practicing addictive behaviors, you are saying that going without your addiction would be worse than those consequences. If you heard someone say the same thing about another addiction, what would you think about his/her behavior?

_____

_____

10. After working through this assignment, you may have a clearer idea of what hitting bottom would mean to you when it comes to addictive behaviors, and you may also have changed some of your thinking about the role such a behavior has played in your life.

   a. Please write about any change in your views on your own behavior.

   _____

   _____

   _____

   _____

b. What will you do if you experience one of the consequences that you said in question 7 would mean hitting bottom to you?

_____

_____

_____

_____

Be sure to bring this handout back to your next session with your therapist, and be prepared to talk about your thoughts and feelings about the exercise.

AM I HAVING DIFFICULTY LETTING GO?

GOALS OF THIS EXERCISE

1. Maintain a program of recovery free from addiction and unresolved grief.
2. Resolve feelings of anger, sadness, guilt, and/or abandonment surrounding a loss, and make plans for the future.
3. Accept a loss and increase social contact with others.
4. Develop and demonstrate coping skills by renewing old relationships and forming new ones.
5. Identify any areas in which the client will need additional assistance in achieving resolution.

ADDITIONAL PROBLEMS FOR WHICH THIS EXERCISE MAY BE USEFUL

- Adult-Child-of-an-Alcoholic (ACOA) Traits
- Borderline Traits
- Childhood Trauma
- Dependent Traits
- Posttraumatic Stress Disorder (PTSD)

SUGGESTIONS FOR PROCESSING THIS EXERCISE WITH THE CLIENT

The "Am I Having Difficulty Letting Go?" activity is designed for clients having trouble understanding their issues of unresolved grief or loss. It also can be useful with clients who are very aware that they have grief issues to resolve but don't know how to begin. The exercise can be tailored to address losses other than bereavement. It is important to examine the client's views about death, dying, and loss in general, as these are influenced by cultural factors. Follow-up can include processing the exercise with the therapist/group, designing and conducting a mourning and letting-go ritual, and the "Moving on with My Life" exercise. ***Note: You must intervene immediately and effectively if a client reports suicidal ideation, intent, or behavior.***

AM I HAVING DIFFICULTY LETTING GO?

Grief and sorrow can be related to the death of a loved one, the end of a relationship, the loss of a job, a catastrophic illness, a major financial loss, or any other serious personal setback. The loss may have been either expected or unexpected. For people coping with addictions, these losses might be related directly to their addictive behaviors and lifestyles, or unrelated. Sometimes these losses occur well into a person's recovery, and inability to cope with loss can increase the risk of relapsing into addictive behavior to deal with painful emotions. Additionally, losses that occurred while we were actively engaged in addictive behaviors may not be resolved for us and may act as relapse triggers in early, late, or middle recovery if healing does not occur. While very personal and painful, healthy resolution of loss requires and begins with assessing whether we have losses that are unresolved. This exercise will guide you through the process of reflecting on whether unresolved grief is a recovery or treatment issue for you and what your unresolved losses might be.

1. Below is a list of signs that may indicate that you are dealing with an unresolved loss (old or new). These are normal, not abnormal, reactions to loss. Please check all those that apply to you.

    ☐ Inability to stop talking about the loss

    ☐ Avoiding talking or thinking about certain subjects that remind you of the loss

    ☐ Replaying what you believe you should have done differently

    ☐ Feeling or believing that if you express any emotion about the loss, it will take over (e.g., feeling that if you start crying you won't be able to stop, or that if you express your anger you'll go out of control)

    ☐ Disbelief that the loss occurred

    ☐ Withdrawing from others or isolating

    ☐ Becoming overwhelmed and disorganized

    ☐ Having trouble sleeping or eating

    ☐ Feeling apathetic or numb

    ☐ Having difficulty concentrating

    ☐ Feeling guilty about the loss

    ☐ Feeling as if you're "falling apart"

☐ Feeling hopeless about the situation, or your feelings, ever changing

☐ Feeling a lack of control in other areas of your life

☐ Feeling betrayed

☐ Having suicidal thoughts *(If you are thinking about killing or hurting yourself, share this with your therapist immediately and ask for help to stay safe—these thoughts will pass if you do whatever it takes to avoid acting on them.)*

☐ Feeling anger and resentment

☐ Feeling dissatisfied with everything or everyone

☐ Feeling a lack of purpose

☐ Having a sense of failure or worthlessness

☐ Others:

_____

_____

2. What loss or losses do you believe are related to the signs you checked in question 1?

_____

_____

_____

_____

3. What methods of coping with these losses have worked for you? How did they help and how did they not help?

_____

_____

_____

_____

_____

_____

_____

4. What has been the most difficult aspect of thinking about letting go (e.g., do you feel you would be abandoning or betraying someone you lost if you let yourself heal)?

_____

_____

5. Please list any fears you may have about letting go.

   _____

   _____

   _____

   _____

6. On which item that you chose from the list above would you like to begin working first?

   _____

   _____

Be sure to bring this exercise back to your next session with your therapist, and be prepared to discuss your thoughts and feelings about the exercise.

MOVING ON WITH MY LIFE

GOALS OF THIS EXERCISE

1. Normalize the experience of grief.
2. Learn that grief can be addressed and resolved in a number of ways.
3. Resolve feelings of anger, sadness, guilt, and/or abandonment surrounding a loss and make plans for the future.
4. Accept a loss and obtain increased social support from others.
5. Develop and demonstrate coping skills by renewing old relationships and forming new ones.

ADDITIONAL PROBLEMS FOR WHICH THIS EXERCISE MAY BE USEFUL

- Childhood Trauma
- Posttraumatic Stress Disorder (PTSD)

SUGGESTIONS FOR PROCESSING THIS EXERCISE WITH THE CLIENT

The "Moving on with My Life" activity is suited for clients experiencing loss or losses. It offers suggestions for action to resolve grief and loss. Grief over a particular loss can be new or old. This activity asks the client to take an active role in determining how he/she will continue living his/her life and regain as much quality of life as possible in spite of the loss. It can be helpful to process family and cultural issues and identify barriers and resources specific to the client's situation. This exercise may be useful for skill training in individual and/or group settings—that is, the therapist would teach a skill in session, then have the client or group practice the new skill as homework for a set length of time and report the outcomes at a future session.

MOVING ON WITH MY LIFE

Many feelings and thoughts may be attached to loss. Grief is a normal and natural reaction to losing someone or something important; depending on how meaningful a loss is, the feelings related to it may vary from mild to very intense, and may be easy or difficult to resolve. Unresolved grief can keep us from participating in our own day-to-day lives. Part of recovery is learning to manage our feelings, both pleasant and painful, with positive skills and without addictive behaviors. Until we are willing to resolve any loss, it can remain a trigger for relapse. It is important to remember that recovery is about action, and just waiting for time to pass will not heal what's unresolved. Further, to recover from loss, we must expect to recover. It does not mean to push ourselves and try to force instant resolution, either; this can be just as dangerous. It is therapeutic and recovery-focused action over time that resolves grief and loss. We aren't taught these skills in school growing up. This exercise gives you a series of suggestions for resolving grief—it will give you alternatives to leaving a loss unresolved and avoiding dealing with it or staying stuck in grief. It will guide you through steps that others have found useful, so that you can generate your own personal plan for moving on with your life.

Exercises for Grief and Loss
Caution: If you become overwhelmed during this assignment, stop and take care of yourself. After you've calmed down, write in a journal about what is causing you difficulty so you can work with your therapist on moving past any especially painful parts of this process.

1. Please record in a journal or write in letter form all the messages or lessons you have been taught by, or that you've learned from, the loved one who has died or left, or the other person or part of your life that you've lost. This activity helps with feeling abandoned.

2. Give your pain a voice by recording or listing all the ways you feel the pain. This activity helps express and release some of your pain.

3. Write a letter to the person or other part of your life for which you are grieving, telling how you feel about what has happened and the ways in which the loss has affected your life. Be sure to include any questions that remain in your mind about this loss. Second, write a letter back to yourself from the person or part of your life you are grieving, answering your questions. You may want to do this exercise in two parts and with the help of your therapist.

4. Practice the following relaxation strategy of deep breathing to calm stress, sadness, anxiety, and pain: Breathe in, counting to 10, breathing from your diaphragm and not your chest (your belly will rise and fall rather than your chest). Exhale, counting to 10. Repeat 10 times. You can visualize yourself doing this in a relaxing setting.

5. Practice visualization to calm yourself. First, practice item 4 until you feel relaxed. Then picture yourself making whatever positive changes you want to make in your life. Think of who will be in your life, where you will be, and what you will be doing on a daily basis.

6. Spend time with understanding and supportive people. Find and join a bereavement support group and/or work with your sponsor. Reconnect with old, positive acquaintances.

7. Write positive, nurturing memories about your loved one or your previous experience. Grieving doesn't mean forgetting the good stuff.

8. Add a pet or a plant to your environment so you can take care of and nourish life.

9. Lean on spiritual beliefs or philosophies that give you comfort.

10. Remember how you've coped in positive ways with past losses. Write about how you did this and what you can do again to help you with a loss that remains unresolved.

My Moving on Plan

1. Using suggestions from above or others you have gathered on your own, please make a simple plan for how you will live your life dealing with the losses you have experienced.

   _____

   _____

   _____

   _____

2. What suggestions would you make to others who are either beginning to grieve a loss or are avoiding dealing with a loss?

   _____

   _____

   _____

   _____

3. What was the hardest part in completing this activity?

   _____

   _____

4.   What questions do you still have? What barriers?

   _____

   _____

   _____

   _____

5.   Sometimes we have thoughts that nothing can be done to resolve the loss or that
   we'll never feel better because the loss is too great. Please record any thoughts like
   this here so that you can check them out for accuracy with your therapist, a spiritual advisor, and/or someone else who has also experienced a loss but seems to be
   doing better.

   _____

   _____

   _____

   _____

   Be sure to bring this exercise with you to your next therapy appointment. This may
be an exercise that you will have to work on and then rework more than once as you
address each loss. Please write about and then discuss with your therapist any problems you encounter and your general feelings about this activity.

A DIFFERENT APPROACH

GOALS OF THIS EXERCISE

1. Maintain a program of recovery free from impulsive behavior and addiction.
2. Learn to stop, think, and plan before acting.
3. Learn self-observation skills to identify patterns of impulsive behavior.

ADDITIONAL PROBLEMS FOR WHICH THIS EXERCISE MAY BE USEFUL

- Attention Deficit Disorder, Inattentive Type (ADD)
- Attention Deficit/Hyperactivity Disorder (ADHD)
- Suicidal Ideation

SUGGESTIONS FOR PROCESSING THIS EXERCISE WITH CLIENT

The "A Different Approach" activity is designed for clients who would benefit from observing their own behavior, assessing it, and developing and implementing new behavioral approaches. It may be useful to work through a few of the exercises together in session and have the client practice alternative coping methods outside the session and record the results. You may or may not want to give the example provided until the client has worked through one successfully on his/her own. If a client gets stuck, you may show video clips of people acting impulsively (e.g., from TV programs or popular films) and walk through the steps with him/her regarding the characters in the clips. Many times the outcome of impulsive behavior is positive in the short-term, but the long-term consequences are negative. The goal is to get the client to improve his/her insight regarding achieving desired outcomes with fewer negative returns.

A DIFFERENT APPROACH

Impulsivity means having difficulty resisting urges or delaying behavior. Some people think of it as being impatient or not thinking things through. Acting impulsively can cause social, legal, academic, relationship, work-related, and other types of problems. It can lead to physical fights, addictive behavior, and alienation from others. Acting and reacting less impulsively is a skill that can be learned and used to avoid these painful consequences and to get the outcomes you desire. Acting less impulsively involves two components: First, it requires being able to observe your own behavior. Second, it involves developing self-management skills. This exercise will help you work through the steps of self-observation and find ways to get what you want without the painful consequences that often accompany acting without thinking first.

1. Choose a situation, recently or some time ago, in which you acted impulsively. You may want to select an event related to your addiction, since this is often connected with acting impulsively. Describe that event in the following format:

    a. What happened first?

    _____

    _____

    b. Then what?

    _____

    _____

    c. What next?

    _____

    _____

    d. Next, and so on to its conclusion?

    _____

    _____

    _____

    _____

2. Now assess your motivation for your behavior by asking yourself, "What did I want to have happen? What was the purpose of this behavior?"

    _____

    _____

3. Third, finish analyzing the consequences by asking yourself, "What were the outcomes or results of this behavior?" and "Were they what I wanted to happen?"

    _____

    _____

    _____

    _____

4. Assess alternatives. Ask yourself, "What else could I have done to get what I wanted?" List as many other options as you can think of.

    _____

    _____

    _____

    _____

5. Last, pick one alternative and identify five actions you will take to practice this alternative.

    _____

    _____

    _____

    _____

Be sure to bring this worksheet back to your next therapy session, and be prepared to discuss any questions you may have and to talk over your thoughts and feelings about this activity.

HANDLING CRISIS

GOALS OF THE EXERCISE

1. Maintain a program of recovery free from impulsive behavior and addiction.
2. Reduce the frequency of impulsive behavior and increase the frequency of behavior that is carefully thought out.
3. Gain confidence in ability to handle or prevent crises without addictive coping behaviors.
4. Create a written quick reference for use in a crisis.

ADDITIONAL PROBLEMS FOR WHICH THIS EXERCISE MAY BE USEFUL

- Anxiety
- Grief/Loss Unresolved
- Medical Issues
- Suicidal Ideation

SUGGESTIONS FOR PROCESSING THIS EXERCISE WITH CLIENT

The "Handling Crisis" activity is a relapse prevention tool for clients who feel that they might be unable to cope with some crisis without returning to addiction. It guides the client in anticipating crises that might occur and planning healthy responses for each. Follow-up can include sharing crisis management plans with the therapist, a treatment group, and sponsor; keeping a journal and reporting on preparations made; and keeping a journal and reporting back about crises that do occur and how the client copes with them. This assignment is useful in conjunction with the activities titled "Relapse Prevention Planning" and "Personal Recovery Planning."

HANDLING CRISIS

Dealing with unexpected, uncomfortable, and stressful events is a normal part of life; these things will occur throughout the recovery process and the rest of our lives. Some crises are preventable, and all crises can be managed without returning to addictive behaviors. For many people dealing with substance abuse issues or other addictive pattern, their addictions have played a key role in coping with crises, and in recovery a crisis can put them at risk to return to their old patterns. Crisis often evokes feelings of being overwhelmed by intolerable stress. Further, mood swings and emotionality often accompany the early recovery process, making any stressful situation more likely to feel like a crisis. This exercise will help you think ahead today to prevent and/or cope with crisis so that you have a completed quick-reference action plan.

1.   Often, a crisis is not a total surprise. Sometimes it builds over time, and there are signs that things are beginning to get overwhelming. What physical, emotional, and behavioral signs have you noticed in yourself in past situations that could tell you when a crisis was building?

     _____

     _____

2.   Please list three events that would be particularly distressing and overwhelming for you, and how you plan to cope with them if and when they happen.

     Event   **Plan**

     _____   _____

                                    _____

     _____   _____

                                    _____

     _____   _____

                                    _____

3. Often, situations that are easily manageable if we face them early become crises because we procrastinate and neglect doing things we know we will have to do sooner or later, such as leaving bills unpaid. Are there situations and feelings you are avoiding dealing with or other ways you are setting yourself up for crises? If so, what are they?

_____
_____
_____
_____

4. What steps can you take today to prevent crises from building up in your life?

_____
_____
_____
_____

5. Think of someone you know who handles crises well. How does that person do it—what methods and resources does he/she use?

_____
_____
_____
_____

Can you use some or all of the same methods? If so, which ones? If not, why not?

_____
_____
_____
_____

6. If you encounter a life event that is so unexpected, uncomfortable, or distressing that it is a crisis for you, what specific steps will you take to defuse the crisis? Include people you will contact and what help you can get from them, places you may go, and resources, skills, or information you will use.

   a. _____
   _____
   b. _____
   _____
   c. _____
   _____

d. _____

_____

e. _____

_____

f. _____

_____

g. _____

_____

h. _____

_____

Be sure to bring this handout back to your next therapy session, and be prepared to talk about your thoughts and feelings about the exercise.

HANDLING TOUGH SITUATIONS
IN A HEALTHY WAY

GOALS OF THIS EXERCISE

1. Maintain a program of recovery free from addiction and legal conflicts.
2. Accept responsibility for legal problems without blaming others
3. Learn to cope with the uncertainty that is associated with legal problems.
4. Identify nonaddictive coping strategies to deal with any outcome of legal problems.
5. Create a plan to cope with each possible legal outcome.
6. Decrease antisocial behaviors and increase prosocial behaviors.

ADDITIONAL PROBLEMS FOR WHICH THIS EXERCISE MAY BE USEFUL

•   Antisocial Behavior

SUGGESTIONS FOR PROCESSING THIS EXERCISE WITH THE CLIENT

The "Handling Tough Situations in a Healthy Way" activity is designed for the client who is having difficulty coping with current legal issues (pending or resolved) or legal issues that have been left unresolved. It can be used as an adjunct activity to basic problem-solving strategies or to a cost/benefit analysis.

HANDLING TOUGH SITUATIONS
IN A HEALTHY WAY

A big part of recovery from addictions and a healthy coping skill is taking responsibility for past and current behaviors. If you are working a 12-Step program, this is also part of your Step work. Handling legal problems without resorting to old negative coping patterns is a vital part of your recovery. Sometimes the outcomes of legal issues are not in our hands, and we must learn to deal with the possibility of serious consequences (e.g., prison time), without returning to addictive behaviors. Other times the consequences of legal situations are known—fines, child support/alimony, loss of a driver's license, and so on. Whether the outcome is known or unknown, you may feel anxiety, worry, depression, confusion, guilt, shame, fear, and a host of other emotions. Handling pending, current, or unresolved legal situations in healthy ways is possible by using new skills. The goal of this exercise is to help you look at the legal issues you face, explore your feelings about them, identify some techniques to help cope with those legal issues, and begin to plan to maintain your recovery no matter what happens.

1. List the legal charges you have pending, your known current legal issues, and the legal issues that have not been resolved.

   _____

   _____

   _____

   _____

2. What are the known consequences for the items you've listed in question 1 (e.g., jail, criminal record, stigma, court-ordered treatment, probation, parole, etc.)?

   _____

   _____

3. What are your worries and fears about your pending legal issues or the legal issues you have not resolved?

   _____

   _____

   _____

   _____

4. With whom could you consult to get more information and insight regarding what you are facing (e.g., probation, attorney, police, court official, etc.)?

_____

_____

5. For each legal issue that you have pending or unresolved, what would be the best and worst possible outcome? For all these outcomes, what is a strategy to deal with each?

Legal Issue	Best Outcome	Worst Outcome	Strategy
_____	_____	_____	_____
_____	_____	_____	_____
_____	_____	_____	_____
_____	_____	_____	_____

6. How can you begin to assume responsibility for your legal problems? Name one action you can take for each legal problem.

_____

_____

_____

_____

7. How does failing to address these unresolved legal issues put you at risk for relapse?

_____

_____

8. List five ways you can show you're taking responsibility for your life in spite of legal uncertainties.

_____

_____

_____

_____

9. Write a beginning plan for how you will cope with possible painful consequences of future legal problems without relapsing.

_____

_____

_____

_____

10. How would you benefit from living without the stress of legal problems?

_____

_____

_____

_____

11. Talk with people who've had legal problems and resolved them without returning to addictive behaviors. Ask them how they were able to do it and list three things they did that could work for you in dealing with your current legal issues.

_____

_____

_____

_____

Be sure to bring this handout to your next therapy session, and be prepared to discuss questions, thoughts, and feelings you may have had in completing it.

WHAT'S ADDICTION GOT TO DO WITH MY PROBLEMS?

GOALS OF THE EXERCISE

1. Maintain a program of recovery free from addiction and proactively address any legal conflicts resulting from past addictive behaviors.
2. Accept responsibility for legal problems without blaming others.
3. Identify the connections between legal problems experienced and addictive behaviors.
4. Identify thought patterns that created legal difficulties.
5. Understand the need to maintain abstinence from addiction and to remain free of negative consequences that include legal problems.
6. Decrease antisocial behaviors and increase prosocial behaviors.

ADDITIONAL PROBLEMS FOR WHICH THIS EXERCISE MAY BE USEFUL

- Antisocial Behavior
- Living Environment Deficiency
- Occupational Problems
- Substance-Induced Disorders
- Treatment Resistance

SUGGESTIONS FOR PROCESSING THIS EXERCISE WITH THE CLIENT

The "What's Addiction Got to Do with My Problems?" activity aims to help clients focus on the connections between addictive behavior and legal or other problems. It is useful, when clients assess the outcomes of their actions, to point out ripple effects (e.g., going to jail is a primary consequence, which in turn interferes with holding a job, which makes it harder to earn income needed for bills). This exercise is useful as a group activity—the group gives feedback and input. Follow-up may include "Analyzing Acting-Out Behavior" and "Relapse Prevention Planning."

WHAT'S ADDICTION GOT TO DO WITH MY PROBLEMS?

The consequences of addiction often include legal trouble. It's important to remember that legal difficulties (e.g., jail/prison, fines, probation) tend to cause problems in other areas including self-worth, relationships, work, and finances. It is also important to remember that taking responsibility for the decisions that led to illegal acts, and the acts themselves, is a necessary part of recovery. Neither is easy. Sometimes we want to blame people, circumstances, or our addictions rather than being accountable. We also may not want to admit that our illegal activities are related to our addictive behaviors. If we don't want to keep having legal problems, though, we have to do things differently. This exercise will help you look at your legal problems, the painful consequences you've experienced, the patterns that have led to your breaking the law or not accepting responsibility, and strategies for avoiding legal difficulties in recovery.

1. In the left-hand column below, list your legal history including past and current legal issues. In the right-hand column, list how the illegal behavior is related to addictive behavior. Keep in mind that the relationship may be direct (e.g., was high when stole a car or stole money from work to continue gambling) or indirect (e.g., stole money to pay bills which went unpaid due to gambling behavior).

    Legal Problems   **Relationship to Addiction**

    _____   _____
    _____   _____
    _____   _____
    _____   _____
    _____   _____

2. What are the consequences you've experienced as a result of legal difficulties? List all the types of unpleasant results you've suffered due to the legal problem(s) listed in question 1.

    _____
    _____

_____

_____

3. Have you tried to deny your actions or to blame something or someone else for your current or past legal problems? If so, how?

    _____

    _____

    _____

    _____

4. What thoughts helped you support or justify engaging in illegal activities?

    _____

    _____

    _____

    _____

5. How would continued addictive behavior complicate your current legal difficulties or those legal difficulties that remain unresolved?

    _____

    _____

    _____

    _____

6. Following is a sample list of prosocial behaviors. Please list specific ways you can practice each in recovery. For example, for _honesty,_ be more specific than "tell the truth"—describe how you'll be honest in a situation where you've been dishonest in the past.

Prosocial Behaviors	What I Will Do
Honesty	_____
Helping Others	_____
Reliability	_____
Consistency	_____
Dependability	_____
Acting responsibly	_____
Respecting rules even if I disagree with them	_____

7.   What do you foresee as the biggest obstacle in preventing future legal problems?

_____

_____

8.   List at least five strategies for meeting your social, emotional, and financial needs in recovery without criminal activity or addictive behavior.

_____

_____

_____

_____

   Be sure to bring this activity with you to your next therapy session, and be prepared to talk about any questions, thoughts, and feelings about the exercise.

ASSESSING MY NEEDS

GOALS OF THIS EXERCISE

1. Maintain a program of recovery free from addiction and the negative impact of a deficient living environment.
2. Understand the negative impact of the current environment on recovery from addiction.
3. Identify connections between living environment deficiencies and addictive life-styles.
4. Improve social, occupational, financial, and living situations sufficiently to increase the probability of successful recovery from addiction.
5. Prioritize needs for correcting environmental deficiencies and set goals to improve each.
6. Develop a peer group that is supportive of recovery.

ADDITIONAL PROBLEMS FOR WHICH THIS EXERCISE MAY BE USEFUL

- Medical Issues
- Self-Care Deficits—Primary
- Self-Care Deficits—Secondary

SUGGESTIONS FOR PROCESSING THIS EXERCISE WITH THE CLIENT

The "Assessing My Needs" activity encourages clients in early recovery to become more aware of their living environments and how those environments support or undermine their recovery, assess what they may need to change to reduce their risk of relapse, plan strategies for those changes, and get feedback. This exercise can be used as an individual or group activity. Follow-up with these clients could include sharing feedback received from program sponsors or others, tracking and reporting on progress on plans made, and other assignments such as "Personal Recovery Planning" and "Relapse Prevention Planning."

ASSESSING MY NEEDS

Addictive behavior and lifestyle may directly cause deficiencies in one's living environment. These can include limited support for recovery, social isolation, abuse or violence, financial problems, and/or inadequate food and shelter. Sometimes people are trying to work their recovery programs in environments that undermine abstinence and recovery. They work very hard to succeed with these factors holding them back, when other ways are less risky and difficult. A big step for many is asking for help before external stressors trigger a relapse. In this exercise you'll assess how your current environment may sabotage your recovery or cause other problems for you; decide what you want to work on first and then develop a plan to work on each unmet need.

1. What are the problems in your living environment in the following areas?
    Family life: _____

    _____

    Social: _____

    _____

    Occupational: _____

    _____

    Financial: _____

    _____

    Spiritual: _____

    _____

    Recovery support: _____

    _____

    Necessities of daily life (food, shelter, clothing, etc.): _____

    _____

2. List five ways your current living environment hinders your recovery efforts.

    _____

    _____

    _____

    _____

3. In what ways do your peers and family increase your risk of relapse (e.g., are they actively using, angry with you due to past behaviors, unsupportive of your recovery, etc.)?

    _____

    _____

4. What other problems do you experience in your current living environment (e.g., abuse, violence, etc.)?

    _____

    _____

5. Pick the three most important deficiencies in your environment to work on first.

    _____

    _____

    _____

    _____

6. What are five actions you can take to improve things in the areas you listed in question #5 as your most important deficiencies? The actions don't have to be dramatic—think of small steps. If you cannot think of five on your own, consult with your sponsor or someone in recovery or treatment you trust for other alternatives.

    _____

    _____

    _____

    _____

    _____

Be sure to bring this handout with you to your next therapy session, and be prepared to discuss your thoughts and feelings about the exercise with your therapist.

WHAT WOULD MY IDEAL LIFE LOOK LIKE?

GOALS OF THE EXERCISE

1. Maintain a program of recovery free from addiction and the negative impact of a deficient living environment.
2. Understand the negative impact of the current environment on recovery from addiction.
3. Develop a peer group that is supportive of recovery.
4. Clarify and prioritize life values and goals.
5. Increase awareness of the effects of addictive behavior on achieving values and goals.

ADDITIONAL PROBLEMS FOR WHICH THIS EXERCISE MAY BE USEFUL

- Suicidal Ideation
- Treatment Resistance

SUGGESTIONS FOR PROCESSING THIS EXERCISE WITH CLIENT

The "What Would My Ideal Life Look Like?" activity is written for clients who are having difficulty establishing concrete goals for life in recovery. Its approach is to guide the client in establishing what his/her ideal would be in each of several life domains, then determining the difference between the current situation and that ideal and what action is necessary to achieve the ideal. The exercise then leads the client in thinking about whether addictive behaviors will help or hinder him/her in achieving these ideals and challenges rationalizations, working to increase cognitive dissonance and break down denial and minimization. Follow-up could include establishing plans and timelines for some of the actions defined in this exercise and keeping a journal and sharing outcomes of those plans with the therapist and treatment group. *As this exercise is also recommended for clients experiencing suicidal ideation, it is critical to ask directly about urges or intent to harm self or others at each therapeutic contact, and take whatever therapeutic action is necessary to keep the client safe.*

WHAT WOULD MY IDEAL LIFE LOOK LIKE?

This assignment will help you identify the benefits of sobriety that mean the most to you personally. It will also help you set some goals above and beyond recovery and focus on what changes in your life would make you happiest.

1. Do you have a clear idea of what your ideal life would be like? Please think about this a moment, then fill in the following sections with short descriptions of your ideal life in each area.

    a. Where would you live? _____ _____

    b. What would your marital/family situation be? _____

    _____

    c. What would your work be? _____

    d. What would be your proudest achievements? _____

    e. What would your hobbies and leisure activities be? _____

    _____

    f. How would other people think of you? _____

    _____

2. Now, let's see what it would take to get from where you are today to where you want to be.

    a. Where would you live?

Situation Now	Ideal Situation	What Change Is Needed?
_____	_____	_____
_____	_____	_____

    b. What would your marital/family situation be?

Situation Now	Ideal Situation	What Change Is Needed?
_____	_____	_____
_____	_____	_____

c. What would your work be?

Situation Now	Ideal Situation	What Change Is Needed?

d. What would be your proudest achievements?

Situation Now	Ideal Situation	What Change Is Needed?

e. What would your hobbies and leisure activities be?

Situation Now	Ideal Situation	What Change Is Needed?

f. How would other people think of you?

Situation Now	Ideal Situation	What Change Is Needed?

3. Concentrating on the changes needed, please consider the impact of abusing alcohol or other drugs, or engaging in other addictive behavior, on your chances of making those changes.

	Addictive Behavior Will Help	Addictive Behavior Will Interfere	No Difference Either Way
a. Where you would live:			
b. Marital/family:			
c. Work:			
d. Hobbies/leisure:			
e. What others think:			
TOTAL:			

4. This time, let's look at the effects of being clean and sober.

		Sobriety Will Help	Sobriety Will Interfere	No Difference Either Way
a.	Where you would live:	_____	_____	_____
b.	Marital/family:	_____	_____	_____
c.	Work:	_____	_____	_____
d.	Hobbies/leisure:	_____	_____	_____
e.	What others think:	_____	_____	_____
	TOTAL:	_____	_____	_____

5. Some final questions:

   a. If drinking, using drugs, or other addictive behaviors will interfere with your chances of achieving your most cherished dreams, but you keep on practicing the addictive behaviors anyway, what conclusions do you draw from this?

   _____

   _____

   b. If someone you knew put an addictive behavior ahead of his/her dreams and ideals, what would you think it meant about his/her relationship with that behavior?

   _____

   _____

   c. If this is happening in your life, do the people who know you think you have a problem? _____ If they think you have a problem but you feel you don't, how do you explain this discrepancy?

   _____

   _____

Be sure to bring this handout back to your next therapy session, and be prepared to talk about your thoughts and feelings about the exercise.

COPING WITH ADDICTION AND MOOD DISORDERS OR BEREAVEMENT

GOALS OF THE EXERCISE

1. Maintain a program of recovery that is free of manic/hypomanic behavior and addiction.
2. Understand the relationship between manic/hypomanic states and addiction.
3. Understand the biopsychosocial aspects of manic/hypomanic states and addiction and accept the need for continued treatment, including medication.

ADDITIONAL PROBLEMS FOR WHICH THIS EXERCISE MAY BE USEFUL

- Depression
- Grief/Loss Unresolved
- Substance Abuse/Dependence
- Suicidal Ideation

SUGGESTIONS FOR PROCESSING THIS EXERCISE WITH CLIENT

The "Coping with Addiction and Mood Disorders or Bereavement" activity is meant for dually diagnosed clients suffering from depression, dysthymia, bipolar disorder, or cyclothymia, or for clients coping with both addiction and serious loss in their lives. It guides clients to awareness of the role of self-medication for emotional distress in their addictions and to exploration of healthier alternatives. Follow-up could include bibliotherapy related to the client's mood disorder(s), homework assignments to engage in healthy alternative activities identified through this exercise and then report back to the therapist and/or a treatment group on the results, and assignment to a treatment/support group for a mood disorder.

COPING WITH ADDICTION AND MOOD DISORDERS OR BEREAVEMENT

What is the connection between substance abuse or nonchemical addictions and emotional issues? Many people suffer from both addictive problems and mood disorders such as depression or bipolar disorder and are unable to overcome either problem alone. Others find that when they are faced with a death of someone close to them, a divorce, or some other painful loss, they feel they can't cope without blocking their pain with alcohol, another drug, or some addictive behavior. This exercise will help you identify and plan for these issues.

1. People who abuse alcohol or other drugs are more likely to suffer from depression or other mood disorders, because they can become depressed or manic as a result of their drinking or drug use. Please describe any ways you feel substance use has caused problems with your moods.

   _____

   _____

2. Sometimes the connection between addiction and moods works in the other direction: The mood problems come first, and when people do things to try to improve their mood or escape their emotional pain they end up getting hooked, either on a chemical or on a behavior such as gambling or high-risk sex. Please describe how your mood problems may have led you to behave addictively.

   _____

   _____

3. Many people believe that there are experiences they couldn't handle without drinking, using, or acting out in some way. If there are situations you think would make you relapse, what are they?

   _____

   _____

4. If you know people who have succeeded in overcoming both addiction and mood problems or great losses, could you use some of their methods? What did they do?

_____

_____

_____

_____

5. Many people find that some of the methods they use to overcome chemical dependence and other addictions, such as participating in recovery programs, learning new coping skills, and finding replacement activities, also help them with mood problems. What recovery tools might help you deal with mania, depression, other mood problems, or a serious loss?

_____

_____

6. On the other hand, there are some techniques used with mood disorders that may seem not to fit into recovery from substance abuse, such as the use of prescribed mood-altering medications.

   a. If you are under a doctor's instructions to take medications for a mood disorder, have you talked about your substance abuse issues with the doctor who prescribed the medications? If you have, what did the doctor tell you about this?

   _____

   _____

   _____

   _____

   b. If you haven't, what keeps you from sharing this information, and what is the potential risk to your recovery efforts of your keeping this secret?

   _____

   _____

7. If you are taking prescribed mood-altering medications, what might happen to you and your recovery from addiction to substances or behaviors if you stopped taking those medications?

_____

_____

8. Have you also talked about this with your sponsor or other people working with you on your addictive issues? If so, what did these people tell you?

_____

_____

9. If you are participating in a 12-Step recovery program, do you know about the policies those programs have developed about the use of prescribed mood-altering medications? What do you believe those programs have to say about this?

_____

_____

Actually, the official position of Alcoholics Anonymous is that if your doctor knows your history of addiction, is experienced in working with patients with addictions, and you are taking your medications exactly as prescribed, you are doing what you need to do to stay sober. Other programs have similar policies. If anyone in your 12-Step group challenges this, they don't know their own program. If you have questions, check the official literature.

10. Do you know others in your 12-Step program who take prescribed mood-altering medications? How do they avoid the trap of substance abuse?

_____

_____

_____

_____

11. Please describe the tools you will use to cope with the combined problems of substance abuse and mood disorders or grief and loss.

_____

_____

_____

_____

Be sure to bring this handout back to your next therapy session, and be prepared to talk about your thoughts and feelings about the exercise.

EARLY WARNING SIGNS OF MANIA/HYPOMANIA

GOALS OF THE EXERCISE

1. Maintain a program of recovery that is free of manic/hypomanic behavior and addiction.
2. Understand the importance of early detection and intervention in manic/hypomanic episodes.
3. Identify early warning signs of mania/hypomania, create plans to self-monitor for these early warning signs, and get help if they occur.

ADDITIONAL PROBLEMS FOR WHICH THIS EXERCISE MAY BE USEFUL

- Dangerousness/Lethality
- Impulsivity
- Relapse Proneness

SUGGESTIONS FOR PROCESSING THIS EXERCISE WITH CLIENT

The "Early Warning Signs of Mania/Hypomania" activity is useful for clients diagnosed with bipolar disorder/cyclothymia, or for those at risk for these disorders (e.g., clients diagnosed with depression, ADHD, or ADD) who may be having manic/hypomanic symptoms. *It is crucial to watch for these signs in patients starting antidepressant medications! These medications may trigger previously latent mania which can lead to behaviors that endanger the client or others.* This exercise identifies warning signs related to (1) thinking and emotions, and (2) observable behaviors. It offers a checklist for both types of warning signs and helps the client create a plan for routine self-monitoring and an action plan for use if he/she experiences one or more early warning sign(s) for longer than one day. Follow-up can include referral to support groups and reviewing outcomes with the therapist and group.

EARLY WARNING SIGNS OF MANIA/HYPOMANIA

Mania and hypomania can be hard to detect when they start, and they can feel so good we don't *want* to do anything about them. However, the time to get help is before they lead to actions with painful results. Another reason to catch a manic or hypomanic episode early: If it runs its course, it usually ends with a sudden plunge into dangerous depression. This exercise will help you spot the warning signs so you can get some help before your mania or hypomania leads you to grief. This problem can look different in different people, or in the same person at different times, so you probably won't experience all the early warning signs on this list. If you experience more than one for a day, call your therapist or physician and talk about what is going on.

1. Some of the early warning signs of mania or hypomania are changes in our *thoughts and emotions*. Be alert for any of the following in your own thinking—you may notice them yourself, or someone close to you may point them out. Use this handout as a checklist.

    _____ Suddenly improved mood when nothing in your life is significantly better

    _____ Suddenly feeling more irritable and impatient than usual

    _____ A sudden burst of creative thinking, with lots of new ideas

    _____ Feeling more restless than usual

    _____ Your mind jumping from one subject to another more than usual

    _____ Becoming more easily distracted by things going on around you

    _____ Suddenly feeling more impulses to do things that feel good (using alcohol/other drugs, sex, spending, etc.)

    _____ A sudden and significant increase in self-confidence and self-esteem

2. Other early warning signs show up as changes in our *behavior*. These are the ones other people may be more likely to see and comment on:

    _____ Suddenly feeling more energetic and needing less sleep than usual

    _____ Increased sex drive and sexual activity

    _____ Talking more/faster, interrupting more, having a harder time than usual being quiet

    _____ Snapping at people or blurting out things you wouldn't usually say

_____ Unusual bursts of physical activity such as walking, pacing, exercise, fidgeting

_____ Decreased appetite and eating less

_____ Increased impulsive behavior in areas like spending money

_____ Suddenly working harder and becoming more productive at work, school, or hobbies

3. Please describe your plan for monitoring the early warning signs listed above.

    _____

    _____

    _____

    _____

4. Please describe your plan of action if you see two or more of these things happening for longer than a day.

    _____

    _____

    _____

    _____

Be sure to bring this handout back to your next therapy session, and be prepared to talk about your thoughts and feelings about the exercise.

COPING WITH ADDICTION AND OTHER MEDICAL PROBLEMS

GOALS OF THE EXERCISE

1. Understand the relationship between medical issues and addiction.
2. Reduce the impact of medical problems on recovery and relapse potential.
3. Reduce the risk of relapse by using therapeutic strategies to cope with both addictive problems and other illnesses or injuries.
4. Participate in the medical management of physical health problems.

ADDITIONAL PROBLEMS FOR WHICH THIS EXERCISE MAY BE USEFUL

- Chronic Pain
- Opioid Dependence
- Substance Abuse/Dependence

SUGGESTIONS FOR PROCESSING THIS EXERCISE WITH CLIENT

The "Coping with Addiction and Other Medical Problems" activity is designed for clients with, as the title indicates, serious medical problems apart from their addictive issues. It addresses issues of self-medication as a factor in addiction, the possible causal role of addictive behaviors in having suffered injuries or illnesses, and coping strategies to achieve the best practicable quality of life for these clients. Follow-up could include referral to additional support groups that are focused on the specific medical problems that clients are experiencing. Another suggestion is bibliotherapy involving books such as *Kitchen Table Wisdom* by Rachel Naomi Remen, M.D., which addresses the interaction between spirituality and coping with physical trauma from the perspective of a therapist, physician, and client.

COPING WITH ADDICTION AND OTHER MEDICAL PROBLEMS

Some people suffer from both substance abuse problems and other medical problems that may be very serious, even life-threatening. If you are working to recover from both an addiction and another serious or painful medical problem, this assignment will help you use the same tools for both tasks where possible and guide you in coping with some special challenges in this situation.

1. What is the connection between addictions and other medical problems? Sometimes there is no connection. It's just coincidence or bad luck that the same person is both having a problem with alcohol, another drug, or an addictive behavior, and is also badly hurt or sick. However, it's also true that people who engage in addictive behaviors are much more likely than others to get hurt or sick, and people with debilitating injuries and illnesses are at higher-than-average risk to have problems with addictions. In some cases, people's injuries or illnesses are directly caused by their drinking, drug use, or other high-risk behavior (e.g., a heroin addict becoming infected with hepatitis C through a shared needle or a person contracting HIV from unsafe sex). This is not pointed out to blame anyone, but merely to acknowledge the role of cause and effect. Please describe any ways your addictive behavior caused or contributed to your becoming injured or ill.

    _____

    _____

2. Sometimes the connection between addiction and medical issues works in the other direction. The medical problems come first, and then people medicate themselves for their pain or other symptoms—then they end up with addictions as well as the injuries or diseases they started with. When people use drugs (street drugs or prescription medications) to try to control or cope with their medical symptoms, they may become dependent on those drugs. Please describe how your medical problems may have led you to addictive behaviors in the search for relief.

    _____

    _____

3. If you know other people who have succeeded in recovering from both addictions and serious medical problems at the same time, what did they do? How could you use some of their methods?

_____

_____

_____

_____

4. Many people find that some of the same methods they use to overcome chemical dependence can also help them to deal with injuries or diseases that sharply limit their physical capabilities. These can be things like participating in support groups, learning new coping skills, and finding replacement methods and activities for things they can't do any more. What drug and alcohol recovery tools might help you deal with your own medical problems, and how would they help?

_____

_____

_____

_____

5. On the other hand, there are some treatment approaches used for medical problems that may not seem to fit into recovery from substance abuse, such as the use of narcotics and other powerful drugs for pain management. If you are under a doctor's instructions to take medications for your sickness or injury, have you talked about your substance abuse issues with the doctor who prescribed the medications? If you have, what did the doctor tell you about this? If not, what keeps you from sharing this information, and what results might keeping this secret have for your recovery from both issues?

_____

_____

_____

_____

6. What might happen to you and your recovery if you stopped taking those medications, or didn't take them as prescribed?

_____

_____

7. Have you also talked about this with people working with you on your addictive issues? If so, what did these people tell you?

_____

_____

If you are participating in a 12-Step recovery program, are you aware of the policies such programs have developed about the use of prescribed medications? Actually, the official position of Alcoholics Anonymous is that if your doctor knows your history with addiction, is experienced working with people with addictions, and has prescribed medication with that knowledge, and you are taking it exactly as prescribed, you are doing what you need to do to stay sober. Other programs have similar policies. If anyone in your group challenges this, they don't know their program. If you have questions, check the official literature.

8. Do you know others in a 12-Step program who take powerful prescribed medications? How do they avoid the trap of substance abuse?

_____

_____

_____

_____

9. Please use this space to describe the tools, methods, and resources you will use to cope with the combined challenges of an addiction and a serious injury or illness. If you haven't thought this far ahead yet, what questions and concerns do you have about this issue?

_____

_____

_____

_____

_____

Be sure to bring this handout back to your next therapy session, and be prepared to talk about your thoughts and feelings about the exercise.

PHYSICAL AND EMOTIONAL SELF-CARE

GOALS OF THE EXERCISE

1. Understand the connections among medical issues, self-care, and addiction.
2. Reduce the impact of medical problems on recovery and relapse potential.
3. Understand and participate in the medical management of physical health problems.
4. Examine daily use of time and identify both healthy practices and areas for improvement.

ADDITIONAL PROBLEMS FOR WHICH THIS EXERCISE MAY BE USEFUL

- Borderline Traits
- Chronic Pain
- Depression
- Eating Disorders
- Posttraumatic Stress Disorder (PTSD)
- Relapse Proneness
- Self-Care Deficit—Primary

SUGGESTIONS FOR PROCESSING THIS EXERCISE WITH CLIENT

The "Physical and Emotional Self-Care" activity is for clients who neglect this area and are at greater risk of relapse as a result. It focuses the client's attention on self-care and guides him/her in assessment of needs, habits, and resources, then in creating a structured self-care plan. Follow-up activities can include keeping a self-care log, reporting back on progress, surveying role models on self-care practices, and the "Personal Recovery Planning" activity.

PHYSICAL AND EMOTIONAL SELF-CARE

There's a link between taking poor care of oneself and relapse. When we abuse substances or practice other addictions, we often neglect our needs, physical (nutrition, sleep, exercise) and emotional (safety, competence, sense of value, acceptance, sense of control). This exercise will help you see what you're doing now to take care of yourself and where you can improve.

1. What things are you doing today to take care of yourself physically?

   _____

   _____

2. Physical self-care tracking chart (please keep a record for the next 7 days).

Date	What I Planned to Do	What I Did	What Helped	What Got in the Way	How I Can Overcome in Future
Ex.	Take a walk	No exercise		Procrastinated	Do first thing in A.M.
Ex.	Eat balanced meal	Ate breakfast	Planned meal		
___	_____	_____	_____	_____	_____
___	_____	_____	_____	_____	_____
___	_____	_____	_____	_____	_____
___	_____	_____	_____	_____	_____
___	_____	_____	_____	_____	_____

3. Please answer these questions about your emotional self-care.

   a. What emotional needs do you have which are not being met today?

   _____

   _____

b. What emotional needs did you try to meet with addictive behaviors in the past?

_____

_____

c. What methods or resources now help you provide for your emotional needs?

_____

_____

d. What additional methods or resources do you need for emotional self-care, and where and how can you learn these methods or get these resources?

_____

_____

_____

_____

Be sure to bring this handout back to your next therapy session, and be prepared to talk about your thoughts and feelings about the exercise.

BEING GENUINELY UNSELFISH

GOALS OF THE EXERCISE

1. Develop a realistic sense of self without narcissistic grandiosity, exaggeration, or excessive sense of entitlement.
2. Understand the relationship between narcissistic traits and addiction.
3. Develop empathy for other people, particularly victims of the client's narcissism.
4. Identify a role model and examine that person's life for unselfish behavior.
5. Identify and plan ways to become less selfish in daily life.

ADDITIONAL PROBLEMS FOR WHICH THIS EXERCISE MAY BE USEFUL

- Antisocial Behavior
- Oppositional Defiant Behavior
- Peer Group Negativity

SUGGESTIONS FOR PROCESSING THIS EXERCISE WITH CLIENT

The "Becoming Genuinely Unselfish" activity targets self-centeredness, one of the core traits of both narcissism and addiction. It does so by examining the benefits of becoming unselfish in terms of enhanced self-esteem and improved relationships, guiding the client in identifying a role model and examining the ways that person models unselfish actions, and planning specific strategies to implement unselfish behavior in daily life. Follow-up could include videotherapy using films such as *Amelie* or others recommended in the book *Rent Two Films and Let's Talk in the Morning* by John W. Hesley and Jan G. Hesley, also published by John Wiley & Sons, as well as keeping a journal on the outcomes of actions planned in this exercise.

BEING GENUINELY UNSELFISH

What's the point of being unselfish? In a way, it seems like a contradiction to ask, "If I'm unselfish, what's in it for me?" However, it can be answered. For many reasons, being truly generous and unselfish helps people break addictive patterns and stay sober. This exercise will help you to decide whether this is worthwhile for you and why, and if you want to become a less selfish person, to find some ways to work on it.

1. Why do you think it might help you live a happier life to become more unselfish?

   _____

   _____

   _____

   _____

   Some answers might include: increased self-respect, better relationships with other people, less frustration and envy, and a better connection with your spiritual values. Do any of these make sense to you and sound like what you want? _____

2. Name a person that you trust, admire, would go to for help with a problem, and want to be like: _____. Now give some examples of ways this person is unselfish.

   _____

   _____

   Which of these things could you do?

   _____

   _____

3. The word "genuinely" in the title of this activity means that the unselfishness has to be real, not for show to impress people or manipulate them. The best way to do this is to practice doing at least one generous thing a day and not letting anyone else know about it. What are some generous things you could do each day without anyone else knowing, including the people you do them for?

   _____

   _____

_____

_____

4. How do you think it would change your thoughts and feelings about yourself to do this?

_____

_____

5. Do you think this would make a difference in your ability to live the life you want to live? If so, how?

_____

_____

6. Use this space to describe your plan to become more unselfish in your daily life.

_____

_____

_____

_____

_____

_____

_____

_____

_____

_____

_____

_____

Be sure to bring this handout back to your next therapy session, and be prepared to talk about your thoughts and feelings about the exercise.

GETTING OUT OF MYSELF

GOALS OF THE EXERCISE

1. Develop a realistic sense of self, without narcissistic grandiosity, exaggeration, or excessive sense of entitlement.
2. Understand the relationship between narcissistic traits and addiction.
3. Develop empathy for other people, particularly victims of the client's narcissism.
4. Identify past experiences of helping others and their positive effects.
5. List skills and abilities the client has that could be helpful to others.
6. Identify organizations or groups the client could help.
7. Create and carry out a plan to assist a group or organization of the client's choice.

ADDITIONAL PROBLEMS FOR WHICH THIS EXERCISE MAY BE USEFUL

- Antisocial Behavior
- Depression
- Relapse Proneness
- Suicidal Ideation

SUGGESTIONS FOR PROCESSING THIS EXERCISE WITH CLIENT

The "Getting Out of Myself" activity is based on the 12-Step principle of service work. One tenet of Alcoholics Anonymous and other 12-Step programs is that when nothing else works to help a person stay sober, intensive work to help another alcoholic/addict will succeed. This exercise presents this concept to the client, then guides him/her in identifying benefits of past experiences of helping others. It guides a client in identifying special skills or abilities the client has to offer, and groups he/she might want to assist, then creating a plan to engage in some form of formal or informal helping activity to reduce isolation, increase self-esteem, and get the client's emotional focus balanced between his/her own issues and those of others. This exercise is suitable for individual or group use, in session or as homework. Follow-up can include keeping a journal about ongoing experiences with helping activities, discussing outcomes of these activities, and videotherapy using films such as *Pay It Forward* or others recommended in the book *Rent Two Films and Let's Talk in the Morning* by John W. Hesley and Jan G. Hesley, also published by John Wiley & Sons.

GETTING OUT OF MYSELF

Human connections have a healing power that helps us with many problems. Whether we are struggling with addictive patterns, depression, anxiety, grief, or physical illness, emotional isolation is often one of the sources of our problems and always makes it worse. Connecting emotionally with others on a meaningful level, doing things that get our focus off our problems and pain, can help both us and them. It reduces our feelings of isolation, boosts our self-esteem, gives us the benefit of others' insights and experience, and lets us experience their interest in and regard for us. This exercise will guide you in connecting with other people in ways that will enhance your recovery.

1. Think back to a time when you got involved with helping others in some way—raising money for a good cause, helping friends move, helping a child do homework, helping an elderly person with day-to-day tasks. What prompted you to get involved? What did you do and how did you feel about it?

    _____

    _____

2. Are you involved with any helping activities now, including service work in a 12-Step program? _____ If so, what are you doing, what led you to get involved with this activity, and how does it contribute to your life today?

    _____

    _____

    _____

    _____

3. Use this space to list any special talents or training you have to offer (e.g., building or repairing things, teaching a skill, being multilingual, being artistic, being a good listener).

    _____

    _____

4. What organizations or groups of people could you volunteer to help out? If you don't know of any, how could you find them?

    _____

    _____

5. When during your typical day and week would you have some time to help others out?

    _____

    _____

6. Use this space to make a plan to contact a group that could use your help, find something you can do to help them, and make a schedule for this activity.

    _____

    _____

    _____

    _____

Be sure to bring this handout back to your next therapy session, and be prepared to talk about your thoughts and feelings about this exercise. After you've been acting on your plan and helping out in the way you've chosen for two weeks, talk with your therapist about how it's affecting your recovery.

AVOIDING NICOTINE RELAPSE TRIGGERS

GOALS OF THIS EXERCISE

1. Establish and maintain total abstinence from nicotine products while increasing knowledge of the addiction and the process of recovery.
2. Increase awareness of development and maintenance factors for nicotine dependence.
3. Develop personal reasons for working on a recovery plan for nicotine dependence.
4. Identify known triggers or cues for nicotine relapse and develop strategies to maintain abstinence from nicotine.

ADDITIONAL PROBLEM FOR WHICH THIS EXERCISE MAY BE USEFUL

*   Relapse Proneness

SUGGESTIONS FOR PROCESSING THIS EXERCISE WITH THE CLIENT

The "Avoiding Nicotine Relapse Triggers" activity is designed to help the client plan for successful cessation of nicotine use. It is designed to be the client's creation. This exercise works well for individual therapy but can also be useful for groups. The three larger tasks outlined in the exercise—getting prepared, setting up supports, and identifying alternative coping methods—can be broken into smaller segments and assigned over several sessions.

AVOIDING NICOTINE RELAPSE TRIGGERS

No one starts using nicotine because they want to get addicted. Some don't think about it at all. Most people who use nicotine become addicted very quickly, and many deny that they are addicted. While everyone's experience is unique, there are both common physical factors (i.e., physical pleasure and cravings, biological processes) as well as social (i.e., what your peers see as normal) and psychological factors (i.e., relaxation, pleasure) that play important roles in maintaining the addiction. Giving up nicotine requires taking a realistic look at this addiction and why it is so hard to quit. You can gain useful information from attempts you may have already made to quit (what worked, what didn't?). This exercise will help you to plan the three basic components of a successful smoking/chewing cessation plan: (1) increasing your motivation, (2) finding and using supports, and (3) learning and using alternative coping skills.

Preparation/Getting Ready

1. What signs of addiction do you see in your use of nicotine (e.g., increased use, multiple attempts to quit, tolerance, withdrawal, use despite negative consequences)?

   _____

   _____

   _____

   _____

2. What denial statements have you used to rationalize continuing to use (e.g., "Life is too stressful now," "I'm not mentally prepared to quit," "I'll probably fail if I try to quit now")?

   _____

   _____

   _____

   _____

   _____

   _____

   _____

   _____

3. What are the top three reasons you want to give up nicotine, as of today?

    _____

    _____

    _____

4. What family, social, and emotional challenges will you face in your recovery plan?

    _____

    _____

    _____

    _____

5. Part of a successful recovery plan is identifying your doubts and fears about quitting, to prevent setting yourself up for defeat even before you start. What are your doubts and fears about quitting?

    _____

    _____

    _____

    _____

6. If you've quit before, what worked for you, and what led to your return to using nicotine?

    _____

    _____

    _____

    _____

7. Please set a start date to begin carrying out your plan.

    _____

8. How and when will you tell your family, friends, and coworkers about your plan?

    _____

    _____

    _____

    _____

9. What triggers will you have to watch out for (e.g., certain people, places, situations, feelings, association with daily activities or habits, times of the day, events)?

_____

_____

_____

_____

10. Of these triggers, which can you avoid?

_____

_____

_____

_____

11. What is your plan to cope with the triggers you can't avoid?

_____

_____

_____

_____

_____

_____

_____

12. Which of the following methods or sources of support will you use to deal with triggers and cues to smoke or chew nicotine?

a. Self-help groups

b. Acupuncture

c. Medications

d. Hypnosis

e. Publications and reading material

f. Smoking cessation clinics and program

g. Online support

h. Other: _____

13. How will you handle cravings and other withdrawal symptoms? (Remember, they're temporary and will pass, and the longer you abstain, the more your withdrawal symptoms will lessen in both frequency and intensity.)

_____

_____

_____

_____

14. What rewards will you give yourself for abstinence, and when?

_____

_____

Be sure to bring this handout with you to your future therapy sessions, and be prepared to discuss your thoughts and feelings about this exercise as you begin your recovery plan.

USE OF AFFIRMATIONS FOR CHANGE

GOALS OF THE EXERCISE

1. Learn how self-talk influences self-image and moods.
2. Substitute positive self-talk for negative self-talk to improve self-perception and ability to cope with difficult situations.
3. Learn to use subject-specific affirmations to change behaviors and achieve or maintain abstinence from addictive patterns.

ADDITIONAL PROBLEMS FOR WHICH THIS EXERCISE MAY BE USEFUL

- Borderline Traits
- Chronic Pain
- Depression
- Gambling
- Posttraumatic Stress Disorder (PTSD)
- Relapse Proneness
- Substance Abuse/Dependence
- Substance Intoxication/Withdrawal

SUGGESTIONS FOR PROCESSING THIS EXERCISE WITH CLIENT

The "Use of Affirmations for Change" is an evidence-based activity, relying on two cognitive principles—first, that when people are presented with information repeatedly, they are likely to accept it as correct, altering their cognitions more each time they're exposed to it; and second, that when people find their actions in conflict with their cognitive construct, it causes cognitive dissonance, which is usually resolved in turn by modifying the behavior rather than the belief system, especially if the belief system continues to receive reinforcement. In this activity, this process is used with the aim of shifting the client's cognition and behavior. This exercise empowers the client, guiding him/her through a first use of a structured stress-management meditation, with the client choosing the goal and designing his/her own affirmation. Follow-up can include keeping a journal and reporting back to the therapist and treatment group, after 3–4 weeks, about changes experienced as a result of consistent daily use of affirmations.

USE OF AFFIRMATIONS FOR CHANGE

All of us have negative beliefs about ourselves because of painful experiences or things others have said to us. When we talk to ourselves, silently or aloud, what we say is often critical and negative. This negative self-talk molds our thoughts, feelings, and actions, and overcoming it takes work. However, when we do this work, we learn to think of ourselves in ways that are more balanced and realistic, that support our recovery efforts and feelings of self-worth, and that help us stop self-destructive behaviors. This exercise will help you identify the harmful messages you give yourself and increase your ability to replace them with positive self-statements.

1. We all talk to ourselves as we go through the day, either aloud or silently in our thoughts. Over the next week, pay attention to the things you say to yourself, about yourself, and your actions. Also, notice when anyone else gives you messages about yourself (e.g., your boss, coworkers, family members, or friends). When you find yourself saying negative things in your self-talk, or when others are negative or critical to you, note here what negative messages you repeat to yourself or hear from others most often. Then rewrite them to express your desired situation and self-view in reasonable but positive terms, and imagine what it would be like to hear these positive messages instead of the negative ones.

    Negative Self-Statements

    Positive Self-Statements (in Present Tense)

    Ex.: I can't stay sober.

    I like being clean and sober.

    Ex.: I'm weak and this is too hard.

    I am learning new skills and getting better.

    _____   _____

    _____   _____

    _____   _____

    _____   _____

    _____   _____

2. Think about a situation in your life that bothers you. List the negative self-statements that accompany this situation, then describe your feelings when you think about these negative statements. Create positive self-statements to replace those negative messages.

Situation: _____

_____

Negative Statement	Feelings	Positive Replacement Statement
_____	_____	_____
_____	_____	_____
_____	_____	_____
_____	_____	_____
_____	_____	_____

3. Does this situation seem more manageable to you after doing this? If so, what's different?

_____

_____

4. Here's a specific way to use positive self-statements to solve a problem or make a change in your life, such as quitting smoking. This is based on two scientific principles. The first is that if we hear something over and over, we start to believe it—why do you think negative messages have so much power? If this wasn't true, advertisers wouldn't spend their money to make sure we hear their messages again and again. The second principle is that when there is a mismatch between our actions and what we believe, it makes us uncomfortable and we tend to change our actions to match our beliefs. This activity is designed to change your beliefs about a situation in your life so your actions will change to match the new beliefs. Name a problem or change you'd like to make here.

_____

_____

5. Now think about the way you want things to be in this situation, and describe it in one short sentence. Use the present tense, and use only positive terms—talk about what will be going on, not what won't be. For our example of quitting smoking, the sentence could be something like "I love living smoke free and breathing fresh air." Write your sentence here.

_____

_____

6. Now create a mental picture to go with that sentence, which is called an affirmation. For our example, you might picture yourself strolling along a beach taking deep breaths of clean salty air, or in a pine forest in the mountains smelling the breeze through the trees. Close your eyes, picturing this mental scene as clearly as you can for 10 or 15 seconds, and repeat your affirmation in a quiet voice. What is this like for you—what feelings and thoughts come up?

    _____

    _____

7. Now write your affirmation on small cards or pieces of paper and put them where you will see them several times a day, in places like your bathroom mirror, your wallet or purse, your car's dashboard, your desk, your refrigerator, and so on. For one month, make it part of your routine to stop what you're doing ten times a day for 30 seconds to close your eyes, visualize your mental picture, and repeat your affirmation to yourself. You may even want to write it out before or after you do this. This will only take five minutes out of your day and you can do it almost anywhere, so it won't be hard to do. Don't try to use more than two affirmations in the same month, or they won't work very well.

8. Answer this question after a month of testing your affirmation: What changes do you see in your behavior from the time you started using this affirmation until now?

    _____

    _____

    _____

    _____

    Be sure to bring this handout back to your next therapy session, and be prepared to talk about your thoughts and feelings about the exercise.

BARRIERS AND SOLUTIONS

GOALS OF THIS EXERCISE

1. Understand the relationship between the stress of occupational problems and addiction.
2. Identify connections between occupational problems and addictive behaviors.
3. Identify behavioral changes that would help resolve occupational problems.
4. Identify self-defeating thoughts and feelings associated with current and past work problems.

ADDITIONAL PROBLEMS FOR WHICH THIS EXERCISE MAY BE USEFUL

- Borderline Traits
- Legal Difficulties

SUGGESTIONS FOR PROCESSING THIS EXERCISE WITH THE CLIENT

The "Barriers and Solutions" activity is suited for clients who have consistently had behavioral problems at work. For those unable to see the connection between addictive behavior and work problems, this exercise will increase insight. For the client who can recognize a relationship between addiction and work problems but needs help identifying relapse risk factors, it will increase awareness and help with solutions. The activity helps clients identify feelings, thoughts, and behaviors that may be barriers to employment and helps them generate possible solutions. Awareness and personal responsibility for behavior are two critical aspects of recovery. Addressing workplace problems and their relationship to addictive behaviors requires dealing with the associated denial, minimization, or blaming. For clients who are not currently employed, it can be used to assess past difficulties so that future employment is geared toward success.

BARRIERS AND SOLUTIONS

Occupational problems take many forms: problems with authority, conflict with coworkers, stressful work environments, addictive behavior being supported or encouraged, adjustment to retirement or lay-off, underemployment or unemployment due to poor performance or attendance problems, and so on. Cause-and-effect connections between addictions and problems at work run both ways. Addictive behavior may cause work problems, and the work environment may contribute to addiction and relapse. This exercise will help you identify relationships between difficulties you've had with work and with addictive behavior and create solutions.

1. List the last four jobs you've held and the problems you've had in each job.

    _____

    _____

    _____

    _____

    _____

    _____

    _____

    _____

2. List the common problems you have had in work environments in the left-hand column below. In the right-hand column, identify the connections to addictive behaviors or ways these problems are recovery issues. We've given you some examples.

Problem	**Relationship to Addiction/Recovery**
Fired for insubordination	*Conflicts with authority figures*
Lack of meaning to life after retirement	*Used addictive patterns to cope*
_____	_____
_____	_____
_____	_____
_____	_____

3. If you are currently working, how does your work environment place you at risk of relapse (e.g., coworker's addictions, job dissatisfaction, long work hours)?

_____
_____
_____
_____

4. What is your plan to address each of the risks you identified in question 3?

_____
_____
_____
_____

5. What discouraging thoughts or self-talk have you had, or do you have now, about your work situation (e.g., "I can't do this job," "I'll fail like the other times," "No one will hire me")?

_____
_____
_____
_____

6. For each negative thought you identified in question 5, write a more realistic, positive replacement thought (e.g., "I'm as capable as the other people doing this job, if they can do it so can I," "I've learned from past mistakes and am better prepared").

_____
_____
_____
_____

7. What behavior changes do you need to make to solve or avoid problems you've had at work in the past? It may help to ask others you trust to make suggestions.

_____
_____
_____
_____

8. What will you do this week to address one of the problems you listed for question 3?

_____
_____

9. What will you do during the next month to address this problem?

    _____

    _____

10. After completing questions 7, 8, and 9 and carrying out the actions you said you would take, record your evaluation of how you did.

    _____

    _____

    _____

    _____

    Please bring this handout with you to future therapy sessions and talk over any questions or ideas you have, and be prepared to talk about this assignment with your therapist or your group.

INTEREST AND SKILL SELF-ASSESSMENT

GOALS OF THE EXERCISE

1. Assess personal interests and abilities and identify ways to apply existing personal skills in work situations.
2. Understand the relationship between the stress of occupational problems and addiction.
3. Plan ways to bring more meaning and fulfillment to work life.
4. Identify relapse risk factors in work situations and plan strategies to cope with them.

ADDITIONAL PROBLEMS FOR WHICH THIS EXERCISE MAY BE USEFUL

*   Attention Deficit Disorder, Inattentive Type (ADD)
*   Attention Deficit/Hyperactivity Disorder (ADHD)
*   Depression
*   Spiritual Confusion

SUGGESTIONS FOR PROCESSING THIS EXERCISE WITH THE CLIENT

The "Interest and Skill Self-Assessment" activity is designed to help clients gain clarity about their interests and priorities and identify things they do well. It provides encouragement to explore new ways to apply interests and skills in occupational pursuits. It guides the client through an interest self-assessment, a skill self-assessment, a recovery assessment, and a plan for implementing changes to his/her existing work situation or choosing what he/she may pursue in the future. It may be helpful for clients to visualize what their work lives would look like if they were truly fulfilling their lives' purposes. If the new insights lead them to decide to change their existing jobs or careers, it might be useful to have them work with career counselors.

INTEREST AND SKILL SELF-ASSESSMENT

If you feel unsatisfied with your current occupation, feel the need to change your work environment because it puts your recovery at risk, or have lost your job, it may help to analyze where your interests lie and what you do well before you decide what to do about your future employment. When you do something you enjoy and are good at, it improves the quality of your life. It's also vital to choose work that supports your recovery, or at least doesn't interfere with it. This exercise will guide you in determining your own interests and skills.

Interests Self-Assessment

1. What parts of your current job are interesting and what parts do you like most? What do you dislike?

   _____

   _____

   _____

   _____

2. What work would you choose if you could do what you truly enjoyed? (For the purpose of this exercise, eliminate money/family/other responsibilities as factors.)

   _____

   _____

3. Of the items listed below, circle those that give your life the greatest meaning.

Satisfaction with family life	Friendship
Good health	Spiritual awareness
Helping others	Connection with others
Material success	Educational achievement
Creative outlet/expression	Personal growth/awareness
Career advancement	Integrity

   Other(s): _____

   _____

Skill Self-Assessment

4. What are your strongest skills or abilities?

     _____

     _____

5. Do you use them in your current job? If so, how?

     _____

     _____

6. If not, what work or employment would let you put those skills or qualities to good use?

     _____

     _____

7. What's the most important thing for you in choosing a profession and enjoying it (e.g., interest, skill, items in question 3)?

     _____

     _____

Recovery Assessment

8. In what ways is your recovery supported by your current work environment, coworkers, work schedule, etc.?

     _____

     _____

9. How does your current work environment put your recovery in jeopardy (e.g., addictive actions encouraged, stressful work conditions, prevents meeting/treatment attendance)?

     _____

     _____

Putting-It-All-Together Plan

10. In reviewing your answers to the above questions, what parts of your current work situation are acceptable, and what are the things that you would like to change?

     _____

     _____

     _____

     _____

11. What are you willing to do to work toward implementing these changes in:

    a. The next month? _____

          _____

    b. The next year? _____

          _____

Be sure to bring this handout to your future therapy sessions to discuss your questions, thoughts, and feelings with your therapist or group as you continue this activity.

MAKING CHANGE HAPPEN

GOALS OF THE EXERCISE

1. Acquire the necessary skills to maintain long-term recovery from all addictive behaviors.
2. Strengthen motivation for change by identifying areas of life impacted by drug use and alternatives available in recovery.

ADDITIONAL PROBLEMS FOR WHICH THIS EXERCISE MAY BE USEFUL

- Relapse Proneness
- Substance Abuse/Dependence

SUGGESTIONS FOR PROCESSING THIS EXERCISE WITH THE CLIENT

The "Making Change Happen" exercise can be used with a client who is entering treatment for the first or fifth time. It can be used with clients in any stage of recovery when motivation wanes, self-doubt increases, or relapse indicators surface. Before assigning this exercise, it is helpful to educate clients about the process of change and explain that the purpose of this activity is to help them see where they are in this process. Follow-up can include regular check-ins to track both progress and motivation and to continue educating the client about the process of change.

MAKING CHANGE HAPPEN

Drug use and abuse can begin for one reason and continue for others. The same is true of other, more positive changes we decide to make in our lives—sometimes the reasons we decide to enter treatment change along the way. People working to overcome addictions often go to professionals to find help and support for other changes too. This exercise will help you get a clear picture of where you've been, where you are, and where you want to go, as well as how to get there. After completing this exercise and following through by making some changes in your behavior, you and your therapist may find it useful to go on to the activity titled "A Working Recovery Plan," which will help you continue defining how to get where you want to go.

1. Please identify the psychological factors that led you to use alcohol, other drugs, or other addictive behaviors (e.g., self-medication for physical or emotional pain, avoidance of problems, attempts to feel normal, pleasure-seeking).

    _____

    _____

2. Please list the social, cultural, and environmental reasons for your engaging in addictive behaviors (e.g., family norms, family history, availability of the drugs, activities, acceptability of use among people close to you, use among your peer group).

    _____

    _____

3. Please describe the progression of your addiction from experimentation to dependence. If there are other addictions that you need to address in treatment along with substances, identify them in the space below.

    _____

    _____

4. Have you tried to quit this behavior or gone into treatment before? If so, what were the reasons you went back to practicing the behavior?

    _____

    _____

5. How have each of the following life areas been affected by your addictive behavior?

    a. Health: _____

    _____

    b. Social: _____

    _____

    c. Educational/career: _____

    _____

    d. Legal: _____

    _____

    e. Financial: _____

    _____

    f. Relationships/family: _____

    _____

    g. Spiritual: _____

    _____

    h. Self-image and self-esteem: _____

    _____

    i. Emotional: _____

    _____

6. As you think over your history, what factors do you think helped maintain your addiction?

    _____

    _____

7. What is your motivation for seeking treatment now?

    _____

    _____

    a. What increases your motivation? _____

    _____

    b. What challenges it? _____

    _____

    c. What fears do you have right now about your treatment and recovery?

    _____

    _____

8. If you've tried to quit before either on your own or through treatment, what have you learned from those attempts that can help you in treatment this time?

    _____

    _____

9. A medical evaluation is a significant part of successful long-term healing and recovery from substance abuse or dependence. How will you find and work with a doctor and/or other professionals for a complete physical exam and any necessary treatments and/or medications?

    _____

    _____

    a. What questions do you want to have answered for you?

        _____

        _____

    b. What fears might block you from following through with this?

        _____

        _____

10. For what other areas of your life do you need to include goals when you make a change plan (refer back to question 5)?

    _____

    _____

11. With your therapist, please identify a primary area of your life where you will begin working for change, and plan what behavioral steps you will take to address that area. Be sure to write about what factors will help increase your motivation and what potential barriers could decrease it.

    _____

    _____

    _____

    _____

    Be sure to bring this handout to your next therapy appointment, and be prepared to discuss your thoughts and feelings about the exercise.

A WORKING RECOVERY PLAN

GOALS OF THE EXERCISE

1. Establish a sustained recovery that is free of addictive behaviors.
2. Identify challenges to recovery and learn about recovery resources and supports available in the community.
3. Attend to successes and increase motivation to continue positive changes.

ADDITIONAL PROBLEMS FOR WHICH THIS EXERCISE MAY BE USEFUL

- Living Environment Deficiencies
- Relapse Proneness
- Self-Care Deficits—Primary
- Self-Care Deficits—Secondary
- Substance Abuse/Dependence
- Substance-Induced Disorders
- Substance Intoxication/Withdrawal
- Treatment Resistance

SUGGESTIONS FOR PROCESSING THIS EXERCISE WITH THE CLIENT

The "A Working Recovery Plan" exercise is designed to help the client maintain his/her motivation for healthy behavioral change by tracking successes and highlighting areas for ongoing work. It may be useful to divide major goals into smaller steps to model manageability and realistic goal-setting and to provide the experience of success sooner and more often.

A WORKING RECOVERY PLAN

The challenges of overcoming addiction are many, though the rewards of daily and long-term recovery are great. If you've completed the exercise "Making Change Happen," you have a good foundation for a recovery plan. This exercise will help you assess areas of your life that need ongoing work, acknowledge your successes, identify resources in your community to help you, and spell out what you will continue to address. By doing these things, you'll improve your chances of avoiding or coping with relapse triggers and succeeding in living a recovering life.

Here are five life areas involved in addictive lifestyles. Managing these will be crucial to your maintaining a recovering lifestyle. Please review each area and answer the questions that follow.

1. Managing life stress
    a. What are your main sources of stress?

    _____

    _____

    b. What positive tools or methods do you use to manage stress?

    _____

    _____

    c. What other tools would be important to learn to help you manage stress better, and where can you seek help in your community?

    _____

    _____

2. Breaking unhealthy connections with using associates and places
    a. What positive changes have you made in this area of your life?

    _____

    _____

    b. What is left to do and what makes it hard for you to do it?

    _____

    _____

c. What resources are available to you for help in this area?

_____

_____

3. Addressing emotional concerns (e.g., depression, anxiety, pain, anger, loneliness)
   a. Which emotions are challenges to your recovery?

   _____

   _____

   b. What have you done to make positive change in this area?

   _____

   _____

   c. What is left for you to do in this area, and what resources are available to you for help in this area?

   _____

   _____

4. Regaining physical health
   a. In what positive ways are you currently addressing your physical health?

   _____

   _____

   b. What steps have you taken related to medications (e.g., withdrawal and/or maintenance, learning which prescribed medications you can and cannot use, alternate methods of pain management)?

   _____

   _____

   c. What aspects of recovering physical health are most challenging for you, and what resources are available in your community to help you in this area?

   _____

   _____

   d. Outline a daily or weekly health regimen (e.g., sleeping and waking times, balanced meals, exercise, medical appointments, time for relaxation).

   _____

   _____

   _____

   _____

5. Overall stability and social, legal, family, occupational, and spiritual problems

For each item below, identify those that are challenges for you, the positive steps you have taken to begin working on them, what you have left to do in each area, and what resources are available in your community to assist you.

a. Family relationships and living situation:

_____

_____

b. Finding suitable work/educational pursuits:

_____

_____

c. Financial responsibilities:

_____

_____

d. Spiritual activities:

_____

_____

e. Enjoyable activities and social outlets:

_____

_____

f. Legal responsibilities:

_____

_____

Be sure to bring this handout to your next appointment with your therapist/case worker so that you can research resources and work on developing tools for the challenging areas. It is also a good idea for you to talk about your plans and community resources and options with your sponsor for additional feedback.

ANALYZING ACTING-OUT BEHAVIOR

GOALS OF THE EXERCISE

1. Decrease the frequency of occurrence of angry thoughts, feelings, and behaviors.
2. Gain insight into patterns of self-defeating impulsivity.
3. Learn to recognize patterns leading to impulsive self-sabotage and stop them before they lead to serious consequences.

ADDITIONAL PROBLEMS FOR WHICH THIS EXERCISE MAY BE USEFUL

*   Anger
*   Antisocial Behavior
*   Attention Deficit Disorder, Inattentive Type (ADD)
*   Attention Deficit/Hyperactivity Disorder (ADHD)
*   Dangerousness/Lethality
*   Eating Disorders
*   Impulsivity
*   Peer Group Negativity
*   Sexual Promiscuity

SUGGESTIONS FOR PROCESSING THIS EXERCISE WITH CLIENT

The "Analyzing Acting-Out Behavior" activity is written primarily for clients with patterns of impulsively engaging in oppositional, antisocial, and/or self-defeating behavior with little thought of the consequences. It works to heighten motivation for change by focusing the client on emotional discomfort at not understanding his/her own behavior, then offers a guided analysis of the client's mental and emotional state just before the behavior, the trigger, and the acting-out process. It further prompts the client to engage in self-monitoring in future acting-out situations. Finally, it asks the client to list strategies to stop impulsive acting-out upon realizing that "I'm doing it again." This is intended to break the cycle of unthinking acting out by triggering awareness of consequences and the fact that the behavior is self-defeating, and diverting the client to an alternative strategy he/she has chosen. This exercise is useful for individual or group homework and discussion. Follow-up can include reporting back to the therapist and group.

ANALYZING ACTING-OUT BEHAVIOR

Do you ever find, when someone asks you why you did something that led to trouble, that the only honest answer you can give is, "I don't know?" If so, you know that response doesn't satisfy people. You may have asked yourself the same question before they did; this is a common problem. Impulsive and self-destructive actions, ones we later regret, are part of addiction. It helps to get a better understanding of our own thoughts and feelings when we're doing those things, so we can cut the process short when it starts. This exercise will help you learn to do that.

1. Think about the last time you did something impulsive that got you into serious trouble or caused you to feel strong regrets later. Briefly describe that situation.

    _____

    _____

    _____

    _____

2. The next step is to carefully study what was going on inside you at the time. What were you thinking just before you took the action that caused you problems?

    _____

    _____

3. What emotions were you feeling?

    _____

    _____

4. If you know what triggered the impulse you acted on, what was that trigger?

    _____

    _____

5. One of the best ways to analyze this kind of impulsive behavior is to carefully teach someone else how to do it. This sounds strange to many people, but it often helps

people gain greater understanding. Please explain in detail how you act out impulsively, just as you did in the situation you're writing about. If you need extra paper, feel free to attach more pages.

_____

_____

_____

_____

_____

_____

_____

_____

_____

_____

_____

_____

6. It may be hard to explain your acting-out process well enough to teach someone else how to do it. If so, the next time you find yourself starting to act on a thought or feeling that's likely to result in problems, pay close attention to what you're thinking, feeling, and doing, and write it down here as soon as you can. Try to capture as clear a set of "instructions" as you can on how to do what you do when you act out.

_____

_____

_____

_____

_____

_____

_____

_____

_____

_____

_____

7. If you realize that you're starting to have the same kinds of thoughts and feelings that have led you to act self-destructively before, what can you do to stop the process before you get in trouble or end up doing something you later wish you hadn't? List at least five strategies.

_____

_____

_____

_____

_____

_____

_____

_____

Be sure to bring this handout back to your next therapy session, and be prepared to talk about your thoughts and feelings about the exercise.

LEARNING TO ASK INSTEAD OF DEMAND

GOALS OF THE EXERCISE

1. Understand the effects on others of different forms of expression.
2. Decrease the frequency of angry or overbearing thoughts, feelings, and behaviors.
3. Practice asking for things instead of demanding them in one relationship and evaluate the results.
4. Create a plan to adopt a respectful style of communication.

ADDITIONAL PROBLEMS FOR WHICH THIS EXERCISE MAY BE USEFUL

- Family Conflicts
- Narcissistic Traits
- Partner Relational Conflicts

SUGGESTIONS FOR PROCESSING THIS EXERCISE WITH CLIENT

The "Learning to Ask Instead of Demand" activity is designed for clients whose communication and relationship styles frequently present as disrespectful or inconsiderate. Its approach is to examine reasons people may resist asking for what they want rather than demanding it, then shift to a pragmatic view with the aim of finding the communication style that will work best. It then asks the client to select a relationship on which to conduct a one-week experiment with a more respectful style and report on the outcome. Follow-up for this exercise could include ongoing discussion with the therapist or treatment group on the impacts of communication styles in other relationships.

LEARNING TO ASK INSTEAD OF DEMAND

Why should you work at learning to ask people for what you want instead of demanding it? One reason is that it works better. Think about your own reactions. How do you feel when someone asks you for something, compared to when they demand it? Most of us prefer to be asked.

1. One reason many people try to tell others what to do, rather than requesting, is that they don't feel right asking, especially if they feel others owe them respect. They may feel they would look weak or unsure of themselves if they asked others for things rather than telling them what to do. This may be due to family or cultural traditions or other reasons. When you picture yourself asking someone to do something rather than telling them, what feelings does that bring up for you?

    _____

    _____

2. Actually, some of the most powerful people in history have also been very polite to those around them. Great leaders like Abraham Lincoln have been known for being respectful to everyone they talked with. Many people believe that truly strong people are more likely to be gentle, because they don't need to prove their strength by pushing people around. Think of a strong person who is polite and considerate to others. What is your general impression of that person?

    _____

    _____

3. No matter how we feel about being respectful, to get cooperation in a relationship we need to put ourselves in the other person's place. Think about situations where others order you around—parents or other family members, bosses, or teachers. Now imagine how you'd feel if they asked you politely rather than telling you what to do. What's the difference, based on how that person approached you?

    _____

    _____

4. There is always more than one message in everything we say—one message in our words, and also at least one message in the way we say it. When we ask others for things (e.g., simply saying "please" and "thank you," saying "Would you . . ."), we're also saying, *I respect your feelings and your dignity, you matter, and I care how you*

feel. When we leave these things out and simply order people around, the unspoken message is, *Your feelings and dignity aren't important. I don't have to be polite to you, and I don't care how you feel.* You may actually care very much about that other person's feelings, but that is the message you may be sending without meaning to.

It might be useful to test this. If you have a relationship in which you're used to simply telling the other person what to do, why not try switching the way you do things for a week, asking this person for what you want instead of demanding it? You might tell them you're doing this experiment. You can explain that you're practicing a new way of communication to show that they're important to you, and that you're going to try asking for things instead of demanding them. You may slip into the old way during the week. Habits are hard to break. You can *ask* them to remind you, and they can do that by *asking* you to rephrase what you've said. How does it feel to imagine doing this?

_____

_____

5. After trying this experiment for one week, please describe the results here.

_____

_____

6. If you feel this experiment was worthwhile, please use this space to describe a plan to practice this more respectful approach to dealing with people in all your relationships. What would some of the challenges be? Some of the rewards?

_____

_____

_____

_____

Be sure to bring this handout back to your next therapy session, and be prepared to talk about your thoughts and feelings about the exercise.

AM I TEACHING MY CHILDREN ADDICTIVE PATTERNS?

GOALS OF THE EXERCISE

1. Understand the relationship between addictive behavior and parent–child conflicts.
2. Understand how parental behaviors contribute to multigenerational cycles of addiction.
3. Improve parenting skills by learning to role model healthy and nonaddictive behaviors.

ADDITIONAL PROBLEMS FOR WHICH THIS EXERCISE MAY BE USEFUL

*   Adult-Child-of-an-Alcoholic (ACOA) Traits
*   Childhood Trauma
*   Family Conflicts
*   Treatment Resistance

SUGGESTIONS FOR PROCESSING THIS EXERCISE WITH CLIENT

The "Am I Teaching My Children Addictive Patterns?" activity is intended for clients at risk of transmitting addictive behavior patterns to their children. It aims to increase motivation for recovery by helping clients see how these behaviors increase the risk of the next generation falling into similar patterns. It lists patterns of addictive thinking and behavior and asks clients to provide examples and then think of ways to model healthy alternatives. This activity is suitable for use as an individual or group exercise, in session or as homework. Follow-up can include tracking strategies for change identified in the exercise, as well as videotherapy with films such as *Riding In Cars With Boys* or others recommended in the book *Rent Two Films and Let's Talk in the Morning* by John W. Hesley and Jan G. Hesley, also published by John Wiley & Sons.

AM I TEACHING MY CHILDREN
ADDICTIVE PATTERNS?

For just about all parents, one of our most cherished hopes is to give our children good childhood experiences. Many of us who grew up in families with problems promised ourselves we'd do better than our parents were able to do. One of the worst things about addictive patterns is that they, with their complications, tend to be passed on to our children. Think back on your own family history. How many generations back do the patterns go? Do you suppose the generations before you felt the same way, not wanting to pass the problems on to their children? Why did it happen anyway? It seems simply wanting to do better isn't enough.

First, we can't teach what we haven't had the chance to learn. Second, it may not be obvious that these patterns of thinking, feeling, and behavior are connected with addiction, so we may be setting our children up to repeat our problems without knowing we're doing it. In this exercise we'll look at attitudes and habits of thought that seem to be built into addictive lifestyles, so you can work to break the generational cycle. Please take a look at these patterns, list ways you may have been role-modeling them for your children, and decide what you will do to change each one.

1. *Dishonesty*. Lying to ourselves and others, stealing, putting on a front, and mind games (e.g., denial, blaming, rationalizing, focusing on looking good over inner qualities).

   Ways I've modeled or taught dishonesty to my children: _____

   _____

   Ways I'll model and teach honesty: _____

   _____

2. *Self-centeredness and using people.* Putting our own wants ahead of the well-being and feelings of others; manipulation, controlling, and objectifying others. This includes being careless about hurting other people; not trying to see things from the other person's point of view; treating others as tools by conning, bullying, "kissing up," deliberate button-pushing, etc.

   Ways I've modeled or taught self-centeredness and using people to my children:

   _____

   _____

Ways I'll model and teach consideration and respect for others: _____
_____

3. *All or nothing thinking.* Seeing ourselves, others, and situations in over-simplified extremes—perfectionism, calling ourselves or others stupid or bad for normal mistakes, feeling we are either better or worse than everyone else, over-dramatizing normal problems into disasters.

   Ways I've modeled or taught all or nothing thinking to my children: _____
   _____

   Ways I'll model and teach realistic, "shades-of-gray" thinking: _____
   _____

4. *Doing things to excess.* Going overboard with using, drinking, eating, spending, work, greed, or any activity, often leading to painful consequences.

   Ways I've modeled or taught going to excess to my children: _____
   _____

   Ways I'll model and teach moderation: _____
   _____

5. *Impulsiveness.* Lack of self-control, not enough attention to the consequences of our actions.

   Ways I've modeled or taught impulsiveness to my children: _____
   _____

   Ways I'll model and teach maturity and self-control: _____
   _____

6. *Impatience and unrealistic expectations.* Expecting instant gratification—intolerance for frustration or delays; wishful thinking, perfectionism.

   Ways I've modeled or taught impatience to my children: _____
   _____

   Ways I'll model and teach patience: _____
   _____

7. *Isolation from others.* Lack of trust, poor communication, loneliness, judging ourselves by different standards (usually harsher) than we apply to everyone else, refusal to ask for help.

   Ways I've modeled or taught isolation to my children: _____
   _____

   Ways I'll model and teach connection to others: _____
   _____

8. *Shame.* Low self-esteem, feeling that we are defective/stupid/ugly/crazy/bad, feeling that if we fail at something or do bad things we're bad people.

    Ways I've modeled or taught shame to my children: _____

    _____

    Ways I'll model and teach self-respect: _____

    _____

Be sure to bring this handout back to your next therapy session, and be prepared to talk about your thoughts and feelings about the exercise.

WHAT DO I WANT FOR MY CHILDREN?

GOALS OF THE EXERCISE

1. Identify impacts of the client's addictive behaviors on his/her children.
2. Compare client's childhood experiences to those he/she is passing on to the next generation.
3. Decrease parent–child conflict and increase mutually supportive interaction.

ADDITIONAL PROBLEMS FOR WHICH THIS EXERCISE MAY BE USEFUL

*   Adult-Child-of-an-Alcoholic (ACOA) Traits
*   Anger
*   Childhood Trauma
*   Family Conflicts
*   Impulsivity
*   Substance Abuse/Dependence

SUGGESTIONS FOR PROCESSING THIS EXERCISE WITH CLIENT

The "What Do I Want for My Children?" activity is aimed at clients whose children are adversely affected by the clients' addictive patterns. It aims to refresh and reinforce the client's ideals as a parent and increase cognitive dissonance between those ideals and addictive behavior. Follow-up can include bibliotherapy with books such as *My Daddy Was A Pistol and I'm A Son of a Gun* by Lewis Grizzard and videotherapy using films such as *When A Man Loves A Woman*, *The Great Santini*, or others as recommended in the book *Rent Two Films and Let's Talk in the Morning* by John W. Hesley and Jan G. Hesley, also published by John Wiley & Sons.

WHAT DO I WANT FOR MY CHILDREN?

This assignment will help you strengthen your motivation for recovery by focusing on how your actions affect your children's lives, both positively and negatively.

1. Think back to your childhood. All of us looked at some of the things our parents (or whoever raised us) did and told ourselves, "I want to do the same thing with my children someday." All of us also looked at some of their actions and promised ourselves, "I would never do that with my kids." List your personal top five items in each category:

   a. "I want to do the same thing with my children someday."

   _____

   _____

   _____

   _____

   b. "I would never do that with my kids."

   _____

   _____

   _____

   _____

2. Now think about the day you first found out you were going to be a parent, or if you haven't had children, your thoughts on this subject now. List your top five goals in adulthood for things you did and didn't want to do with your children.

   a. "I want to do these things with my children."

   _____

   _____

   _____

   _____

   b. "I would never do these things with my children."

   _____

   _____

_____

_____

3. If you were strongly affected as a child by the addictive behavior of one or both of your parents, or of some other adult who played an important role in your life, please write briefly about what happened and how you felt about it then.

_____

_____

_____

_____

4. Please list any ways you intend do better as a parent, present or future, than you have done because of your drinking, drug use, or other addictive behavior.

_____

_____

_____

_____

5. Now list any parental goals you have which drinking or using might interfere with.

_____

_____

_____

_____

6. If you see that your addictive behavior will interfere with your chances of giving your children the kind of childhood you want them to have, but you keep drinking or using anyway, what does that tell you about your priorities? If you're acting as if alcohol, another drug, or another addictive pattern is more important to you than your children, please describe your thoughts about this conflict.

_____

_____

_____

_____

_____

7. If someone you knew put an addictive behavior ahead of his/her ability to be his/her best as a parent, how would you explain it?

_____

_____

8. If your children feel you have a problem and you feel you don't, how would you explain this conflict between your values and your actions to them if they asked?

_____

_____

_____

_____

Be sure to bring this handout back to your next therapy session, and be prepared to talk about your thoughts and feelings about the exercise.

COMMUNICATION SKILLS

GOALS OF THE EXERCISE

1. Understand the relationship between addiction and partner relational conflicts.
2. Develop and maintain effective communication and sexual intimacy with a partner.
3. Identify ways the client succeeds and fails in communicating with important others.
4. Identify better ways to communicate and learn to use them.
5. Learn to teach and use effective communication strategies with others in the client's life.

ADDITIONAL PROBLEMS FOR WHICH THIS EXERCISE MAY BE USEFUL

- Borderline Traits
- Family Conflicts
- Occupational Problems
- Parent-Child Relational Problem
- Social Anxiety

SUGGESTIONS FOR PROCESSING THIS EXERCISE WITH CLIENT

The "Communication Skills" activity is intended for clients whose relationships are troubled due to poor communication skills on the part of the clients themselves or others. This is critical to relapse prevention, as the most common relapse trigger is relationship conflict and the most common source of relationship problems is poor communication. Follow-up for this exercise could include guided practice in group, couples, or family therapy; keeping a journal about the outcomes of this assignment; and reporting back to the therapist and treatment group on outcomes.

COMMUNICATION SKILLS

Saying what you mean clearly and in a way that is respectful both to yourself and to others is a skill that must be learned. So is hearing what others are trying to tell you. Effective communication takes two basic skills: (1) expressing yourself clearly and (2) listening actively. In this exercise you will learn how to communicate more effectively, and how to teach this to others.

1. Please list two people with whom you have the most trouble communicating, and why you think this happens. Then do the same for people with whom you find it easy to communicate.

    **People with Whom It's
    Hard to Talk**   **Why It's Hard**

    _____   _____

    _____   _____

    **People with Whom It's
    Easy to Talk**   **Why It's Easy**

    _____   _____

    _____   _____

2. Now we'll look at communication styles and how they work. We each have a favored style we use most; please think about your habits and those of others in your life.

    a. *Aggressive.* Expressing yourself with little regard for others' rights, thoughts, or feelings. Aggressive communication can be abusive and judgmental. It may include name-calling, yelling, interrupting, sarcasm, ridicule, and hostile body language.

    b. *Passive-aggressive.* Not expressing yourself openly. Hinting; talking behind others' backs; sarcasm; constant complaining; expecting others to know what you think, feel, or want without telling them; refusing to talk even when others can see you're upset.

    c. *Passive.* Not expressing yourself in ways you fear might upset others, or possibly any way at all. Giving short, uninformative answers; agreeing with whatever others say.

    d. *Assertive*. Expressing your thoughts, feelings, and wishes clearly without ignoring those of others; being able to say "no" in a way that respects both others and yourself.

    Which of the styles described above best describes your style of communication? Please choose one and give some examples of how you use this style.

_____

_____

3.   In your relationships with family members, friends, and coworkers, what happens when you disagree with someone or they disagree with you?

_____

_____

4.   Think about the last time you disagreed with someone close to you. How did you handle the situation, and how did the other person? What was the result?

_____

_____

5.   Now we'll look at specific elements of effective communication and how you can use them:

    a. *Avoid mind-reading*. Don't try to tell other people what they think and feel or what their reasons are for things they do. None of us like it when others tell us what we think or feel, and this often triggers arguments. Think about a time when someone did this to you. Describe that situation, how you felt, and whether it helped the communication between you and the other person.

_____

_____

_____

_____

    b. *No name-calling*. When we are upset with others it is because of what they did or didn't do: in other words, their actions. Calling people names is not referring to their actions. It is labeling who and what they are, things they can't change. Name-calling is one of the most assured ways to turn a discussion into an argument or fight. Think about a time when someone called you names. Describe the situation, how you felt, and whether it helped communication between you and the other person.

_____

_____

_____

_____

c. *No interrupting/No long speeches.* These two guidelines go together. When we cut others off or finish their sentences for them, the message is, "What you have to say is not important enough for any more of my time." Also, we're often wrong about what people mean to say when we finish sentences for them. Of course, for one person to let another talk uninterrupted, they both have to know that they'll have a chance to speak, which is why long speeches cause problems. Think about a time when someone went on and on in a conversation or kept interrupting you. Describe that situation, how you felt, and whether it helped the communication between you and the other person.

_____

_____

_____

_____

d. *Be specific.* When we say "You always _____" or "You never _____," we're labeling the person more than we are describing a specific action. We're also wrong. Even if they *very often* or *very seldom* do something, it is unlikely that they *always* or *never* do it—no human being is that consistent. If we tell others they always or never do things, they'll think of exceptions right away. They'll probably feel hurt that we don't recognize those exceptions. This leads to an argument about the "always/never" statement, not to a useful talk about changes we want in others' actions. Think about a time when someone generalized about your behavior. Describe that situation, how you felt, and whether it helped the communication between you and the other person.

_____

_____

_____

_____

e. *Talk about one thing at a time.* We may have many problems to work out with another person, but if we bring them all up at once he/she will feel overwhelmed. Most of us want to get along with others, and we want to know what they want from us. When we start bringing up one issue after another in a discussion, it is sometimes called "kitchen-sink fighting" because it seems to other people that we are throwing everything at them including the kitchen sink. Think about a time when someone "threw the kitchen sink" at you in a discussion by piling issue upon issue. Describe that situation, how you felt, and whether you feel it helped the communication between you and the other person.

_____

_____

_____

_____

f. *Claim your own feelings and actions.* A near-guaranteed way to pick a fight is to blame someone for your own feelings or actions, by saying "You made me feel _____" or "You made me do _____." Other people can't make us do anything, unless they use physical force. They can't make us feel or think a certain way. Turn it around: Do you want to be blamed for someone else's actions and feelings? To solve a problem instead of starting a fight, it works better to say things like "When you did <u>(action)</u>, <u>(result)</u> happened, and I felt <u>(emotion)</u>." Think about the last time someone blamed you for their feelings or actions. Describe that situation, how you felt, and whether it helped the communication between you and the other person.

    _____

    _____

    _____

    _____

g. *Respond to both the spoken and unspoken parts of the message.* As well as listening to other people's words, we need to respond to the emotions they express through facial expressions, body language, and tone of voice. It always helps if others see we are paying attention and trying to understand them. Think about a time someone acknowledged your feelings as well as your words. How did they let you know? How did you feel about it?

    _____

    _____

    _____

    _____

h. *Use a structured communication method.*

    1) Agree to talk about the issue at a specific time in the near future and at a place that is practical for both people and as free of distractions as possible.

    2) Agree on who will talk first and who will listen first (you'll trade places often).

    3) The first person makes a short statement, using this format:

        EVENT / RESULT / FEELINGS

        "When (*event*) happened, you did (*action*), it caused (*result*), and I felt (feelings)."

        Think of a time when you were upset with someone. How could you have expressed your viewpoint in this format?

        _____

        _____

4) The listener then says something like, "If I understand what you're telling me, you're saying . . . (the listener paraphrases the message, expressing it in his/her own words). This is key because sometimes the same words mean different things to two people.

5) The first person either agrees that the second person got the message right, or restates any part that was left out or mixed up, or deletes anything that got added.

6) Trade places and repeat the process. After the first time, you can switch to telling one another what you would like the other person to do or stop doing. Just say "I would like you to _____." The feedback works the same as before.

7) If you are not willing or able to do what the other person wants, tell them so in plain English: "I'm not willing to _____. I can't _____ because _____." If possible, offer a compromise. Think about a time someone wanted you to do something you were unable or unwilling to do. How could you have expressed this to the other person?

_____

_____

8) Keep repeating this process until you both feel you clearly understand each other's perceptions, feelings, wants, and what you are willing to do for each other.

6. These techniques can seem awkward at first but get easier with repetition. It helps to practice with important people in our lives. Part of this exercise is to talk about this with at least two important people in your life, practice these skills with them, and talk about the results with your therapist and/or your therapy group. After practicing these communication techniques, what questions/challenges do you have about continued improvement of your communication skills?

_____

_____

Be sure to bring this handout back to your next therapy session, and be prepared to talk about your thoughts and feelings about the exercise.

IDENTIFYING PROVEN PROBLEM-SOLVING SKILLS

GOALS OF THE EXERCISE

1. Understand the relationship between addiction and partner relational conflicts.
2. Develop the skills necessary to maintain open, effective communication, sexual intimacy, and enjoyable time with a partner.
3. Clarify and more effectively use innate strengths and resources in the community and environment to achieve and maintain recovery from addiction.
4. Reframe both addiction and conflict as problems to be solved, having much in common with other problems already solved in the past.

ADDITIONAL PROBLEMS FOR WHICH THIS EXERCISE MAY BE USEFUL

- Family Conflicts
- Parent-Child Relational Problem
- Suicidal Ideation

SUGGESTIONS FOR PROCESSING THIS EXERCISE WITH CLIENT

The "Identifying Proven Problem-Solving Skills" activity is intended for clients who suffer from learned helplessness or low self-esteem and as a result fail to use available resources and abilities to achieve and maintain recovery and productive relationships. It guides the client in a systematic self-assessment to identify problem-solving skills he/she has successfully used in other situations and plan strategies for using these skills to address current issues. Follow-up can include keeping a journal and reporting back on successes and lessons learned.

IDENTIFYING PROVEN PROBLEM-SOLVING SKILLS

This assignment will strengthen your recovery quickly. Everyone has problem-solving skills, and we each have a combination of talents. This exercise will help you look at your successes in all areas to find resources you already have.

1. Often in addiction treatment we hear unfamiliar terms. People use words like dependence, abstinence, surrender, Higher Power, and others in unfamiliar ways; it can seem like learning a new language. Please list words that are new or being used in ways that are new to you.

    _____

    _____

2. We may also get the impression that we'll have to learn a whole new set of skills to solve the problems that brought us into treatment. When staff and fellow clients talk about what has to be done to stay clean and sober, these terms are often equally unfamiliar. Please list any tasks or actions you've heard people talking about that seem foreign and unfamiliar.

    _____

    _____

3. None of us grow up without learning ways to solve problems. Using addictive behaviors was one of our problem-solving tools, and that one obviously won't work here, but you've used other methods. Please list three situations where you have solved problems or achieved goals.

    _____

    _____

    _____

    _____

4. Now please examine this list of problem-solving/goal-accomplishing skills and traits, and check off the ones you used in the three situations you just listed.

    _____ Asking for help

    _____ Attention to details

    _____ Being alert

_____ Being decisive

_____ Being persistent

_____ Brainstorming—generating lots of ideas then picking out the best ones

_____ Breaking a big problem down into small steps

_____ Courtesy

_____ Explaining and teaching things to others

_____ Finding alternative ways to do things

_____ Flexibility

_____ Following instructions

_____ Humor

_____ Learning by watching others

_____ Listening carefully

_____ Mastering new information

_____ Negotiating

_____ Open-mindedness

_____ Organizing/working with other people

_____ Patience

_____ Planning use of time

_____ Practicing a difficult task until it gets easy

_____ Practicing an easy task, then working up to hard ones

_____ Recognizing patterns

_____ Researching needed info (e.g., asking people, using books, the Internet, etc.)

_____ Taking notes

_____ Trial and error

_____ Working alone

5. The items from this list that most people find most useful are all of the above! However, each of us uses them differently. Please go over the list in question 4, and pick three items you use most often in solving problems, then write about how you can use them during your recovery. For example, if you picked _researching needed information_, you could read books on the problem, talk to people who succeed at the task, find web sites with useful information, etc.

Problem-Solving Skill or Trait   **How I Can Use It in Recovery**

_____   _____

_____   _____

_____   _____

_____   _____

6. Many alcoholics and addicts, once they're no longer impaired, are smart, creative, funny, hard-working, loyal, generous people. How many of those words fit you? What qualities do others value in you? Please ask three people who know you well what qualities and abilities of yours they think will be most helpful in staying clean and sober. Write their answers here.

_____

_____

How can you apply those same qualities and abilities to other problems?

_____

_____

Here are some ways in which some particular skills and strengths can help people in recovery. If you have these skills or strengths, here are ways you can use them:

a. *Communication skills*. Work with others—staff, others in recovery, clergy, friends, family—to improve relationships.

b. *High energy and determination*. Keep working your program even if you're temporarily discouraged; help others.

c. *Sense of humor*. Cope with difficult or painful times, avoid self-pity or false pride, enjoy fellowship with other recovering people.

d. *Spirituality*. Improve a relationship with a Higher Power; stay clear on what your values are; have faith to carry you through hard times.

e. *Creativity*. Find new ways to help oneself and others and new uses for old tools.

7. Think about the hardest or most nerve-wracking parts of getting and staying clean and sober. Pick a situation that has you worried, and briefly describe how you'll use these methods and qualities to tackle the issue. After you finish this handout, talk it over with your therapist.

Problem: _____

_____

How I Can Tackle It: _____

_____

_____

_____

Above all, remember, whatever questions or problems you face in recovery, someone else has faced them before you. If they succeeded, so can you; pick out some people a lot like you who overcame similar problems, find out what they did, and try doing the same things.

Be sure to bring this handout back to your next therapy session, and be prepared to talk about your thoughts and feelings about the exercise.

WHAT DO I NEED AND HOW DO I GET IT?

GOALS OF THE EXERCISE

1. Maintain a program of recovery free of addiction and negative influences from peers.
2. Understand that continued association with a negative peer group increases risk of relapse.
3. Develop a new peer group that supports working a recovery program.
4. Address fears related to giving up the former peer group.
5. Find healthier ways to meet needs that old peer relationships fulfilled.

ADDITIONAL PROBLEMS FOR WHICH THIS EXERCISE MAY BE USEFUL

- Dependent Traits
- Legal Problems
- Living Environment Deficiencies

SUGGESTIONS FOR PROCESSING THIS EXERCISE WITH THE CLIENT

The "What Do I Need and How Do I Get It?" activity is for clients whose recovery efforts are undermined by peer interactions. It guides clients to assess this for themselves and draw conclusions based on data they collect. Clients may not feel ready to cut ties with old peer groups. They may not believe that peer associations affect recovery negatively. Multiple efforts may be needed to work through the resistance, ambivalence, fear, and grief related to ending peer relationships even if the client understands that their influence is negative. It may help to role-play ways to distance or end unhealthy relationships and initiate healthy new ones. It may also be useful to help the client educate his/her family and supportive friends about addiction and the recovery process.

WHAT DO I NEED AND HOW DO I GET IT?

Some of the hardest challenges people face in early recovery are relationships with family members, significant others, and friends who continue to engage in addictive behavior or illegal activities, don't understand or support recovery, mock or ignore treatment and recovery, and encourage addictive behaviors. As you get healthier physically, emotionally, and spiritually, you may find you have less and less in common with some of the people who were closest to you before you got into recovery. Each of us has the right and the responsibility to choose with whom we will associate. We deserve to have the people in our lives support our recovery and respect our decision to live free of addiction. We need to eliminate risks that lead back toward addictive lifestyles and behaviors, and this may include people with whom we've shared important parts of our lives. To maintain recovery, we need to increase our contact with positive people who support nonaddictive lifestyles. This exercise will help you assess your peer group for risks, identify the benefits of being around people who support your recovery, and begin identifying what you are willing to do for yourself to create a more recovery-oriented support system.

1. Please list some situations when peers encouraged you to engage in addictive behavior or illegal activity.

   _____

   _____

2. We are responsible for our own choices, but the people we associate with can be a powerful influence. Does your current peer group support addictive behavior (e.g., do they encourage use, use around you, act unsupportive of your recovery), and if so how?

   _____

   _____

3. What are some things you've said, or heard others say, to deny that peers influence their thinking or behavior? What do you think about those statements?

   _____

   _____

4. Does continued involvement with your peer group increase your risk of relapse? If so, how do your peers undermine your success in treatment? List up to five ways.

_____

_____

_____

_____

_____

5. What worries do you have about breaking off your connections with current peers and making new contacts?

_____

_____

6. What are the main advantages and disadvantages of changing your peer group from one that increases your risk of relapse to one that encourages a nonaddictive lifestyle?

Advantages   **Disadvantages**

_____   _____

_____   _____

7. What needs does your peer group fulfill for you (e.g., fun, excitement, second family, sense of belonging, etc.)?

_____

_____

8. Imagine explaining to your peer group your need to distance or end your relationship for your own well-being. What would you want them to know?

_____

_____

9. If a friend told you he/she needed to stop spending time with you for his/her own good, would you respect your friend's decision? If so, what are your thoughts about making the same decision for yourself?

_____

_____

10. To increase the likelihood of staying in recovery, each of us needs to develop a new peer group that is free of addictive behaviors and supports working a program of recovery.

   a. How can you increase opportunities for fellowship with positive peers?

   _____

   _____

b. What are the benefits to you if you do these things?

_____

_____

11. What skills do you need in order to develop new friends? What do you foresee as potential barriers?

_____

_____

12. How can each member of your family help you in your recovery?

_____

_____

13. Write a brief plan to start identifying and making new social contacts, keeping in mind your answers to questions 7 and 10.

_____

_____

_____

_____

Be sure to bring this handout back to your next therapy session, and be prepared to talk over your thoughts and feelings about this topic with your therapist or with your group.

WHAT DO OTHERS SEE CHANGING?

GOALS OF THE EXERCISE

1. Maintain a program of recovery free of addiction and negative influences from peers.
2. Learn the skills necessary to develop a new peer group that is addiction-free and supportive of working a program of recovery.
3. Become more aware of positive changes and progress in treatment by getting feedback from other people.
4. Increase emotional support from others.

ADDITIONAL PROBLEMS FOR WHICH THIS EXERCISE MAY BE USEFUL

- Depression

SUGGESTIONS FOR PROCESSING THIS EXERCISE WITH CLIENT

The "What Do Others See Changing?" activity is intended to correct distorted self-perceptions that feed into social isolation, depression, and low self-esteem, and to lead the client into connecting with others in healthy ways. Its approach is to guide the client in selecting several people from whom to get feedback on changes as a result of recovery work, log their responses, and share that information with the therapist, group, and program sponsor. Follow-up may include repeating this activity at set intervals, perhaps quarterly, and again sharing the responses, as well as discussing differences between the client's self-perception and the way he/she is perceived by peers.

WHAT DO OTHERS SEE CHANGING?

Sometimes it's hard to measure change in our lives. Feedback from others can help us see our own progress more clearly. This exercise will guide you in gathering feedback from people who are close to you, who support your recovery efforts, and whom you trust.

1. List four people you will ask for feedback about changes they see in you and your life.

    _____

    _____

    _____

    _____

2. You might want feedback about your relationships, work or school performance, moods, appearance, or health. How will you ask them about changes they've noticed? Write your questions here.

    _____

    _____

    _____

    _____

3. Record the feedback you received here.

WHO I ASKED	WHAT THEY TOLD ME

4. After reviewing what others said, some of the information may not surprise you but some may. Jot down your thoughts related to the information you've gathered.

    _____

    _____

    _____

    _____

5. Identify some preliminary ways this information will be useful for your recovery efforts.

    _____

    _____

Be sure to bring this handout back to your next therapy session, and be prepared to talk about your thoughts and feelings about the exercise.

COPING WITH ADDICTION AND PTSD
OR OTHER ANXIETY DISORDERS

GOALS OF THE EXERCISE

1. Understand posttraumatic stress symptoms and how they can lead to addiction.
2. Learn coping skills to bring posttraumatic stress symptoms and addiction under control.
3. Promote healing and acceptance and reduce relapse risk by using coping strategies for both addictions and problems related to anxiety disorders.

ADDITIONAL PROBLEMS FOR WHICH THIS EXERCISE MAY BE USEFUL

- Anxiety
- Borderline Traits
- Childhood Trauma
- Grief/Loss Unresolved
- Medical Issues

SUGGESTIONS FOR PROCESSING THIS EXERCISE WITH CLIENT

The "Coping with Addiction and PTSD or Other Anxiety Disorders" activity is for clients suffering from unresolved trauma, panic attacks, and other anxiety disorders. It addresses self-medication and risky behaviors as factors in trauma, and offers healthier ways to cope with the combined challenge of trauma and addiction. Follow-up can include referral to support or therapy groups for PTSD or other anxiety disorders, assignments to try alternative coping strategies, and reporting back to the therapist and/or treatment group on outcomes.

COPING WITH ADDICTION AND PTSD OR OTHER ANXIETY DISORDERS

Many people suffer from both substance abuse problems and posttraumatic stress disorder (PTSD), panic attacks, or other anxiety disorders. What is the connection between addiction and anxiety disorders? People who abuse alcohol or other drugs are more likely than others to suffer from PTSD or other anxiety disorders, and people with anxiety disorders are at a higher-than-average risk to have problems with substance abuse due to self-medication in their efforts to relieve their anxiety. Some find that when they go through a traumatic experience in recovery, they feel they can't cope without alcohol or another drug. This exercise will help you identify and plan to cope with issues of this kind.

1. In some cases, people find themselves in traumatic situations as a result of their drinking, drug use, or other high-risk addictive behaviors. Please describe any ways you feel your addictive patterns have led to you suffering traumatic experiences.

   _____

   _____

2. Sometimes the connection between addiction and anxiety works in the other direction: The traumatic experiences or other anxiety problems come first, and when people use chemicals or intense experiences to try to block out the pain they end up getting hooked. How have painful experiences led you to drink, use, or otherwise act out addictively?

   _____

   _____

3. If you know others who have succeeded in overcoming both addiction and anxiety disorders, could you use some of their methods? What did they do?

   _____

   _____

   _____

   _____

4. Many people find that some of the same methods they use to overcome addictions, such as participating in recovery programs, learning new coping skills, and finding replacement activities for substance use, also help them deal with anxiety disorders. What recovery tools might help you deal with PTSD, panic attacks, or other anxiety disorders?

_____

_____

_____

_____

5. On the other hand, some techniques that are often used with anxiety disorders that may not seem to fit into recovery from substance abuse, such as the use of anti-anxiety drugs and other prescribed mood-altering medications. If you are under a doctor's instructions to take medications for an anxiety disorder, have you talked about your substance abuse issues with the doctor who prescribed the medications? If so, what did the doctor tell you about this? If not, what keeps you from talking to your doctor about this recovery issue, and what effect might keeping this secret have on your ability to avoid relapse?

_____

_____

_____

_____

6. What has your doctor told you might happen if you stopped taking those medications?

_____

_____

_____

_____

If you are participating in a 12-Step recovery program, do you know your program's policies about the use of prescribed mood-altering medications? Actually, the official position of Alcoholics Anonymous is that if your doctor knows your history of addiction, is experienced in working with people with addictions, and has prescribed medication with that knowledge, and you are taking it exactly as prescribed, you're doing what you need to do to stay sober. Other programs have similar policies. If anyone in your 12-Step group challenges this, they don't know their program. If you have questions, check the official literature.

7. Do you know others in a 12-Step program who take prescribed mood-altering medications? How do they avoid the trap of substance abuse?

_____

_____

_____

_____

8. Please describe the tools you will use to cope with the combined problems of substance abuse and PTSD or other anxiety disorders.

_____

_____

_____

_____

Be sure to bring this handout back to your next therapy session, and be prepared to talk about your thoughts and feelings about the exercise.

SAFE AND PEACEFUL PLACE MEDITATION

GOALS OF THE EXERCISE

1. Learn the coping skills necessary to bring posttraumatic stress symptoms and addiction under control.
2. Learn and practice a healthy method to achieve deep relaxation that can be used in many situations.
3. Improve ability to cope with stress in a healthy way.
4. Learn to achieve quick relief from posttraumatic stress symptoms.
5. Recognize the first signs of anger and use behavioral techniques to control it.

ADDITIONAL PROBLEMS FOR WHICH THIS EXERCISE MAY BE USEFUL

*   Anxiety
*   Borderline Traits
*   Childhood Trauma
*   Chronic Pain
*   Grief/Loss Unresolved
*   Substance Intoxication/Withdrawal

SUGGESTIONS FOR PROCESSING THIS EXERCISE WITH CLIENT

The "Safe and Peaceful Place Meditation" activity is useful for managing stress and anxiety, particularly if these are chronic. It is also useful for pain management and coping with insomnia. This exercise guides the client in a personalized multisensory imagery exercise in which he/she creates a mental construct of a safe and peaceful place and practices temporarily withdrawing from engagement with stressors. With practice this exercise can become a very effective method of achieving quick relaxation. This exercise can be used in individual or group therapy and as an opening routine for treatment groups. Follow-up can include practice at home, teaching the exercise to someone else, and reporting on outcomes.

SAFE AND PEACEFUL PLACE MEDITATION

Do you sometimes wish you could just get away from whatever situation you're in, or from whatever you're thinking and feeling? This is a normal and healthy wish. It may not be practical to actually leave a situation right away, though, and sometimes it's hard to leave our own thoughts and feelings behind even when we do physically go somewhere else.

This exercise will teach you how to get away even when you can't go anywhere. It will guide you through a process of creating a mental picture of a safe and peaceful place where you can temporarily relax, so that you can come back to your situation calm and refreshed. Practice is important. The more you practice this, the better you'll get at it and the better it will work for you. With enough repetition, people have used this to achieve calm and inner peace very quickly even in the midst of great pain, anger, and anxiety.

For many people, it works best to do this with their eyes closed, so you may want to have someone you trust and feel safe with read this to you while you follow the instructions, or record it in your own voice to play back and listen to.

1. *Image.* What is a place that makes you feel calm, peaceful, and safe to think about? Please think of the place that best fits this description for you and form a mental picture of this place. It may be a real place you've been—anything from a favorite beach to your grandparents' kitchen, a place you've heard about and would like to go, or an imaginary place. Whatever is relaxing for you is right for you. Briefly describe this safe and peaceful place.

    _____

    _____

    _____

    _____

2. *Emotions and sensations.* Focus on this image or mental picture. What emotions do you feel? What pleasant physical sensations do you feel, and where are they located in your body?

    _____

    _____

_____

_____

3. *Enhancement.* Please explore this imagery in more detail. Take a few moments to savor it with all your senses and enjoy the idea of being in this safe and peaceful place. When you look around in this place in your mind's eye, what do you see happening? What do you hear? Is it warm or cool? What does the air feel like against your face? Is there a distinctive aroma? Please describe these sensory details.

_____

_____

_____

_____

_____

_____

_____

4. *Cue or key word.* Please think of a single word to represent this picture, and keep this word in mind while you again bring up the mental picture, the sights, the sounds, and all the sensations of peace and safety and pleasure of this place you've created for yourself. Focus on whatever pleasant things come to each of your senses in turn, keeping this key word in mind. Now let your mind dwell on those pleasant sensations and repeat the key word to yourself over and over. Try blanking out the pleasant place you have been thinking of, then thinking of the key word, and see how the image comes back to you quickly and vividly. Notice how your body is feeling relaxed.

5. *Coping with mild stress.* Let's test this as a way for you to relax and overcome negative feelings. Blank out your safe and peaceful place again. Now think of a minor annoyance, a situation or person that isn't a big problem but gets on your nerves. What kinds of negative physical sensations are coming to you when you think of this annoyance? Where are they located in your body?

_____

_____

_____

Now think of your key word. Again, think of the safe and peaceful place in your mind's eye that goes with the key word. Think of the visual image, the scenery, the sounds, and the pleasant physical sensations. As you think of this, how does your body feel? What is happening to the negative sensations you felt in your body?

_____

_____

6.   *Practice.* For the next two weeks, practice this at least twice a day, and use it when you find yourself getting irritated or anxious. You can also use it when you are feeling physical pain or discomfort, or if you have trouble sleeping. As you practice, keep noticing anything about your mental image of the peaceful and safe place that makes it more vivid and more relaxing for you, and keep those details in mind for future times when you do this exercise. As an added help to learning to use it, try teaching it to someone else and see how it works for them.

Use this space to record anything you notice or learn about using this meditation exercise.

_____

_____

_____

_____

_____

_____

_____

   Be sure to bring this handout back to your next therapy session, and be prepared to talk about your thoughts and feelings about the exercise.

COPING WITH ADDICTION
AND THOUGHT DISORDERS

GOALS OF THE EXERCISE

1. Gain an understanding of the interaction between addictions and thought disorders.
2. Develop adaptive methods to cope with symptoms and seek treatment when necessary.
3. Stabilize cognitive functioning adequately to allow treatment in an outpatient setting.

ADDITIONAL PROBLEMS FOR WHICH THIS EXERCISE MAY BE USEFUL

- Depression with Psychotic Features
- Mania with Psychotic Features
- Self-Care Deficits—Primary
- Self-Care Deficits—Secondary
- Substance Abuse/Dependence

SUGGESTIONS FOR PROCESSING THIS EXERCISE WITH CLIENT

The "Coping with Addiction and Thought Disorders" activity is designed to help the client with schizophrenic symptoms cope with the challenges of this dual diagnosis. Its approach is to examine issues of self-medication and the possible role of substance abuse in the development of thought disorders and to offer strategies for integrating recovery work on both problems. Follow-up may include referral to Double Trouble or another dual-diagnosis recovery/support program or to a support group specifically focused on thought disorders. Another suggestion is to give homework assignments to use coping strategies identified through this exercise in a structured way and report back on the outcomes.

COPING WITH ADDICTION AND THOUGHT DISORDERS

Some people suffer from both substance abuse problems and what are called psychoses or thought disorders, most often schizophrenia. If you are working to overcome both of these problems, the purpose of this assignment is to help you use the same tools for both tasks where possible, and to guide you in handling the special challenges of this type of mental health issue.

How are substance abuse and thought disorders connected? People who abuse alcohol or other drugs can suffer from thought disorders, and people with thought disorders are at higher-than-average risk to have problems with substance abuse.

1. In some cases, people find their thought disorder's beginnings seem to be connected to their drug use, particularly with hallucinogenic drugs or with prolonged use of stimulants like methamphetamine. Please describe any ways you feel your substance use has led to your thinking becoming distorted.

    _____

    _____

2. Sometimes the connection between addiction and thought disorders works in the other direction: The hallucinations, false beliefs, or other symptoms of psychosis come first, and when people use drugs (either street drugs or prescription medications) to try to control or cope with these symptoms, they become dependent on those drugs. Please describe how your thought disorder's symptoms may have led you to drink or use other drugs in the search for relief from those symptoms.

    _____

    _____

3. If you know any people who are succeeding in overcoming both addictions and thought disorders, what are they doing that is helping them?

    _____

    _____

4. Many people find that some of the same methods they use to overcome addictions, such as participating in recovery programs, learning new coping skills, following a recommended treatment plan, and finding replacement activities for substance use, also help them deal with thought disorders. What recovery tools might help you deal with your thought disorder symptoms?

   _____

   _____

5. On the other hand, some techniques that are used with thought disorders may not seem to fit into recovery from substance abuse, such as the use of antipsychotic drugs and other prescribed medications. If you are under a doctor's instructions to take medications for a thought disorder, have you talked about your substance abuse issues with the doctor who prescribed the medications? If so, what did the doctor tell you about this? If not, what keeps you from talking to your doctor about this recovery issue?

   _____

   _____

6. What did your doctor tell you might happen if you stopped taking your medications or didn't take them as prescribed?

   _____

   _____

   If you are participating in a 12-Step recovery program, do you know your program's policies about the use of prescribed mind-altering medications? The official position of Alcoholics Anonymous is that if your doctor knows your history of addiction, is experienced in working with people with addictions, and you are taking it exactly as prescribed, you are doing what you need to do to stay sober. Other programs have similar policies. If others in your group challenge this, or if you have questions about this, check the official literature.

7. Do you know others in 12-Step programs who take prescribed mind-altering medications? How do they avoid the trap of substance abuse?

   _____

   _____

8. Please describe the tools you will use to cope with the combined problems of substance abuse and a thought disorder.

   _____

   _____

   Be sure to bring this handout back to your next therapy session, and be prepared to talk about your thoughts and feelings about the exercise.

PLANNING FOR STABILITY

GOALS OF THE EXERCISE

1. Identify early warning symptoms of decompensation to get help as quickly as possible.
2. Stabilize cognitive functioning adequately to allow treatment in an outpatient setting.
3. Develop adaptive methods to cope with symptoms and seek treatment when necessary.

ADDITIONAL PROBLEMS FOR WHICH THIS EXERCISE MAY BE USEFUL

*   Impulsivity
*   Mania/Hypomania

SUGGESTIONS FOR PROCESSING THIS EXERCISE WITH THE CLIENT

The "Planning for Stability" activity is for the client who experiences psychotic symptoms as a result of mental illness, a co-occurring disorder, or chemical addiction and is working toward developing a comprehensive recovery plan. It is designed to be the client's creation. The clinician must work from the client's perspective. It may require that, of the various things the client suggests as components of the plan, the clinician clarify which he/she can assist and support. Recovery is both defined and carried out by the client. Essential elements include instilling hope, education, receiving support, personal responsibility, and learning to advocate for oneself. It may be useful to have supportive family members attend a session so the client can share the plan with them and educate them regarding their roles in the plan. You can also include family members as active participants in the planning process. Family and others often have information that is useful and information that the client may or may not be aware of himself/herself.

PLANNING FOR STABILITY

The relationship between thought-disordered symptoms and addiction can vary. Thought-disordered symptoms may be a direct result of chemical use or abuse; the use of substances may make already-existing symptoms worse; or people may use chemicals to self-medicate the negative symptoms. In any case, most people want troublesome symptoms to go away and they want to feel better. In addition to managing symptoms, you will need to find ways to cope with the feelings associated with thought-disordered/psychotic symptoms (e.g., inadequacy, fear of dependency on others, fear of being intruded upon). Recovery means working toward having more to life than coping with symptoms or the illness itself. This exercise will help you design a safety and recovery plan so that you can reach your goals and plan to avoid problems or cope with them if they arise.

With your therapist, caseworker, sponsor, or another trusted supportive person, write out your stability plan. When your plan is complete, keep one copy at home, one with you when you're away from home, and give one to your therapist or caseworker. Please make sure to include each of the following in your stability plan:

1. Your daily routine (what your day-to-day schedule will look like).
2. Your medications (what they are, the dosages, and when they are to be taken).
3. Your diet (what will it include and things to avoid or limit).
4. Your sleep plan (include a bedtime ritual describing how you will get ready for bed).
5. Activities for fun.
6. Supportive people (nonfamily members) and how to contact them.
7. Supportive family members and how they can be helpful to you.
8. Your personal goals (what you'd like to accomplish, both short and longer term).
9. Topics about which you or your family members need more information.
10. Barriers that could get in the way of maintaining stability (feelings related to taking medications, dealing with side effects of medications, fears, limited support, etc.), with simple strategies to avoid or overcome each barrier.
11. A list of thoughts, feelings, and behaviors that indicate your symptoms are getting worse.

12. For each warning sign you listed for question 11, please write instructions for yourself about what to do, including names and phone numbers of people you will contact. Also, please write instructions about what those supportive people you've identified in questions 6 and 7 can do to be of assistance.

13. A list of techniques and resources that have worked before to help you stabilize your symptoms, your moods, or your urges to return to addictive behaviors.

14. A crisis intervention plan: (This should be developed when you are not in crisis and before it happens!) Include what you know already works, who you'd like to be involved, what is not helpful, and other suggestions for the people who will help you when a crisis occurs.

Be sure to bring this handout to your next therapy session, and be prepared to ask for assistance when needed and talk over your thoughts and feelings about this exercise with your therapist.

EARLY WARNING SIGNS OF RELAPSE

GOALS OF THE EXERCISE

1. Develop coping skills to use when experiencing high-risk situations and/or cravings.
2. Increase awareness of personal early warning signs of relapse.
3. Learn that relapse is a process and how a person can prevent that process from continuing to its completion in his/her life.

ADDITIONAL PROBLEMS FOR WHICH THIS EXERCISE MAY BE USEFUL

- Eating Disorders
- Gambling
- Nicotine Dependence
- Opioid Dependence
- Substance Abuse/Dependence
- Treatment Resistance

SUGGESTIONS FOR PROCESSING THIS EXERCISE WITH CLIENT

The "Early Warning Signs of Relapse" activity is intended to help clients in early recovery learn about cognitive, emotional, and behavioral changes often seen in the early stages of relapse (before an actual return to active addiction) and plan strategies to counter these changes if and when they see them. This exercise is also useful to prepare for the "Relapse Prevention Planning" activity. Follow-up can include sharing the information gathered with a program sponsor and keeping a journal to track and record "red flag" symptoms.

EARLY WARNING SIGNS OF RELAPSE

In addition to external pressures to use, our attitudes, thoughts, and behavior play a key role in relapse. Learning about early warning signs can help you avoid going back to drinking, using, or other addictive patterns. This exercise will help you identify your personal warning signs, stop the relapse process, and turn it around before you pick up a drink or drug or return to another addictive behavior.

When a person picks up a drink or drug, walks into a casino, or otherwise returns to an addiction, that's the completion of the relapse process, not its beginning. Before that happens, there are many warning signs. Knowing the warning signs can help you cut the process short and stay in recovery.

1. Relapse-related changes in thinking may include persuading yourself that some new method of controlled drinking, drug use, gambling, etc. will work; remembering the good times and overlooking the problems; thinking of addictive actions as a reward for success or a way to celebrate; or believing that one cannot succeed in recovery. Please list specific examples of how your thinking changed before your last relapse, or similar changes you've seen in others.

    _____

    _____

    _____

    _____

2. Emotions and attitudes also change as a person drifts toward relapse. Determination, optimism, teamwork, and motivation may be replaced by forms of negativity such as apathy, selfishness, and a feeling that being unable to drink, use, gamble, or so on is an undeserved punishment. Please list specific examples of how your attitudes changed before your last relapse, or similar changes you've seen in others.

    _____

    _____

    _____

    _____

3. Another area where there are clear differences between an actively addicted person's lifestyle and that of a recovering person is in how he/she relates to others. Before returning to active addiction, our behavior slips back into patterns such as

self-isolation, manipulation, dishonesty, secretiveness, and being demanding and resentful. Please list specific examples of how your ways of relating to other people changed before your last relapse, or similar changes you've seen in others.

_____

_____

_____

_____

4.   You have probably also seen common behavior patterns in yourself and others who were abusing alcohol or other drugs or practicing other addictions, and seen very different patterns in recovering people. When a person is sliding back toward addiction, his/her behaviors start looking more and more like they did before recovery. Some typical addictive behavior patterns include irregular eating and sleep habits, neglect of health, irresponsibility, recklessness, procrastination, impulsivity, and other patterns showing a loss of self-control and the growth of chaos in one's life. Please list specific examples of how your behavior changed before your last relapse, or similar changes you've seen in others.

_____

_____

_____

_____

5.   Together with the other changes described above, the feelings and moods of actively addicted people tend to be different from those they experience in recovery. Common addictive patterns of feelings and mood include irritability, anxiety, depression, hopelessness, indifference, self-pity, anger, and self-centeredness. Please list specific examples of how your feelings and moods changed before your last relapse, or similar changes you've seen in others.

_____

_____

_____

_____

6.   Now think back, check with others if possible, and identify whatever warning signs from all the areas above that you or others saw in you before your last relapse. If you've never tried to quit before and have no experience of relapse, list the main patterns that were normal for you when you were drinking or using. Either way, please write these red flags down in the order in which they happened.

_____

_____

_____

_____

_____

_____

_____

_____

Once you've completed this exercise, you've gathered the information you need to complete another exercise, "Relapse Prevention Planning."

Be sure to bring this handout back to your next therapy session, and be prepared to talk about your thoughts and feelings about the exercise.

IDENTIFYING RELAPSE TRIGGERS AND CUES

GOALS OF THE EXERCISE

1. Increase awareness of personal situational triggers and cues to relapse.
2. Recognize high-risk situations involving increased risk of relapse.
3. Develop coping skills to use when experiencing high-risk situations and/or cravings.
4. Learn refusal skills to use when tempted to relapse into addictive behavior.

ADDITIONAL PROBLEMS FOR WHICH THIS EXERCISE MAY BE USEFUL

- Eating Disorders
- Gambling
- Nicotine Dependence
- Opioid Dependence
- Posttraumatic Stress Disorder (PTSD)
- Sexual Promiscuity
- Substance Abuse/Dependence
- Treatment Resistance

SUGGESTIONS FOR PROCESSING THIS EXERCISE WITH THE CLIENT

The "Identifying Relapse Triggers and Cues" activity is designed to help the newly recovering client identify environmental and internal relapse triggers and plan strategies to cope with those triggers. Follow-up may include the "Relapse Prevention Planning" activity, keeping a journal, and reporting back on outcomes of strategies identified.

IDENTIFYING RELAPSE TRIGGERS AND CUES

Relapse is common but preventable. To avoid it, we have to stay aware of things that can trigger us to behave addictively. We must be ready to react effectively to such triggers. This exercise will help you identify relapse triggers and make a plan to cope with them.

Risky Situations

1. Relapse is often triggered by sights, sounds, and situations that have gone together with addictive behaviors in your past. Many of us find that unless we stay on guard, our thoughts automatically turn back to old behavior patterns when we are around people with whom we drank, used, gambled, etc. Please describe the people with whom you usually practiced addictive behaviors in the past.

   _____

   _____

2. Addictive behaviors are often part of social activities. You may know people who expect you to continue to do the old things with them. They may not care about your recovery, and may use persuasion, teasing, or argument to try to get you to relapse. Who are the people most likely to pressure you to relapse?

   _____

   _____

3. Many recovering people find that family members, friends, or coworkers have enabled their addictions by helping them avoid the consequences, making it easier for them to keep doing the same things. Please briefly describe how anyone who enabled your addiction did so.

   _____

   _____

4. For each of the groups listed, describe how you will avoid relapse triggered by their actions.

   a. Drinking/using/gambling, etc. companions:

   _____

   _____

b. People pressuring you to relapse:

_____

_____

c. Enablers:

_____

_____

5. Changing focus from people to situations, what are the social situations that you think will place you at greatest risk to relapse?

_____

_____

6. Many people also used addictions to cope with stress, and sometimes relationship issues can be extremely stressful. When you think about your future, how could relationship difficulties put you at risk for returning to addictive patterns?

_____

_____

7. For many of us our addictions had also become a daily routine, something we did at certain times (e.g., just after work). In your daily routine, when are you most vulnerable to relapse?

_____

_____

8. Many people feel the urge to "test" their recovery in challenging situations (e.g., being with drinking friends and going to old hangouts). This is an unnecessary risk and often leads to relapse. Describe any ways in which you've tested your ability to stay in recovery.

_____

_____

9. To guard against stress-induced relapse, please think about current situations and future life events that you need to be ready to handle without escaping into addictions. What are they, and what's your plan to handle these situations? What changes are you willing and able to make to handle the pressures and temptations you may face?

_____

_____

_____

_____

Internal Triggers

10. When you experience urges or cravings to act out addictively, how does your body feel?

_____

_____

11. When you experience urges to act out addictively, what emotions do you usually feel?

_____

_____

12. As mentioned earlier, we've often used addictions to cope with stress (i.e., to change feelings we dislike to ones that are more comfortable). What feelings will place you at greatest risk for relapse?

_____

_____

13. Following are some common feelings for which people have used chemicals to cope. It's important not only to be determined to avoid addictive behaviors, but also to know what you will do instead. If you don't have an alternative to replace substance abuse, your risk of relapse is high despite your willpower, logic, and good intentions. Next to each feeling, describe what you will do instead of acting out addictively to cope with that feeling.

Feeling	What You Will Do to Cope
a. Anger	_____
b. Anxiety	_____
c. Boredom	_____
d. Sadness	_____
e. Fatigue	_____
f. Fear	_____
g. Frustration	_____
h. Loneliness	_____
i. Indifference	_____
j. Self-pity	_____
k. Shame	_____
l. Depression	_____
m. Other feelings	_____

Be sure to bring this handout back to your next session with your therapist, and be prepared to talk about your thoughts and feelings about the exercise.

RELAPSE PREVENTION PLANNING

GOALS OF THE EXERCISE

1. Practice a program of recovery that includes regular participation in recovery group meetings, working with a sponsor, and helping others in recovery.
2. Develop a relapse prevention plan of action using information gathered in previous exercises.
3. Develop coping skills to use when experiencing high-risk situations and/or cravings.
4. Take greater responsibility for recovery and increase chances of success through planning.

ADDITIONAL PROBLEMS FOR WHICH THIS EXERCISE MAY BE USEFUL

*   Gambling
*   Opioid Dependence
*   Peer Group Negativity
*   Substance Abuse/Dependence

SUGGESTIONS FOR PROCESSING THIS EXERCISE WITH CLIENT

The "Relapse Prevention Planning" activity is for clients beginning in recovery or experiencing stresses that raise the risk of relapse. It provides a structured framework drawing on earlier exercises to anticipate relapse triggers and cues, plan coping or avoidance strategies, spot early warning signs of relapse, and identify resources and strategies to use to maintain recovery. For best results, have the client complete "Identifying Relapse Triggers and Cues" and "Early Warning Signs of Relapse" before this activity. Follow-up may include having the client present the plan to the therapist, treatment group, and sponsor; keep a journal; and report on outcomes.

RELAPSE PREVENTION PLANNING

If you have identified your own personal relapse triggers and relapse warning signs, you have a good understanding of your relapse process and how to spot it early, before it leads you to an actual return to your addiction. Now it's time to take this information and plan specific strategies to put it to use. The more work you do on this plan and the more specific you are, the more prepared you will be to deal with day-to-day living and unexpected stressful events without reliance on alcohol, other drugs, or other addictive behavior patterns.

1. First, consider your thoughts and feelings about sobriety. Are you ready to take any action needed, to go to any lengths, and to live your life without using mind-altering chemicals or addictive behaviors to block painful feelings or seek pleasure? Describe your attitude about this.

   _____

   _____

2. What consequences are likely if you relapse?

   _____

   _____

3. Refer to the exercises on relapse triggers and warning signs or draw on whatever information you have about the process of relapse. List what you consider your five most important relapse triggers and warning signs and what you will do to cope with each of them.

   Triggers/Warning Signs   **Specific Plan to Avoid Drinking or Using**

   Ex.: Feeling hopeless   *Review progress, ask others what growth they see*

   Ex.: Urge to use   *Attend meetings, contact sponsor, meditate*

   _____   _____

   _____   _____

   _____   _____

   _____   _____

Work with your therapist, your group, or others to rehearse how you'll handle these situations.

4. Recovery is not a solo process, which is why people who try to quit without help from others usually relapse. Who will you contact for support and assistance? List four people here.

Name   **Phone number**

_____   _____

_____   _____

_____   _____

_____   _____

5. *Emergency planning.* Your relapse prevention plan should include what you will do if you encounter a crisis—a stressful situation that triggers a strong urge to use or drink. This plan should be simple—it should be something you can start doing right away. If you encounter an unexpected event that puts you at risk, your plan of action will be:

_____

_____

6. You should also have some general-purpose strategies ready for use if you encounter relapse triggers or warning signs you hadn't specifically planned for. List three general-purpose strategies to stay clean and sober here.

_____

_____

_____

_____

7. Changing your routine is important in staying sober. How will you begin and end each day?

_____

_____

8. Your plan should include support groups—Alcoholics Anonymous, Narcotics Anonymous, Gamblers Anonymous, and so on. List meetings you will commit yourself to attend regularly.

Name of Group   **Day and Time**   **Location**

_____   _____   _____

_____   _____   _____

_____   _____   _____

9. Do you foresee any obstacles/barriers to implementing this plan? If so, what are they?

   _____

   _____

10. What will you do about these roadblocks to your recovery or any others you experience?

    _____

    _____

11. If your plan isn't enough, and you relapse, what will you do to get back on track in your recovery as quickly as you can?

    _____

    _____

12. Are there parts of this plan that you are already carrying out? What are they and how well are they working?

    _____

    _____

    _____

    _____

13. Now that you have your plan made, it's important to monitor your success with it and correct or add to it as needed. When and with whom will you make regular progress checks?

    Person   **When You Will Talk about Your Progress**

    _____   _____

    _____   _____

    _____   _____

    _____   _____

   Be sure to bring this handout back to your next therapy session, and be prepared to talk about your thoughts and feelings about the exercise.

ASSESSING SELF-CARE DEFICITS

GOALS OF THE EXERCISE

1. Understand the relationship between addictions and problems with self-care.
2. Learn basic skills for maintaining a clean, sanitary living space.
3. Understand and verbalize the need for good hygiene and implement healthy personal hygiene practices.
4. Regularly shower or bathe, shave, brush teeth, care for hair, and use deodorant.
5. Improve self-care and learn about community resources available for assistance.
6. Experience increased social acceptance via improved appearance and/or self-care.

ADDITIONAL PROBLEMS FOR WHICH THIS EXERCISE MAY BE USEFUL

- Chronic Pain
- Living Environment Deficiencies
- Psychosis
- Self-Care Deficits—Secondary

SUGGESTIONS FOR PROCESSING THIS EXERCISE WITH THE CLIENT

The "Assessing Self-Care Deficits" exercise is suited for use with clients, concerned family members, case workers, or guardians. It may be used to identify which self-care deficits are related to addiction and which are related to other mental health or developmental concerns. After identifying the most serious deficits and resolving them, follow-up may consist of using the information generated in this exercise as a basis for a discussion of secondary gains associated with not taking care of oneself and/or as part of a relapse/aftercare plan.

ASSESSING SELF-CARE DEFICITS

Self-care involves many things. Some of it involves taking care of our bodies (e.g., hygiene, grooming, seeking proper medical/dental care, taking medications as prescribed, eating a balanced diet), and some of it involves taking care of our environments (e.g., keeping our living environments sanitary and safe, responding to crisis situations appropriately). Addiction can seriously interfere with our motivation, self-discipline, desire, and available time to do these things. At times, you may have relied on others to do some of these things for you. As you begin the recovery process, you have to assess the areas of self-care you've neglected and the impact of that neglect so that you can begin to take better care of yourself. In turn, you'll feel better about yourself and ultimately your interactions with others will improve. This exercise will help you begin this process. This may be an embarrassing topic to work through, but you can't solve problems of which you aren't aware, and your recovery depends on it.

1. Please use this space to create an inventory of your functioning in these areas of self-care.

   a. Positive aspects of self-care (what you do to promote healthy self-care):

   _____

   _____

   b. Negative aspects of self-care (positive actions you avoid or neglect or negative things you do to interfere with healthy self-care):

   _____

   _____

2. What are the personal, social, occupational, and relational impacts of not taking care of yourself?

   _____

   _____

3. What feedback have people given you about times you've neglected self-care?

   _____

   _____

4. Imagine for a moment the positive changes that can result when you give more attention to your appearance, hygiene, medical care, and a sanitary living environment. Please describe what this will look and feel like for you.

_____

_____

5. Prioritize the self-care areas on which you will focus your efforts first. What will you do differently?

_____

_____

6. Please briefly outline a specific plan for daily self-care (i.e., doing the same things in the same order each day) and attending to your self-care priorities (e.g., making an appointment for a full physical and dental visit).

_____

_____

_____

_____

7. What help do you need to begin to carry out your plan? What resources are available in your community to help you? Who can you ask for help? What are the perceived barriers (e.g., time, motivation, money, significance to you, etc.)?

_____

_____

_____

_____

Be sure to bring this handout to your next therapy session, and be prepared to talk about your thoughts, feelings, successes, and challenges related to the exercise.

RELATING SELF-CARE DEFICITS TO MY ADDICTION

GOALS OF THE EXERCISE

1. Understand the relationship between addiction and self-care deficits.
2. Learn the benefit of addressing self-care and how it relates to recovery.
3. Learn basic skills for maintaining a clean, sanitary living space.
4. Understand and verbalize the need for good hygiene and implement healthy personal hygiene practices.
5. Regularly shower or bathe, shave, brush teeth, care for hair, and use deodorant.
6. Experience increased social acceptance because of improved appearance and/or functioning in the area of self-care.

ADDITIONAL PROBLEMS FOR WHICH THIS EXERCISE MAY BE USEFUL

- Psychosis
- Self-Care Deficits—Secondary
- Substance-Induced Disorders

SUGGESTIONS FOR PROCESSING THIS EXERCISE WITH THE CLIENT

The "Relating Self-Care Deficits to My Addiction" is designed as a follow-up exercise to the first exercise in this section, "Assessing Self-Care Deficits." It can be assigned and processed as a motivational activity. For clients with severe deficits, it is important that they begin to make behavioral changes to their self-care habits and that measurable progress is noted before attempting to achieve further insight into its relationship to their addictive lifestyles. This exercise can also be used to facilitate discussions related to relapse prevention planning.

RELATING SELF-CARE DEFICITS TO MY ADDICTION

Primary self-care activities include behaviors related to hygiene, grooming, proper nutrition, interpersonal social and communication skills, keeping a safe/clean living environment, and responding to crises appropriately. Addictive lifestyles can interfere with functions like these in many ways. This exercise will help you learn more about how addiction has affected your own ability to take care of yourself, and improve your quality of life by correcting deficits.

1. What role do you think your addictive behaviors have played in causing you to neglect your primary self-care activities?

    _____

    _____

2. Secondary gains are benefits we obtain without their being obvious reasons for doing things. What secondary gains have you experienced when you neglected your self-care (e.g., getting others to do things for you, avoiding intimacy or uncomfortable situations)?

    _____

    _____

3. What negative consequences have come from continued neglect of primary self-care activities in your life?

    _____

    _____

4. If you've done the exercise titled "Assessing Self-Care Deficits," you've identified some areas in which you feel you need to make improvements in your self-care. Please refer to your responses from that exercise to help answer these questions.

    a. What benefit(s) will come, or have already come, from improving your self-care in these areas?

    _____

    _____

    b. How does paying attention to these self-care activities support your recovery?

    _____

    _____

c. What progress have you made so far in improving your self-care? What's your next step?

    _____

    _____

d. What is your next step after that?

    _____

    _____

Be sure to bring this handout with you to your next therapy session, and be prepared to discuss your thoughts and feelings about the exercise.

FILLING IN THE GAPS

GOALS OF THE EXERCISE

1. Demonstrate increased organization of, and attention to, daily routines resulting in personal responsibilities being fulfilled.
2. Increase proficiency in daily living skills and knowledge of available community resources.
3. Consistently use available addiction recovery and/or mental health community resources.
4. Prioritize independent activities of daily living (IADLs) upon which to focus efforts and improve functioning.
5. Take responsibility for own IADLs up to the level of the client's potential and develop resources for obtaining help from others.
6. Plan and implement timely, appropriate, and safe responses to emergency situations.

ADDITIONAL PROBLEMS FOR WHICH THIS EXERCISE MAY BE USEFUL

- Living Environment Deficiencies
- Self-Care Deficits—Primary

SUGGESTIONS FOR PROCESSING THIS EXERCISE WITH THE CLIENT

The "Filling in the Gaps" exercise is for clients with secondary self-care skill deficits. As with the exercise "Assessing Self-Care Deficits," this activity may be done with a client, family, caseworker, or guardian, depending on the client's level of functioning. It may be necessary to consider literacy, educational level, cultural differences, family values, gender differences, environmental barriers, and other mental health issues when assessing deficits and working toward solutions. Role-playing can help clients practice skills individually or in a group. Follow-up can include discussion of perceived versus actual barriers and ways to work through each. Knowledge of available community resources will be necessary.

FILLING IN THE GAPS

Sometimes in our daily lives we have to do things we aren't good at or interested in. If we neglect our responsibilities, though, it creates stress and puts our stability and independence at risk. We can't always rely on others to do these things for us. As a result of addiction, we may have managed our responsibilities poorly and/or created additional problems that have become as important as the original responsibilities; we have to include these daily tasks in our recovery plans too. This exercise will help you see what areas you need to address and how you can begin.

1. Below is a sample list of independent activities of daily living and examples of each.

   a. *Financial responsibilities* (e.g., opening accounts, balancing the checkbook, preparing and following a budget, paying bills, addressing debt, paying taxes).

   b. *Medical responsibilities for self and/or children* (e.g., scheduling and attending appointments, filling prescriptions).

   c. *Educational/occupational responsibilities* (e.g., being on time, interacting with coworkers, performing assigned tasks, using study skills, managing time).

   d. *Legal responsibilities* (e.g., keeping court dates, finding counsel, attending required appointments, informing work supervisors about these responsibilities and limitations).

   e. *Accessing community resources* (e.g., dealing with transportation, daycare, support group meetings, financial assistance, church/spiritual activities, planning for emergencies).

2. Review the above list. Please circle any areas in which you see deficits in your life.

3. For the deficits you circled, please decide what barriers keep you from succeeding in those responsibilities (e.g., lack of organization, lack of attention, lack of motivation, need for more information or skills training).

_____

_____

_____

_____

4. List, in order from most to least important, which three of the problem areas from question 2 you need to address soonest.

_____

_____

_____

5. With the help of your caseworker or therapist, create a step-by-step plan for working through the first item you picked for question 4. Please include what you will do, when, how, and what result you expect if you carry out your plan. Be as specific as you can.

_____

_____

_____

_____

6. Select a date to begin your plan and check in with your therapist, caseworker, or group members frequently about your progress and challenges. Remember, some of these skills take practice to master, but they do get easier over time, and each skill you learn makes it easier to learn more skills and tackle additional problems.

Be sure to bring this handout with you to your future therapy sessions, and be prepared to discuss your thoughts and feelings about the exercise.

WORKING TOWARD INDEPENDENCE

GOALS OF THE EXERCISE

1. Develop a program of recovery and increase knowledge of community resources.
2. Demonstrate increased organization of, and attention to, daily routines resulting in personal responsibilities being fulfilled.
3. Consistently use available addiction recovery and/or mental health community resources.
4. Identify relevant community resources and ways to access them for help with independent activities of daily living (IADLs).
5. Take responsibility for own IADLs up to the level of the client's potential and develop resources for obtaining help from others.
6. Plan and implement timely, appropriate, and safe responses to emergency situations.

ADDITIONAL PROBLEMS FOR WHICH THIS EXERCISE MAY BE USEFUL

- Attention Deficit Disorder, Inattentive Type (ADD)
- Attention Deficit/Hyperactivity Disorder (ADHD)
- Dependent Traits
- Psychosis
- Self-Care Deficits—Primary

SUGGESTIONS FOR PROCESSING THIS EXERCISE WITH THE CLIENT

The "Working toward Independence" exercise is designed to help clients who may not be accustomed to seeking help or know how to find and use healthy community resources. Follow-up may include making appropriate referrals and/or guiding the client in investigating resources in his/her community and practicing specific skills in gaining access to them.

WORKING TOWARD INDEPENDENCE

Addictive lifestyles have a negative impact on personal independence. Continuing in an addictive lifestyle can interfere with effectively carrying out independent activities of daily living (e.g., banking, shopping, interacting with others, responding to crisis, organizational skills, utilizing community resources) and can ultimately undermine an individual's ability to live independently. This exercise asks you to take an inventory of your independent daily living skills and will help you make some decisions about areas on which you can begin to work.

1. What positive and negative experiences have you had with your day-to-day activities of independent living while you've been engaging in your addiction?

    _____

    _____

2. What are three ways in which your addiction threatens your personal independence?

    _____

    _____

    _____

3. What problems have you had because you neglected or avoided daily living tasks or relied on others to do them for you while actively engaged in an addictive lifestyle?

    _____

    _____

4. What do you see as the benefits of personally taking responsibility for carrying out daily living tasks in healthy and adaptive ways?

    _____

    _____

5. If you've done the exercise titled "Filling in the Gaps," you identified areas of your life where you believe there are deficits. Do you know what resources in your community

could provide you some help in these areas? With which are you familiar, how will they help you, and which ones do you need help locating?

_____

_____

_____

_____

6.   Of the resources you know, do you use them consistently and when you need them? If not, what interferes (e.g., finances, transportation, day care)?

_____

_____

7.   After identifying your deficits and some resources that could help you with them, think about what personal barriers reduce your desire or ability to follow through (e.g., communication skills, confidence, fear, motivation). Please list them here.

_____

_____

8.   Choose one of the barriers you've identified in question 7. With the help of your therapist, develop a step-by-step plan to begin to face and overcome that barrier. Briefly describe your plan here.

_____

_____

_____

_____

Especially in early recovery, the details of managing day-to-day living, personally healing, and resolving the difficulties created by your past addictive behavior can seem overwhelming. It is important to prioritize things, take things a step at a time, and ask for help when you need it.

   Be sure to bring this handout back to your next therapy session, and be prepared to talk about your thoughts and feelings about the exercise.

IS IT ROMANCE OR IS IT FEAR?

GOALS OF THE EXERCISE

1. Maintain a program of recovery that is free from addictive or high-risk behavior in relationships.
2. Identify and correct thoughts that trigger sexual promiscuity and learn to practice self-talk that promotes healthy sexual behavior.
3. Identify connections between childhood relationships with alcoholic, addicted, or otherwise dysfunctional parents and dysfunctional love relationships in adult life.
4. Achieve insight into the roots of dysfunctional relationships both with alcoholic parents and adult partners in feelings of responsibility for others' behavior.
5. Identify healthy nonromantic relationships to use as models for healthier love relationships.
6. Identify early warning signs to avoid future dysfunctional relationships.

ADDITIONAL PROBLEMS FOR WHICH THIS EXERCISE MAY BE USEFUL

*   Borderline Traits
*   Partner Relational Conflict

SUGGESTIONS FOR PROCESSING THIS EXERCISE WITH CLIENT

The "Is It Romance or Is It Fear?" activity is for clients with patterns of unhealthy relationship dynamics echoing childhood relationships with dysfunctional parents. This exercise is useful when clients present with dissatisfaction with dysfunctional relationships or loneliness and desire to establish new relationships. Follow-up can include bibliotherapy or videotherapy (see the book *Rent Two Films and Let's Talk in the Morning* by John W. Hesley and Jan G. Hesley, also published by John Wiley & Sons).

IS IT ROMANCE OR IS IT FEAR?

Do you repeatedly find yourself in romantic and/or sexual relationships with partners who are abusive, dishonest, neglectful, or otherwise bad for you, relationships that always seem to end in heartbreak, humiliation, fear, or abandonment? Do you find that even knowing you'd be safer and happier with someone who was honest, considerate, and dependable, it's the "bad boys/bad girls" who excite you? This exercise will help you start changing this painful pattern.

1. First, please reflect on the relationship or relationships that stand out in your mind as having been hardest to cope with. For each person that came to mind, think about what was most hurtful. The experiences that hurt most can include verbal and emotional abuse, physical abuse, dishonesty, emotional instability, undependability, abandonment, infidelity, neglect and emotional unavailability, addictive behaviors, and other irresponsible and self-destructive behavior by our partners.

    _____

    _____

    _____

    _____

2. If you thought about more than one relationship, do you see any trends or patterns? For example, some people get into relationships over and over with partners who are unfaithful and involve them in romantic triangles. Others may be repeatedly drawn to alcoholics, or workaholics, or batterers, or sex addicts. Please describe any patterns you see.

    _____

    _____

3. Now we'd like you to think about your experience growing up with alcoholic, addicted, or otherwise dysfunctional parent(s) or other adults. In many families where a caregiver has these problems, children are emotionally neglected. Impaired parents are also more likely than others to be verbally, emotionally, and/or physically abusive; to divorce or abandon their families; to be dishonest, undependable, and emotionally unavailable; and to be unstable and self-destructive.

Look at the patterns you listed for your painful love relationships, and circle any that also describe your childhood relationship with your parents. What patterns are repeated?

_____

_____

4. When those things happened in your childhood family, which of the following emotions did you feel: fear, anger, anxiety, shame, or despair? What about other painful feelings?

_____

_____

5. When the painful things you described happened in your adult love relationships, which of those emotions did you feel?

_____

_____

6. As children, it's normal for us to feel responsible for whatever other people do that affects us. Children often blame themselves for their parents' divorces, depressions, rages, drinking, and other problems. Even if a child doesn't consciously think, "It's my fault that they did that," often he/she thinks "if only I were a better kid, if only I could say or do the right thing, they'd act different." If you felt that way, please list some things your parents did that you felt were somehow your fault.

_____

_____

7. Now, moving back to adolescent and adult love relationships, if you sometimes have that same "if only . . ." feeling, please describe an experience where you felt that way.

_____

_____

8. If you are like most adult children of alcoholics, the partners to whom you've been drawn have had much in common with your parents, and you may have experienced many of the same patterns and feelings. If you are seeing this kind of similarity, please describe the emotions this realization brings up for you, and your thoughts about what you could do about it.

_____

_____

_____

_____

9. One of the most attractive qualities of dysfunctional partners is often the intensity and excitement we feel when we're with them. Another relationship marked by

similar intensity and excitement is that of an addict with his/her drug or other addictive behavior. What other parallels do you see between an addict's relationship with an addiction and yours with your parents, past partners, or both?

_____

_____

_____

_____

10. Take a moment to imagine your ideal partner. Please circle the six qualities from the list below that would best describe the person you'd like to be in a relationship with.

Honest	Humorous	Kind	Healthy	Patient	Intelligent
Positive	Courageous	Spiritual	Loyal	Practical	A Good Parent
Practical	Emotionally Strong	Dependable	Playful	Sensitive	Unselfish

Now think about your closest nonsexual, nonromantic relationship today. This could be with a best friend or a family member. Which of the qualities you circled describe that person?

_____

_____

11. Please compare how it feels to be in that close nonromantic relationship with how it feels or felt to be with your partner in your most painful relationship, then think about which relationship has been more emotionally rewarding and healthier for you. What are your thoughts about this comparison?

_____

_____

What would it be like to be in a romantic relationship with a person whose personality was similar to the person you thought about for question 10?

_____

_____

12. If you would rather be in such a relationship, less exciting but more nurturing, how can you seek out this type of partner?

_____

_____

_____

_____

Be sure to bring this handout back to your next therapy session, and be prepared to talk about your thoughts and feelings about the exercise.

WORKING THROUGH SHAME

GOALS OF THE EXERCISE

1. Maintain a program of recovery that is free of sexual promiscuity and addictive behavior.
2. Recognize and understand issues of shame and negative self-image.
3. Understand connections between negative self-image and addictive behaviors.
4. Build a more positive self-image as part of a recovery program.

ADDITIONAL PROBLEMS FOR WHICH THIS EXERCISE MAY BE USEFUL

- Childhood Trauma

SUGGESTIONS FOR PROCESSING THIS EXERCISE WITH CLIENT

The "Working through Shame" activity is intended to guide clients in correcting distorted perceptions and expectations that generate shame. Its approach is to guide the client in evaluating his/her own behaviors more objectively than in the past and to apply the same standards to himself/herself as to others. Follow-up could include sharing responses and outcomes of the affirmation-style portion of the exercise with the therapist and treatment group, as well as the exercise titled "Using Affirmations for Change" and bibliotherapy using the works of John Bradshaw, Janet Woititz, Claudia Black, and others who have written on this topic.

WORKING THROUGH SHAME

Shame is thinking that as a person, you are bad, inadequate, defective, unworthy, or less than other people. It results in feeling hopeless, helpless, and unable to change or succeed. Shame frequently accompanies addictive behavior. There's a difference between guilt and shame. Guilt is feeling that an *action* is unacceptable, but shame is feeling that *we ourselves* are unacceptable. We can deal with guilt by correcting our actions, but shame is destructive because we can't change who we are. If left unresolved, this puts us at high risk of returning to drinking, using, or other addictive and self-destructive behaviors. Shame convinces us that we can't get better and don't deserve to feel better. This exercise will help you identify and correct shame in your beliefs about yourself. You deserve to heal!

1. In the first column below, please list some mistakes you have made and things you have done wrong as a result of alcohol, other drug use, or other addictive patterns. In the second column, list things you should have done, but didn't do because your addiction(s) interfered.

   Mistakes and Wrong Actions　　　　**Things Not Done**

   _____

   _____

   _____

   _____

2. What kinds of shaming things do you say to yourself about the things you listed? Describe any thoughts in which you call yourself bad, weak, stupid, lazy, evil, or other negative labels.

   _____

   _____

   _____

   _____

3. What true and positive messages do you want to repeat to yourself about the things you listed in question 1, to replace these shaming messages (i.e., what might you say to a good friend who was in your situation)?

    _____

    _____

    _____

    _____

4. Each night for the next two weeks, please write your answer to the following questions, and talk with your therapist about what you write and any changes you see in your beliefs about yourself.

    "Of everything I did today, what do I feel the best about?"
    "What kind of person acts that way?"

Be sure to bring this handout back to your next therapy session, and be prepared to talk about your thoughts and feelings about the exercise.

UNDERSTANDING MY DEFENSE MECHANISMS

GOALS OF THE EXERCISE

1. Maintain a program of recovery that is free of addictive patterns and excessive anxiety.
2. Increase understanding of psychological defense mechanisms that interfere with progress in treatment and ways they have been demonstrated in past life experiences.
3. Understand the benefits and costs of defense mechanisms.
4. Learn and use healthier alternative ways to cope with difficulties.
5. Interact socially without excessive anxiety.

ADDITIONAL PROBLEMS FOR WHICH THIS EXERCISE MAY BE USEFUL

- Anger
- Antisocial Behavior
- Dangerousness/Lethality
- Narcissistic Traits
- Occupational Problems
- Treatment Resistance

SUGGESTIONS FOR PROCESSING THIS EXERCISE WITH CLIENT

The "Understanding My Defense Mechanisms" activity is designed for clients who are motivated for recovery but lack insight into dysfunctional defense mechanisms that are impeding their progress. The exercise presents information on psychological defense mechanisms and guides clients in self-assessment, then presents a structured cost/benefit analysis for each defense mechanism. It concludes by pointing in the direction of identifying and practicing more functional coping mechanisms as replacements for dysfunctional defense mechanisms. Follow-up can include keeping a journal of thoughts and actions related to defenses identified, continued work with the therapist on alternative coping strategies, studying role models to identify their coping processes, and reporting back to the therapist and treatment group on learning and progress.

UNDERSTANDING MY DEFENSE MECHANISMS

Defense mechanisms are mental and emotional responses we all use, often without knowing we're doing it, to protect ourselves from painful experiences and feelings. These defenses may save us from short-term emotional discomfort, but they can be problems when they keep us from being able to see ourselves, our world, and our behavior accurately. They can block recovery and maintain self-defeating behavior. This exercise will help you look at how your defenses were created and maintained, how they may be hurting you, and the costs of keeping them.

Some common defense mechanisms include:

a. Sense of humor (making light of a serious situation or downplaying its impact on others)

b. Sublimation (channeling feelings into safe and acceptable channels, like an aggressive person who vents anger playing football instead of assaulting his boss)

c. Denial (not being able to see the reality of a current situation, past actions, or the impact of consequences)

d. Projection (seeing other people as having your problem instead of seeing it in yourself)

e. Reaction formation (overcompensating by going to the opposite extreme, such as being extra nice to someone you don't like)

f. Intellectualizing (thinking of situations in nonemotional terms)

g. Displacement (expressing to one person or thing what you feel toward another, like yelling at your kids when you're mad at the police officer who pulled you over)

h. Repression ("forgetting" or putting something out of your conscious mind)

i. Hypochondriasis (thinking you are sick as a way to avoid dealing with a situation)

1. What are some painful or uncomfortable thoughts or situations you've had to deal with during the past year?

_____

_____

_____
_____

2. What defense mechanisms do you believe you may have used to cope with the thoughts or situations you listed for question 2, and how did you use them?

_____
_____
_____
_____

3. How have your defenses kept you from seeing your addictive behaviors realistically?

_____
_____
_____
_____

4. What feedback have others given you regarding your defenses?

_____
_____
_____
_____

5. *Cost/Benefit Analysis:* Choose one of the defenses that are part of your addiction's self-protection system and complete the following analysis.

Benefits of Keeping This Defense	**Costs of Keeping This Defense**
_____	_____
_____	_____
_____	_____

Benefits of Working through Painful/Uncomfortable Situations in a More Realistic Way	**Costs of Working through Painful/Uncomfortable Situations in a More Realistic Way**
_____	_____
_____	_____
_____	_____

6. How can you become aware as quickly as possible that you are using a defense mechanism in an unhealthy way?

_____

_____

_____

_____

7. For any defense mechanisms you've decided to give up, what will you replace them with to deal with the situations that prompted you to use those defense mechanisms? Who can help you develop coping methods that give you better results, and how will you get their help?

_____

_____

_____

_____

Be sure to bring this handout back to your next therapy session, and be prepared to talk about your thoughts and feelings about the exercise.

USING MY SUPPORT NETWORK

GOALS OF THE EXERCISE

1. Maintain a program of recovery that is free of addictive patterns and excessive anxiety.
2. Identify the ways a support network can assist in recovery.
3. Learn to work with others versus trying to sustain recovery alone.
4. Form relationships that will enhance a recovery support system.

ADDITIONAL PROBLEMS FOR WHICH THIS EXERCISE MAY BE USEFUL

- Adult-Child-of-an-Alcoholic (ACOA) Traits
- Chronic Pain
- Dependent Traits
- Depression
- Grief/Loss Unresolved
- Opioid Dependence
- Peer Group Negativity
- Posttraumatic Stress Disorder (PTSD)
- Relapse Proneness
- Sexual Promiscuity
- Self-Care Deficits—Primary
- Self-Care Deficits—Secondary
- Substance Abuse/Dependence
- Substance Intoxication/Withdrawal
- Suicidal Ideation

SUGGESTIONS FOR PROCESSING THIS EXERCISE WITH CLIENT

The "Using My Support Network" activity is for clients who have difficulty with shame and isolation that impedes their seeking and accepting support from others for therapeutic goals. Its approach is to guide the client in identifying potential sources of support from among family members, coworkers, and in other domains of life, and thinking through ways to assertively seek support and help from those people, anticipating and solving problems that may arise in doing so. Follow-up could include homework assignments to talk with the people identified in this exercise and ask for their support, then report back to the therapist and group on the outcomes.

USING MY SUPPORT NETWORK

It is common for people dealing with substance abuse or other addictive patterns to isolate themselves and to feel embarrassed or ashamed about their histories. Also, some feel that since they got themselves into the messes they are in alone, they need to solve their problems alone. However, people embarking on this journey benefit when they seek help from others who care about them, or who are succeeding at the same goals. This exercise will get you started using the support of helpful people to increase your chances of success in making these lifestyle changes.

1. The supportive people I can ask to help me stay in recovery from my addiction are:

    Family: _____

    _____

    Friends: _____

    _____

    Work/School: _____

    _____

    Church/spiritual community: _____

    _____

    Recovery community: _____

    _____

    Other(s): _____

    _____

2. Three benefits I will get from letting these people support what I am doing are:

    _____

    _____

    _____

3. The biggest obstacle or barrier for me in asking for assistance is:

    _____

    _____

4. The best thing that could happen when I ask someone for help is:

_____

_____

5. The worst thing that could happen when I ask someone for help is:

_____

_____

6. What I will tell these people about how I would like them to help me:

_____

_____

Be sure to bring this handout back to your next therapy session, and be prepared to talk about your thoughts and feelings about the exercise.

UNDERSTANDING SPIRITUALITY

GOALS OF THE EXERCISE

1. Broaden the client's understanding of spirituality and how it applies to overcoming addictions.
2. Learn the difference between religion and spirituality.
3. Overcome resistance to 12-Step programs based on antipathy toward religion.
4. Develop a concept of a higher power that is loving and supportive to recovery.
5. Resolve spiritual conflicts, allowing for a meaningful relationship with a higher power.

ADDITIONAL PROBLEMS FOR WHICH THIS EXERCISE MAY BE USEFUL

- Grief/Loss Unresolved
- Substance Abuse/Dependence

SUGGESTIONS FOR PROCESSING THIS EXERCISE WITH CLIENT

The "Understanding Spirituality" activity is written for clients whose therapeutic progress is impeded by antipathy toward spirituality as a resource for recovery based on antipathy toward organized religion or perceived conflicts with personal values. Follow-up could include bibliotherapy including books such as *Where in the World is God* by Robert Brizee.

UNDERSTANDING SPIRITUALITY

This assignment will help you begin working through an issue that troubles many people new to recovery programs. This is a big subject, and there's no way that one handout like this can cover it all, but it can offer some pointers to help you get started.

Why work on spirituality? Because it can make the difference between success or failure in recovery, and therefore possibly the difference between life or death. It's the key to effective use of Alcoholics Anonymous (AA), Narcotics Anonymous (NA), and other 12-Step programs.

When people attend their first meetings of 12-Step programs and find they dislike these programs, the most common reason is discomfort with all the talk about God. This may look like a barrier, making these programs useless to them, but it doesn't have to be.

Many people have good reasons to feel skeptical about religion. They may have had bad experiences with religious people or institutions. Perhaps they just feel that God has not been there in their lives. Hearing God or a Higher Power mentioned in 7 of the 12 Steps may be an immediate turn-off.

However, many people who either do not believe in God or believe that no one could know whether God exists find that they can use AA, NA, and other 12-Step programs to make the changes they want to make in their lives. The key is understanding the difference between *spirituality* and *religion*.

1. Write down your description of *religion*. What do you think of when you hear the word?

   _____

   _____

   _____

   _____

2. Now think about the word *spirituality,* and write your definition for this word.

   _____

   _____

   _____

   _____

3. Are there differences in the meanings of *religion* and *spirituality* for you? If so, what is the biggest difference you see?

_____

_____

A definition of *religion* could be as follows:

A religion *is a specific system of practices and rituals, based on a belief in a specific divine or superhuman power, usually practiced through membership in a specific human organization, usually called a church, temple, mosque, or synagogue.*

A similar definition for *spirituality,* on the other hand, might sound like this: *Spirituality is a focus on the moral aspects of life, on doing what is right and what will help us to become the best people we are capable of being.*

We could say it this way: A religion is a system people create to try to achieve spirituality. We could think of spirituality as water and religion as a bottle, a container to hold water—but other containers can hold water, and some bottles contain other things instead of water.

4. Does this idea make sense to you? _____ What other containers for spirituality can you think of (i.e., other ways to help yourself focus on what is right in life)?

_____

_____

5. At this point, you may be thinking, "Doesn't this definition of religion also describe a 12-Step program? It seems to be a specific system of practices and rituals, and it is practiced through membership in a specific organization!" If you've had the thought that AA, NA, or some other 12-Step program seemed to resemble a religion, what similarities do you see?

_____

_____

_____

_____

6. What differences do you see between 12-Step groups and religions?

_____

_____

_____

_____

Here are three key differences between 12-Step groups and religions:

- *Specific Definitions of God.* A religion offers specific ways to understand God, and may insist no other way is correct. A 12-Step program asks you to think in terms of a power greater than yourself, and leaves it to you to decide what that power is and how it works.

- *Authority*. While a religion almost always has a formal hierarchy and structure of people in charge, in a 12-Step group nobody is in charge. There is no chain of command. Decisions are made by the group through a vote called a "group conscience."

- *Membership Requirements*. Religions may restrict their memberships in many ways—by birth, heritage, or obedience to various rules. By contrast, in any 12-Step program, the 3rd Tradition says that the only membership requirement is a desire to solve the problem that group exists to overcome. Anyone who wants to be a member can do so, and no one can be excluded.

7. Going back to our definition of spirituality, how do you think that paying attention to the moral aspects of life and what is right could help you solve the problems facing you with alcohol, drugs, or other addictive behaviors?

_____

_____

If you see that a focus on these parts of your life could be useful, that's all it takes to begin including spirituality in your recovery work.

Be sure to bring this handout back to your next therapy session, and be prepared to talk about your thoughts and feelings about the exercise.

WHAT DO I BELIEVE IN?

GOALS OF THE EXERCISE

1. Clarify the client's personal values and sense of what is right and wrong.
2. Clarify what goals and parts of life are most important.
3. Compare the client's current circumstances and behavior with professed ideals and values.
4. Create a plan to make the client's life more consistent with professed values and ideals.
5. Resolve spiritual conflicts, allowing for a meaningful relationship with a higher power.

ADDITIONAL PROBLEMS FOR WHICH THIS EXERCISE MAY BE USEFUL

- Suicidal Ideation

SUGGESTIONS FOR PROCESSING THIS EXERCISE WITH CLIENT

The "What Do I Believe In?" activity is intended for the client struggling with cognitive dissonance and shifting values as he/she makes the change from an addictive lifestyle to recovery. Its approach is to guide the client in a process of values clarification addressing both moral values and lifestyle choices, then to prompt him/her to create a plan to begin making choices more consistent with stated values. Follow-up could include the assignment titled "Taking Daily Inventory" as well as keeping a journal and reporting back to the therapist and treatment group on outcomes of plans created in the course of this exercise.

WHAT DO I BELIEVE IN?

Many of us haven't thought hard about what we really believe in for a long time, perhaps our whole adult lives. And yet we do all have beliefs and values, and if our actions don't fit them we feel uneasy and may not know why. An important part of recovery is what people sometimes call "being comfortable in our own skin." We can't feel that way without the self-respect that comes with being true to what we believe. This exercise will help you explore your own beliefs and values and plan ways to live that are true to them.

1. First, please look at this list of personal qualities. Note that all of these are choices, qualities we can develop or learn, rather than things we don't control. Check off the six that are most important to you, in yourself and in other people, in doing what's right.

____ Honest	____ Kind	____ Courageous	____ Hard-working
____ Strong	____ Spiritual	____ Religious	____ Good provider
____ Patient	____ Positive	____ Good parent	____ Good partner
____ Practical	____ Respectful	____ Dignified	____ Good son/daughter
____ Dependable	____ Resilient	____ Good communicator	
____ Humble	____ Generous	____ Self-reliant	____ Self-confident
____ Gentle	____ Loyal	____ Playful	____ Understanding
____ Decisive	____ Tactful	____ Enthusiastic	____ Knowledgeable

2. Why are these things the most important to you? How did you come to value them?

    _____

    _____

    _____

    _____

3. Now review your life in each of the following areas, and make some notes about how your actions have either matched your values or been in conflict with them.

    Marriage/partnership: _____

    _____

Parenting: _____

_____

Other family relationships: _____

_____

Friendships: _____

_____

Work or school: _____

_____

Other important parts of your life: _____

_____

4. Please name one thing you will do in each area during the next week to make your actions more consistent with the values you believe are right.

Marriage/partnership: _____

_____

Parenting: _____

_____

Other family relationships: _____

_____

Friendships: _____

_____

Work or school: _____

_____

Other important parts of your life: _____

_____

5. Now we'll look at choices that aren't about what's right or wrong, just what suits you best.

   a. Which is a higher priority for you, your career or your personal life?

_____

   b. Are you comfortable with a busy life, or do you prefer more leisure time?

_____

   c. Would you rather live in a house with a yard, projects, etc., or an apartment where those things are taken care of by others? _____

   d. Do you like moving and getting to know new places, or do you prefer putting down roots and avoid moving if possible? _____

   e. If you had a two-week vacation, would you rather travel or relax at home?

_____

f. Do you prefer to have a nice home with lots of nice things, or live a simpler life with fewer material things? _____

g. Do you want a family, or would you prefer a life without kids? _____

h. Do you prefer recreational activities that involve groups, or are solitary or involve one or two other people? That are outdoors or indoors? That are structured and planned or more casual? That are competitive or more relaxed?

_____

_____

_____

_____

6. How closely does your life match the preferences you listed for question 4? Please list any discrepancies.

_____

_____

_____

_____

7. Please briefly describe three things you will do in the next month to start making your life more consistent with the lifestyle preferences you listed for question 4.

_____

_____

_____

_____

Be sure to bring this handout back to your next therapy session, and be prepared to talk about your thoughts and feelings about the exercise.

BALANCING RECOVERY, FAMILY, AND WORK

GOALS OF THE EXERCISE

1. Establish a sustained recovery, free of addictive behaviors.
2. Reduce potential family tension and conflicts in early recovery.
3. Avoid work-related difficulties undermining early sobriety.

ADDITIONAL PROBLEMS FOR WHICH THIS EXERCISE MAY BE USEFUL

- Family Conflicts
- Occupational Problems
- Parent-Child Relational Problems
- Partner Relationship Conflict

SUGGESTIONS FOR PROCESSING THIS EXERCISE WITH CLIENT

The "Balancing Recovery, Family, and Work" activity is designed for clients experiencing stress or conflicts in their families, their work, or both due to the demands of early recovery. Its aim is to normalize this experience and help clients see that this is not a failing on their part, to identify and explore in therapy specific issues that often arise, and to provide strategies for addressing these issues. Follow-up can include family therapy and keeping a journal. Clients may also benefit from videotherapy, such as an assignment to watch the film *When a Man Loves a Woman*, or others as suggested in the book *Rent Two Films and Let's Talk in the Morning* by John W. Hesley and Jan G. Hesley, also published by John Wiley & Sons, followed by discussion in later sessions.

BALANCING RECOVERY, FAMILY, AND WORK

One of the most important parts of recovery is balance in our lives. Three of the most important parts of our lives are (1) recovery activities, (2) family life, and (3) work life. We may find them in conflict, and by trying to do all we feel we should in one area we may neglect the others. This may make balance hard to achieve. Why is balance so difficult? Well, one key characteristic of an addictive lifestyle is lack of balance. In other words, in anything we do, we tend to either go overboard or fail to do enough.

1. What are some ways in which you went overboard and did too much in your life before you began your recovery?

    _____

    _____

    _____

    _____

2. What are some aspects of your life that you neglected before recovery, doing too little?

    _____

    _____

    _____

    _____

3. We often go to extremes in recovery programs too, especially in our early sobriety. If you have seen this in your life, what tells you you're going overboard?

    _____

    _____

    _____

    _____

4. Since we may have neglected our families, we may go overboard with them too. This can cause problems—they've gotten used to getting along without much help from us, and now we feel they're shutting us out. On the other hand, our families may feel we continue to neglect them to spend time with our newfound friends and activities in recovery. There may be some truth to this, as some of us get so absorbed in rebuilding our lives at work and in our recovery programs that we still have trouble finding time for our families. If things have gone either way with your family life, please describe how it's out of balance.

_____

_____

_____

_____

5. With work, too, it's easy to get carried away. We want to repair our reputations, and we may also fall into workaholism, a pattern in which we lose ourselves in work the way we used to lose ourselves in drinking, drugging, or other addictions, as a way to numb ourselves. If this happens, we may find we feel we need to put so much into work we resent the demands of both our families and our recovery programs. If you see signs of workaholism in your life, what has happened to make you suspect you are working too much?

_____

_____

_____

_____

6. Our families are among those who know us best, but they may be too emotionally involved to see clearly how we are doing. The more they understand about what we are doing, the more helpful their feedback will be and the more likely they are to be supportive. How well does your family understand your addiction and your recovery? What parts don't they understand?

_____

_____

_____

_____

_____

_____

7. How could they be more helpful to you if they understood more about what you are doing?

_____

_____

_____

_____

_____

_____

8. We may see that our family members could benefit from a support group such as Al-Anon or Ala-Teen. However, they might feel they've been doing a better job of dealing with life than we have, and resent our seeming to tell them what they need to do. Often, our families stay angry or mistrustful of us for a long time after we begin recovery, and they may be skeptical about any aspect of that recovery including 12-Step groups. It's best not to be pushy. Here are ways many people have helped family and friends understand their recovery programs.

   a. Ask them to come to meetings with you—and explain that you need their help to recover.

   b. Introduce them to friends from the program, especially your sponsor.

   c. Take them to program social functions.

   d. Leave program literature where they can find it and read it.

   e. Tell them about meetings.

   f. Introduce them to family members of other members of the program.

   If for a while they don't seem to understand, believe, or appreciate the change in you, be patient. List here some people who might be able to help you in helping your family and friends to understand your 12-Step program.

   _____

   _____

9. Regarding work, this may be easier than you think. Most people with addictions are excellent workers when they are clean and sober, and often find they expect more of themselves than anyone else would ask of them. The chances are that your supervisor already knows about your problem, or at least knows you had some serious problem affecting your work. If you explain what you are doing now to overcome the problem, your supervisor may be supportive, and you might not have to push as hard as you think to regain your good standing on the job, as long as you follow through. List some people who can help you prepare to talk with your supervisor about your recovery and what you need to do to take care of yourself.

   _____

   _____

   Remember, even people who aren't newly recovering from addiction have trouble balancing work, family, and self-care in today's world. The fact that you're having difficulty with this doesn't mean you're doing it wrong, it just means that you're human.

   Be sure to bring this handout back to your next therapy session, and be prepared to talk about your thoughts and feelings about the exercise.

CONSEQUENCES OF CONTINUING ADDICTIVE LIFESTYLES

GOALS OF THE EXERCISE

1. Accept powerlessness over addictive behaviors and the accompanying unmanageability of life and participate in a recovery-based program.
2. Establish and maintain total abstinence while increasing knowledge of the disease of addiction and the process of recovery.
3. Clarify how destructive the negative consequences of substance abuse or other addictive behavior will have to get before they become too bad to tolerate without quitting.
4. Focus attention on the negative consequences of addictive behaviors for self and others.

ADDITIONAL PROBLEMS FOR WHICH THIS EXERCISE MAY BE USEFUL

- Gambling
- Legal Problems
- Occupational Problems
- Opioid Dependence
- Peer Group Negativity
- Relapse Proneness
- Sexual Promiscuity
- Treatment Resistance

SUGGESTIONS FOR PROCESSING THIS EXERCISE WITH CLIENT

The "Consequence of Continuing Addictive Lifestyles" activity is for clients who are in denial or ambivalent about recovery. It aims to break down cognitive distortion. Follow-up can include bibliotherapy with personal stories from the book *Alcoholics Anonymous* or a book from another recovery program, or videotherapy using *Clean and Sober* or another film recommended in the book *Rent Two Films and Let's Talk in the Morning* by John W. Hesley and Jan G. Hesley, also published by John Wiley & Sons.

CONSEQUENCES OF CONTINUING ADDICTIVE LIFESTYLES

This assignment will help you see more clearly what your limits are when it comes to suffering negative consequences of substance abuse or other addictive behaviors. Once you've finished this, it will be helpful to talk about it with your therapist and/or your program sponsor.

1. Have you ever made a *yet list* before, or heard of the idea? A yet list is simply a list of negative consequences of addiction that we know could happen, but which we have not experienced yet. How could a list like this be useful?

   _____

   _____

2. As you may have heard or figured out, a yet list is used to define your personal definition of being out of control. This is a list of experiences you feel would show you that you needed to quit drinking, using, or practicing other addictive behaviors. First, if you truly believed your behavior was out of control, would you quit? Why or why not?

   _____

   _____

3. Now to make your list. Write down all the negative consequences of drinking, using other drugs, or practicing other addictive behaviors that you can think of, which you have *never* experienced. If you have a group to work with, you can have everyone brainstorm and make a shared list.

   Now look at the list. If there are experiences you've simply escaped through luck (e.g., not being caught when driving while impaired), what are they?

   _____

   _____

   _____

   _____

4. What experiences have you never risked (e.g., if you never drive while impaired, you've never been in danger of arrest for DWI)?

_____

_____

5. Which experiences from your list that haven't happened yet would you consider to be definite evidence that your behavior was unsafe or out of control, and why?

_____

_____

6. The experiences you listed for question 5 are your yet list. They've happened to others but haven't happened to you yet. Since you've decided these events would mean your behavior was out of control, what will you do if one of them does happen?

_____

_____

7. If you truly feel that the items on your yet list are unacceptable and would mean you had to quit drinking, using, gambling, or practicing some other compulsive behavior, how do you plan to quit if one of these things does happen as a result of your actions?

_____

_____

8. If you are willing to make a formal commitment to follow through on the decision you wrote about in question 7, how can you get started and how can others help you?

_____

_____

_____

_____

9. Review your responses to questions 5 and 7. Describe the potential benefits of working to address behavior to prevent those negatives from happening all together (not waiting for the negatives before getting started).

_____

_____

_____

_____

10. Who can help you with this? It is a good idea to talk to them ahead of time, now while you're calm and rational, and explain what you are asking them to do for you. We suggest specifically asking them how they would feel if you came to them for help. Use this space to record who you will ask for this help, when, and how.

    _____

    _____

    _____

    _____

Be sure to bring this handout back to your next therapy session, and be prepared to talk about your thoughts and feelings about the exercise.

PERSONAL RECOVERY PLANNING

GOALS OF THE EXERCISE

1. Establish sustained recovery, free from addictive behaviors, while increasing knowledge of the disease of addiction and the process of recovery.
2. Learn to think of recovery as something that involves every aspect of life and can be planned for and approached in a practical way.
3. Participate in the medical management of physical health problems.
4. Verbalize understanding of the need to maintain abstinence to remain free of negative legal and health consequences.
5. Create a recovery plan and a convenient list of people, groups, and techniques to lean on for support or information in times of distress.
6. Develop and articulate a concept of a higher power that is supportive to recovery.
7. Learn and demonstrate healthy social skills by developing a new peer group that is drug-free and supportive of working a program of recovery.
8. Develop and demonstrate coping skills by renewing old healthy relationships and forming new ones supportive of recovery.
9. Learn and demonstrate healthy impulse control skills, avoiding high-risk or addictive behaviors including gambling, overspending, and sexual acting out.

ADDITIONAL PROBLEMS FOR WHICH THIS EXERCISE MAY BE USEFUL

- Nicotine Dependence
- Opioid Dependence
- Relapse Proneness

SUGGESTIONS FOR PROCESSING THIS EXERCISE WITH CLIENT

The "Personal Recovery Planning" activity is intended for clients who are at least somewhat motivated for recovery and need structure and direction. It guides clients in identifying their goals for recovery to frame planning and strengthen motivation, then walks them through several domains of life functioning and prompts them to identify supportive resources and relationships and commit to a plan to use them. Follow-up for this exercise can include the activity titled "Relapse Prevention Planning;" keeping a journal; and reporting back to the therapist, treatment group, and sponsor on the outcomes of activities included in the personal recovery plan.

PERSONAL RECOVERY PLANNING

There are many ways to maintain a healthy lifestyle, free of self-defeating addictive behavior. Your recovery plan will be your creation, not exactly like anyone else's. It won't be a finished product when you're done, but it will give you a method to fall back on when things get difficult and confusing. You may have tried on one or more occasion to cut back or abstain from addictive behavior and discovered that some things work and some things do not. Please draw on that experience as you work through this exercise.

1. When you think about recovery, what do you want to accomplish? Beyond abstinence, some goals may include self-respect and dignity, peace of mind, healthy relationships, improved health, career progress, and improved finances. Please list the three things most important to you.

   a. _____

   b. _____

   c. _____

2. For each goal, how would a return to your addiction affect your chances of success?

   a. _____

   b. _____

   c. _____

3. For each goal, what successful result will show that you've achieved that desired outcome?

   a. _____

   b. _____

   c. _____

4. For each goal, what specific warning signs will tell you if you're getting off track?

    a. _____

    b. _____

    c. _____

5. Success in staying in recovery has positive and negative parts: finding *things to do* that help you remain abstinent, and finding *things not to do* because they may lead to relapse. Drawing on all you have learned and the experiences of others, please fill out the following.

    a. *Recovery activities*

        (1) What individual and/or group treatment sessions will I attend each week? When and where?

        _____

        _____

        (2) What support group meeting(s) will I attend during the week? When and where?

        _____

        _____

        (3) When, where, and for how long will I meet with my sponsor each week?

        _____

        _____

    b. *Creating a daily structure and routine*

        (1) What things will I do as part of my routine each day, and when will I do them?

        _____

        _____

        (2) Each week?

        _____

        _____

        (3) Each month?

        _____

        _____

c. *Basic self-care.* Living compulsively, we often neglect the basics (e.g., proper nutrition, health care, adequate rest, and exercise). Building these into your life will help you cope with stress. What can you do in each of these areas to take care of yourself?

(1) Proper nutrition:

_____

_____

(2) Medical care:

_____

_____

(3) Rest:

_____

_____

(4) Exercise/physical activity:

_____

_____

d. *Relationships and support systems.* Relationships with loved ones and friends can have a tremendous effect on recovery, either helping or hurting. You'll need to analyze past and current relationships and keep some, end some, and develop some new ones.

(1) *Old relationships.* What relationships are likely to support your recovery, and what will you do to strengthen them?

_____

_____

What relationships will probably undermine your efforts, and how will you end or distance them?

_____

_____

(2) *New relationships.* Where can you meet people to start some new, healthy, supportive relationships, and how will you go about finding them?

_____

_____

(3) *How you can get support from relationships.* Please list some people with whom you can talk when you feel troubled, confused, or discouraged, and write about how you will approach each of them to ask for this support.

Name	**How I Will Ask for Support**
_____	_____
_____	_____
_____	_____
_____	_____

e. *Spirituality.* Whether or not you're religious, recovery involves making changes in your values; people who include spiritual resources in recovery are usually more successful.

(1) How will I address this component of my recovery?

_____

_____

(2) What questions do I have about this, and whom can I ask for assistance?

_____

_____

f. *Work.* Your job can be a major source of satisfaction, self-esteem, security, and, sometimes, great stress. Recovering people are prone to workaholism and burnout, either because we want to make up for lost time or because we aren't used to moderation.

(1) What will I do to keep my work within healthy, moderate limits?

_____

_____

(2) What will I do if something about my work is posing a risk to my recovery?

_____

_____

(3) How do I plan on dealing with stress related to work?

_____

_____

g. *Legal issues.* Dealing with the legal consequences of addictions is important to be a responsible person, to reduce long-term stress, and to gain self-respect. What am I doing to get any unfinished legal matters settled?

_____

_____

h. *Finances.* This is another part of life with great impact on self-esteem and stress levels. Many newly recovering people are intimidated by financial problems when they get clean and sober, but with steady effort they can clear the difficulties up faster than expected.

(1) What financial problems do I have and what am I doing to resolve them?

_____

_____

(2) What is my long-term plan for financial stability?

_____

_____

i. *Recreation.* Early recovery is a time to start having healthy fun, with activities you have enjoyed in the past or with new activities, to help you cope with stress and enjoy life.

(1) What old healthy recreational activities will I take up again?

_____

_____

(2) What new activities will I try, and/or am I interested in learning more about?

_____

_____

(3) What steps will I take to incorporate this into my weekly schedule?

_____

_____

j. *Other areas of life.*

(1) What other things do I see that I should focus on?

_____

_____

(2) What is one step I can take today to make progress on one of these issues?

_____

_____

k. *Crisis management.* Your plan must include steps to handle crises. Please list things you'll do to handle an unexpected (or expected) crisis without relapsing into addictive behavior.

_____

_____

6. Finally, please list activities you know you need to avoid as they may lead to relapse. This may mean not going to certain places, seeing some people, or engaging in particular work or recreational activities.

    _____

    _____

    _____

    _____

    Congratulations! You've built a foundation on which to build, and a reference that will come in handy when you're under stress and having trouble thinking clearly. By completing this exercise, you've done much of that thinking in advance.

    Be sure to bring this handout back to your next therapy session, and be prepared to talk about your thoughts and feelings about the exercise and make modifications as needed.

PROBLEM IDENTIFICATION

GOALS OF THE EXERCISE

1. Establish a sustained recovery that is free of addictive behaviors.
2. Increase awareness of personal losses and problems associated with addictive behaviors.
3. Collect objective facts about the impact of alcohol or other drug use or addictive behaviors.
4. Increase motivation for change to avoid further problems brought on by or made worse by addictions.

ADDITIONAL PROBLEMS FOR WHICH THIS EXERCISE MAY BE USEFUL

*   Eating Disorders
*   Gambling
*   Nicotine Dependence
*   Opioid Dependence

SUGGESTIONS FOR PROCESSING THIS EXERCISE WITH CLIENT

The "Problem Identification" activity is suited for individual or group use. This is, in a way, the opposite of the "Consequences of Continuing Addictive Lifestyles" exercise. Whereas the latter guides the client in creating a *yet list* of negative consequences, this activity walks him/her through systematically listing at one time in one place the negative things that have already happened—in a way, conducting a self-intervention. Follow-up to this exercise might include writing about reflections afterward; sharing responses with the therapist, treatment group, and program sponsor; and moving on to the "Personal Recovery Planning" activity.

PROBLEM IDENTIFICATION

People don't usually get treatment or help until they find themselves in some kind of crisis. Crises are good motivators, but they don't usually last as long as the underlying problems. To stay in recovery, we need to look at our addictive behaviors over the long run, beyond the crises that get us to act. If you wonder whether you have a problem with alcohol, another drug, or another addictive behavior, or how serious your problem is, compare the events in your life with each of these categories.

1. Below is a brief, partial list of common experiences that encourage people who are practicing addictive lifestyles to decide that they should change these patterns, that their addictions are causing them problems, and that they want help. Please check all those that apply to you.

   Loss of Important Relationships Because of Addictions

   ____ Divorce or equivalent   ____ Children, parents, siblings alienated

   ____ Loss of close friendships   ____ Loss of respect from coworkers

   Practical Difficulties Resulting from Addictions

   ____ Unpayable debts   ____ Loss of employment

   ____ Loss of a vehicle   ____ Loss of a home

   ____ Loss of professional status   ____ Bankruptcy

   ____ Legal problems (*e.g., arrest, jail, probation, loss of driver's license*)

   Dangerous/Harmful Situations Resulting from Addictions

   ____ Health problems   ____ Recreational accidents

   ____ DUIs, DWIs, or car wrecks   ____ Work injuries, falls, or other accidents

   ____ Fights while under the   ____ Harm to others as a result of one's own
        influence or coming down   actions under the influence

   ____ Suicidal ideation, attempts   ____ Self-injury

   ____ Violence

   Things We Once Thought We Would Never Do

   ____ Letting down friends   ____ Repeatedly breaking promises

   ____ Lying to partners/families   ____ Stealing from partners/families/work

   ____ Letting down employers   ____ Abusing family members

____ Selling drugs   ____ Committing crimes to support addiction

____ Exchanging sex for alcohol   ____ Endangering others, especially children
or other drugs

2. When you think about your life without alcohol, other drugs, or the other addictive behavior, what emotions do you feel?

_____

_____

3. Do you see any other evidence that your use of alcohol, other drugs, or other addictive behavior is causing problems in your life? If you do, what is it?

_____

_____

4. On a scale of 1–10 (1 = not at all and 10 = extremely important), how important is it for you to make changes to your use of alcohol, other drugs, or other addictive behavior at this time?

_____

5. On a scale of 1–10 (1 = not at all and 10 = extremely confident), how confident are you that you could begin to make changes to your alcohol, other drug, or other addictive behavior if you wanted to?

_____

Be sure to bring this handout back to your next therapy session, and be prepared to talk about your thoughts and feelings about the exercise.

WHAT DOES ADDICTION MEAN TO ME?

GOALS OF THE EXERCISE

1. Establish and maintain total abstinence while increasing knowledge of the disease of addiction, how abuse/addiction has affected the client's life, and the process of recovery.
2. Increase awareness of addictive patterns of thought and behavior.
3. Increase client ownership of issues by creating a personal definition of the problem of substance abuse or addiction.

ADDITIONAL PROBLEMS FOR WHICH THIS EXERCISE MAY BE USEFUL

- Gambling
- Opioid Dependence
- Sexual Promiscuity
- Substance-Induced Disorders
- Treatment Resistance

SUGGESTIONS FOR PROCESSING THIS EXERCISE WITH CLIENT

The "What Does Addiction Mean to Me?" activity is for the client who is resistant to accepting a diagnosis of substance dependence or abuse due to mistaken ideas about what the terms mean. It explains the *DSM-IV-TR* criteria (in terms with which the client is familiar) and analyzes how they fit the client's life situation, including any non–drug-using addictive behavior. Follow-up can include bibliotherapy on alcoholism and addiction; keeping a journal about the client's thoughts and feelings about the lessons learned, conclusions, and plans made; and discussion with the therapist and treatment group of all of the above.

WHAT DOES ADDICTION MEAN TO ME?

You may be doubtful about whether you are an alcoholic or addict, no matter what anyone else says. To answer this question for yourself, you need to be able to identify patterns of addictive or abusive use of alcohol, other drugs, or compulsive behavior, and to see whether your life fits these patterns.

1. For each of the following patterns, please write about whether this has happened in your life, and if it has, please think of at least one example.

   a. *Tolerance.* This is needing to use more of a chemical or do more of a behavior (or doing it to a greater extreme) to get the same effect, or feeling less effect if you use or do the same amount.

   _____

   _____

   b. *Withdrawal.* This means either feeling ill or uncomfortable after stopping use of the chemical or the behavior, or using the chemical or practicing the behavior to relieve or avoid feeling ill or uncomfortable.

   _____

   _____

   c. *Loss of control.* This means you use, drink, or practice an addictive behavior for longer or in greater quantity than you intended.

   _____

   _____

   d. *Attempts to control.* This fits if you have had a persistent desire to cut down or stop, or have made efforts to control or cut down your using/drinking/addictive actions, including making rules or bargains with yourself to limit it.

   _____

   _____

   e. *Time spent.* This refers to spending a significant amount of time thinking about using, drinking, or practicing the addictive behavior; planning or preparing for it; using/drinking/practicing; and dealing with the consequences (such as being hung over or coming down, or being broke until payday).

_____

_____

f. *Sacrifices made.* This is talking about giving up or reducing social, work, family, or recreational activities that were important to you because they conflicted with your addictive behaviors—for example, drifting away from friendships with people who won't drink or use with you.

_____

_____

g. *Continued use despite known suffering.* This means continuing to use, drink, or practice another addiction in spite of knowing that you have had major physical, psychological, legal, financial, or relationship problems that were caused or made worse by that behavior.

_____

_____

2. Looking back over these symptoms, what do they tell you about your use of substances or other addictive behaviors?

_____

_____

3. For each of the following stages of addiction, please note whether you have experienced this, and if you have, please think of an example of how your life fits the description.

a. *First stage.* The first experience—when you begin using a chemical or engaging in a behavior and discover that you like the way it makes you feel.

_____

_____

b. *Second stage.* Tolerance and withdrawal appear, and you find that you can use the chemical or behavior to cope with situations or feelings that are difficult or uncomfortable.

_____

_____

c. *Third stage.* You begin deliberately and routinely using the chemical or behavior to cope with stress or other problems. You may feel uneasy about it, and may try to cut down or control use; your normal life is disrupted and others may start thinking that you have a problem.

_____

_____

    d. *Fourth stage.* You come to feel that you can't cope with your life's stresses without the chemical or behavior. You feel that you must pay whatever price comes with continued use; you feel trapped; your life seems to be falling apart; and/or relationships with others are compromised.

    _____

    _____

4. Looking over these four phases in the development of an addiction, what have you learned about your own pattern of use?

    _____

    _____

    Be sure to bring this handout back to your next therapy session, and be prepared to talk about your thoughts and feelings about the exercise.

IDENTIFYING AND USING COMMUNITY RESOURCES

GOALS OF THE EXERCISE

1. Restore daily functioning to healthy norms.
2. Participate in medical management of addictions and substance-induced disorders.
3. Effectively use available resources in personal and family recovery.
4. Reduce emotional and social isolation for self and family.
5. Augment treatment and aftercare with resources that can be used indefinitely without cost.

ADDITIONAL PROBLEMS FOR WHICH THIS EXERCISE MAY BE USEFUL

- Grief/Loss Unresolved
- Legal Problems
- Living Environment Deficiency
- Medical Issues
- Posttraumatic Stress Disorder
- Self-Care Deficits—Primary
- Self-Care Deficits—Secondary

SUGGESTIONS FOR PROCESSING THIS EXERCISE WITH CLIENT

The "Identifying and Using Community Resources" activity is for clients who are not accustomed to asking for help or may not know of available resources. It includes examination of resources for various problems and guides the client in researching and contacting them. Follow-up can include reporting on outcomes and referrals to specific community resources.

IDENTIFYING AND USING COMMUNITY RESOURCES

Alcoholics, addicts, and people who grew up with abuse and neglect may become so self-reliant we just don't ask for help or information. Even in treatment for addictions, we may not seek help in other areas. This exercise will help you find support and help for yourself and your family.

1. *Treatment programs.* You may be in such a program now. There are treatment programs for problems other than addictions that you or your family might benefit from. Here are some issues for which treatment programs exist (check any about which you're curious):

    ☐ Eating disorders (anorexia, bulimia, compulsive overeating)

    ☐ Compulsive gambling

    ☐ Depression, anxiety, bereavement, and other emotional or mental problems

    ☐ Codependency and other relationship problems

    ☐ Physical, sexual, or emotional abuse and trauma

    Although they vary, treatment programs usually have these things in common:

    • They charge for their services (often your health insurance will pay); some are free in return for participating in research or are paid for by government agencies or universities.

    • They are run by professionals (physicians, psychologists, therapists, or social workers).

    • They may be residential (clients or patients live there while in treatment) or outpatient, and they are usually intensive—full-time while you are in treatment.

    • Treatment usually lasts for several days or weeks, then ends.

    If you or someone close to you suffers from one of these problems, how do you feel about knowing these treatment programs exist?

    _____

    _____

2. *Support groups.* Another community resource is the support group. Support groups exist for many problems. Alcoholics Anonymous (AA) and Narcotics Anonymous (NA) are two examples, but there are many others, some of which are also 12-Step programs, and others which have different philosophies. Support groups usually have these things in common:

   - They are normally free of charge although they often accept voluntary donations.

   - Rather than being run by professionals, they are run in a democratic way by their members and often engage in debate and voting to make decisions.

   - They meet daily or weekly in public places (e.g., schools, churches, synagogues, temples, restaurants, or conference rooms at hospitals or other businesses).

   - Members often socialize together outside of meetings.

   - They may organize picnics, potluck dinners, or dances for holidays to give members a place to celebrate without alcohol, other drugs, or other temptations around.

   - You can participate for as long as you want. Some attend for the rest of their lives.

   Here are a few common types of groups—check any that might be useful for you:

   ☐ Family members of alcoholics, addicts, or gamblers

   ☐ Sufferers of emotional and mental illness and their families and friends

   ☐ Family and friends of Alzheimer's disease sufferers

   ☐ Parents whose children have died

   ☐ Widows and widowers

   ☐ Families and friends of people who have committed or attempted suicide

   ☐ Survivors of abuse, assault, rape, and other violent crimes

   ☐ Sufferers of various specific illnesses or injuries and their families and friends

   One or more of these issues has probably affected your life. How would having advice and support from others who had experienced the same things be easier than coping with one of these problems alone?

   _____

   _____

3. *Family support programs.* As well as treatment programs and support groups, many kinds of family support programs are offered by government agencies, worship centers, or schools and universities. Please check off any types of assistance you or your family could use.

   ☐ Transportation for work, shopping, health care, therapy, school, or other purposes

   ☐ Help with free or low-cost food

☐ Clothing

☐ Housing assistance

☐ Parenting skills training

☐ Coping with disabilities

☐ Help for single parents and their children (e.g., Big Brothers/Big Sisters and Parents without Partners)

How could such a group be helpful for you or anyone in your family?

_____

_____

_____

_____

4. *Educational and vocational programs.* These programs, mostly run by colleges, help people learn to read and write, learn English, complete high school or earn GEDs, or learn job skills. Some are free, some are inexpensive, and some are costly. You can usually find GED and high school completion programs free. Training for specific skills (e.g., plumbing, welding, auto mechanics) may be economical or expensive. What would you go to school to learn?

_____

_____

5. *Religious and spiritual programs.* This area may or may not be important to you. Some find that spirituality is very important to them, even if they start into recovery with no interest in it. AA and other 12-Step programs have a spiritual focus, though they don't link it with any religion or denomination. Other places to find religious or spiritual programs, obviously, are churches, synagogues, mosques, and other places of worship. These programs are normally free. They can help people figure out what goals they want to achieve and what is important in their lives. If you're interested in religious or spiritual programs, what do you want to change in your life, and how might such a program help you?

_____

_____

6. *Information sources.* In almost every community, a library offers books, newspapers, and magazines with information on anything you want to accomplish; they often have computers and Internet access. You can also turn to trained people (e.g., doctors, teachers, counselors, or therapists). What sources would you use?

_____

_____

7.   We've looked at a range of community resources. Think about what help you could use, talk with your therapist, and make a plan. What help do you want, where will you go for it, and when?

   _____

   _____

   Be sure to bring this handout back to your next therapy session, and be prepared to talk about your thoughts and feelings about the exercise.

PLANNING AFTERCARE

GOALS OF THE EXERCISE

1. Maintain a program of recovery that is free from addiction and substance-induced disorders.
2. Restore daily functioning to healthy norms.
3. Restore normal sleep pattern, improve long- and short-term memory, and maintain abstinence from addictive behaviors.
4. Participate in medical management of addictions and substance-induced disorders.
5. Increase understanding of the importance of self-evaluation and planning in making lifestyle changes that last.
6. Attend to successes and increase motivation to continue positive change.

ADDITIONAL PROBLEMS FOR WHICH THIS EXERCISE MAY BE USEFUL

- Substance Abuse/Dependence

SUGGESTIONS FOR PROCESSING THIS EXERCISE WITH CLIENT

The "Planning Aftercare" activity is designed for clients in early recovery who will benefit from reinforcement of their original motivations for entering treatment and of their progress. It takes the approach of guiding the client in reviewing his/her state of mind and feelings at the time of entry into recovery and making a current self-assessment for comparison. The exercise goes on to reviewing and revising goals for future recovery and choosing ways to track progress. Follow-up for this activity might include completion of the "Personal Recovery Planning" exercise, sharing the results of these exercises with a recovery program sponsor, keeping a journal on progress and lessons learned, and having the client share his/her experiences with this exercise with a therapy group.

PLANNING AFTERCARE

Early in recovery, our thoughts, time, and energy tend to be focused on abstaining from substance use or other addictive patterns. As we accumulate more clean and sober time, our attention turns to maintaining the changes we've achieved and pursuing other personal goals. This exercise will help you identify how far you've come and where you are today in your recovery efforts, and help you identify where you want to go and how you will get there.

1. Looking back: Where did you begin?

    a. What was the date when you took your last drink or drug, or last practiced your other addiction, and decided to quit or entered treatment?

    _____

    _____

    b. What were the main goals you set for your recovery that day or early in treatment?

    _____

    _____

    _____

    _____

2. Taking stock: Where are you today?

    a. What is the date today? _____

    b. What recovery goals are you now working to accomplish?

    _____

    _____

    _____

    _____

    c. What primary issues or problems are you addressing?

    _____

    _____

    _____

    _____

d. What specific actions and changes are you putting into practice today?

_____

_____

e. What issues do you feel you will need to focus on in recovery during the next year?

_____

_____

_____

_____

f. What relapse trends or self-destructive behavior do you see in yourself today?

_____

_____

g. What successes have you achieved since your last self-evaluation of this kind?

_____

_____

_____

_____

3. Planning for tomorrow: Where do you want to go from here?
   a. Please write the date when you will next re-evaluate your progress.

   _____

   b. What goals do you want to work toward between today and that date?

   _____

   _____

   c. What information and other resources do you need to achieve those goals?

   _____

   _____

   d. What is the first step you will take after today's self-evaluation?

   _____

   _____

   e. What results will tell you that you are succeeding in your goals?

   _____

   _____

   f. What self-destructive behaviors do you have to watch out for in yourself?

   _____

   _____

g. With whom will you discuss this self-evaluation (e.g., your therapist, your support group sponsor, supportive friends, supportive family members)?

_____

_____

Be sure to bring this handout back to your next therapy session, and be prepared to talk about your thoughts and feelings about the exercise.

COPING WITH POST-ACUTE WITHDRAWAL (PAW)

GOALS OF THE EXERCISE

1. Recovery from substance intoxication/withdrawal, and participation in a chemical dependency assessment.
2. Learning about a common syndrome in recovery from chemical dependency which might otherwise lead to demoralization, anxiety, and relapse.
3. Becoming empowered to cope with post-acute withdrawal (PAW) and learn about resources and supports available for assistance.
4. Stabilizing the client's condition medically, behaviorally, emotionally, and cognitively and returning to functioning within normal parameters.
5. Keeping health care providers informed of withdrawal symptoms.
6. Compliance with instructions of health care providers in coping with PAW.

ADDITIONAL PROBLEMS FOR WHICH THIS EXERCISE MAY BE USEFUL

- Depression
- Relapse Proneness
- Substance-Induced Disorders

SUGGESTIONS FOR PROCESSING THIS EXERCISE WITH CLIENT

The "Coping with Post-Acute Withdrawal" activity is intended primarily for clients in early recovery after long-term or heavy abuse of alcohol or barbiturates, but some of the features of PAW may be seen in users of other categories of substances as well including opioids and stimulants. The exercise normalizes the experience of otherwise alarming persistent symptoms and relieves clients' fears that those symptoms are permanent, increasing motivation to remain abstinent. Follow-up for this activity may include discussion of symptoms with the therapist, group, a physician, and a program sponsor; keeping a log of gradual improvement; and planning of coping strategies.

COPING WITH POST-ACUTE WITHDRAWAL

Heavy drinking or drug abuse upsets the chemical balance in a person's body. Although it may only take days or weeks for alcohol or other drugs to leave the system, this chemical balance can take months to get back to normal. This is called post-acute withdrawal, or PAW. While this happens, a recovering person may continue to experience physical, mental, and emotional problems. It is important to know that though these PAW symptoms may hang on for months, they *will* keep gradually getting better if you stay clean and sober! This exercise will help you understand PAW and teach you how to get through these problems without relapsing.

1. Some symptoms of post-acute withdrawal (PAW) are as follows:
   - ☐ Difficulty thinking clearly
   - ☐ Problems with memory, especially short-term memory
   - ☐ Increased feelings of anxiety, depression, and/or irritability
   - ☐ Rapid mood swings that seem to happen for little or no reason
   - ☐ Emotional over-reactivity or numbness
   - ☐ Sleep disturbances
   - ☐ Problems with physical coordination

   Have you repeatedly experienced any of these problems since you stopped using alcohol or other drugs? If so, please check the ones you've experienced.

2. What methods have you tried to cope with these symptoms?

   _____

   _____

   _____

   _____

3. What methods have worked best for you?

   _____

   _____

   _____

   _____

4. Your assignment now is to talk with other people in recovery and ask how they have coped with PAW without returning to using/drinking. Who will you ask, and how will you ask them for this information?

    _____

    _____

5. Based on what you have found works for you and on the experiences of other people, please list five things you can do to cope with PAW if you experience the symptoms listed earlier.

    a. _____
       _____

    b. _____
       _____

    c. _____
       _____

    d. _____
       _____

    e. _____
       _____

    Be sure to bring this handout back to your next therapy session, and be prepared to talk about your thoughts and feelings about the exercise.

USING BOOKS AND OTHER MEDIA RESOURCES

GOALS OF THE EXERCISE

1. Find and make effective use of media resources to assist in personal and family recovery from substance dependence, abuse, and related problems.
2. Reduce shame and emotional isolation by learning that addictive issues affect many other people.
3. Increase the effectiveness of treatment and aftercare by augmenting them with resources that can be used outside the treatment environment.

ADDITIONAL PROBLEMS FOR WHICH THIS EXERCISE MAY BE USEFUL

- Adult-Child-of-an-Alcoholic (ACOA) Traits
- Anxiety
- Childhood Trauma
- Depression
- Grief/Loss Unresolved
- Relapse Proneness
- Spiritual Confusion

SUGGESTIONS FOR PROCESSING THIS EXERCISE WITH CLIENT

The "Using Books and Other Media Resources" activity introduces the client to the use of media to explore personal issues. It invites the client to examine his/her reactions to books, movies, or songs that trigger strong feelings or seem relevant to the client's life issues. Follow-up may include discussion of these reactions and what insights they offer the client. For videotherapy, the therapist may want to use the excellent book entitled *Rent Two Films and Let's Talk in the Morning,* by John W. Hesley and Jan G. Hesley, also published by John Wiley & Sons, Inc. This book, now in its second edition, discusses ways to integrate video-viewing homework into therapy using widely available commercially produced films. The Hesleys provide extensive recommendations for using specific films to address various treatment issues.

USING BOOKS AND OTHER MEDIA RESOURCES

Because they affect so many people and are important parts of every culture, the issues you are working on in treatment have inspired films, TV shows, books, art, and music. Often these materials can give us useful information or inspiration, or they can move us emotionally in a powerful way that can help treatment. This exercise will help you think about how you can use some of this material to help you achieve your own goals.

1. Have you seen films or TV shows, read books, or listened to music that dealt with issues of substance abuse, other addictive problems, or other life situations with which you identified? What artistic work were you exposed to, and what emotions did it bring up for you?

    _____

    _____

2. How do you feel these works could help you or others overcome the problems that brought you into treatment?

    _____

    _____

    _____

    _____

3. A basic way these materials can be useful, especially books, is by providing practical information about how your problems may have developed, obstacles and pitfalls that can endanger your recovery, guidance on actions you can take to get better, and stories of others who have succeeded to inspire and provide examples. Please describe any help of this kind that you've found.

    _____

    _____

    _____

    _____

4. Here are some places you can get these materials. Please check all that are available to you.

Free Sources	**Sources That Cost Money**
_____ Libraries	_____ Bookstores
_____ Internet	_____ Video rental/sales outlets
_____ Community agencies	_____ Movie theaters

5. Talk with your therapist, and choose the first video, TV program, book, or piece of music you will use as part of your therapy. _An important note: Especially if you are in the early stages of your recovery, or if your experiences have been very painful and trigger intense emotions, don't do this without your therapist's guidance! You could expose yourself to overwhelming feelings that would put you at higher risk for relapse._ Once you and your therapist have talked it over and agreed on a plan, please watch, read, or listen to the creative work you've chosen, then write here about whatever emotions, thoughts, and new realizations you have.

_____

_____

_____

_____

Be sure to bring this handout back to your next therapy session, and be prepared to talk about your thoughts and feelings about the exercise.

WHAT DID I WANT TO BE WHEN I GREW UP?

GOALS OF THE EXERCISE

1. Understand the relationship between suicidal ideation and addiction.
2. Identify the impact of substance abuse or other addictions on life goals.
3. Compare an addictive lifestyle with childhood ambitions.
4. Reconnect with old ideals and dreams.
5. Resolve preoccupation with death, find new hope, and enter a program of recovery free of addictive thought and behaviors and suicidal ideation.

ADDITIONAL PROBLEMS FOR WHICH THIS EXERCISE MAY BE USEFUL

- Adult-Child-of-an-Alcoholic (ACOA) Traits

SUGGESTIONS FOR PROCESSING THIS EXERCISE WITH CLIENT

The "What Did I Want to Be When I Grew Up?" activity is intended to strengthen the client's motivation for treatment and help him/her reconnect with early ideals and dreams. It guides the client in reviewing childhood goals and hopes, then comparing them with present-day life and identifying ways to achieve early goals that are still appealing, thereby decreasing perceptions of powerlessness and increasing self-esteem. Follow-up could include assignments to research goals identified through this exercise and plan ways to act on them, keep a journal, and report back to the therapist and treatment group on outcomes.

WHAT DID I WANT TO BE WHEN I GREW UP?

This assignment will help you reconnect with early dreams and ideals about which you may not have thought for a long time. Though we often put childhood dreams aside in adulthood, those daydreaming children are still part of our inner selves, and can tell us a lot about our true identities and nature.

1. Take a moment to think back to your childhood. What is your earliest memory of wanting to do a certain job or play a certain role (be a mom or a dad, etc.)? How old were you, and what did you want to do or be?

   _____

   _____

2. What other jobs or roles did you dream about as you grew older?

   _____

   _____

   _____

   _____

3. What does your life now have in common with the life you dreamed about as a child or teen?

   _____

   _____

   _____

   _____

4. If your youthful dreams still appeal to you, are there things you can do as an adult that would be like those dreams in some way? For example, a person who dreamed of being an explorer could be a reporter or get involved in research. What are some things you can do that are in the spirit of your early dreams?

   _____

   _____

   _____

   _____

5. When you thought about your future while you were growing up, did you think about using alcohol or other drugs in that future? If so, how did you picture yourself drinking or using?

_____

_____

6. Now do an exercise in imagination. Find a quiet place where you can think without being disturbed for a while. Sit in a comfortable position. Close your eyes, and picture yourself at the happiest time of your childhood. Now picture the child that you were, standing in front of you looking at you. In this picture, you've come to talk to this child as a friendly, positive adult who will help him/her in life. As you picture this child meeting the adult you are now, what does the child think and feel? What expression is on his/her face?

_____

_____

7. What would you say to that child? What you would want him/her to know about you, and as a caring adult, what would you want to give to that child?

_____

_____

_____

8. Now put yourself in that child's shoes. Look at this adult who has come to visit you. Imagine hearing the things this person would say to you. What would you, as your childhood self, want to say to this adult? What would you ask him/her?

_____

_____

_____

9. Imagine yourself, as a child, telling your adult self about your hopes and dreams. What answer do you think this adult would give you?

_____

_____

_____

10. Continue the exercise in imagination. Picture the adult you are now, going through your typical day, accompanied by the child you were. Which parts of your day would you be proud to have that child watch? Are there parts of your day, parts of your life, you would rather that child didn't see? If so, what are they, and why do you feel that way? What can you do about this?

_____

_____

_____

_____

11. As part of your therapy, talk with your therapist about this exercise and what it is like for you. It can help you strengthen your connections to your oldest, strongest ideals and dreams to make this exercise a part of your daily or weekly routine.

Be sure to bring this handout back to your next therapy session, and be prepared to talk about your thoughts and feelings about the exercise.

WHY DO I MATTER AND WHO CARES?

GOALS OF THE EXERCISE

1. Accurately assess the client's importance in other people's lives.
2. Examine evidence in others' behavior to identify caring and concern.
3. Create a plan to identify concerned others and reach out for their emotional support.
4. Resolve preoccupation with death, and eliminate addictive or suicidal thought/behaviors.

ADDITIONAL PROBLEMS FOR WHICH THIS EXERCISE MAY BE USEFUL

- Borderline Traits
- Depression

SUGGESTIONS FOR PROCESSING THIS EXERCISE WITH CLIENT

The "Why Do I Matter and Who Cares?" activity is aimed at clients at risk for suicidal gestures or attempts, and at others suffering from interpersonal isolation and feelings of worthlessness. It leads clients to correct distorted perceptions of their worth by having them survey situations in which they are valued. It includes an assessment of actions by others indicating that they care about the client, and creation of a safety plan the client will use to reach out for support. This exercise is suitable for individual or group use, in session or as homework. Follow-up can include keeping a journal and reporting to the therapist and group on outcomes of plans developed in this exercise, as well as bibliotherapy tapping the extensive literature on depression, and videotherapy using films like *Ordinary People* recommended in the book *Rent Two Films and Let's Talk in the Morning*, by John W. Hesley and Jan G. Hesley, also published by John Wiley & Sons.

WHY DO I MATTER AND WHO CARES?

When we are experiencing depression, we often feel worthless. We may become convinced that our lives don't matter and no one understands or cares how we feel, or even that others would be better off without us. These feelings and perceptions are normal in depression, but they aren't accurate, and they can be dangerous. This exercise will help you get a true picture of whether your life matters and others truly care about you, and create a plan to form stronger connections with people to whom you are important and get their emotional support.

1. First, think of things that others have done for you that have been helpful and important in your life. These others may have been family members, friends, teachers, faith leaders, employers, team coaches, or anyone else who has really helped you along the way. Please give three examples, describing who they were, what they did for you, and why it mattered.

    _____
    _____
    _____
    _____
    _____
    _____
    _____
    _____

2. Now reflect on whether you've done similar things for others. Name three people whose lives you've touched in a good way, and describe what you did.

    _____
    _____
    _____
    _____
    _____
    _____
    _____
    _____

3. What do you think these people would say if someone asked them whether your life is important to them?

    _____

    _____

    _____

    _____

4. Ask three other people (friends or family members) the following question, and record their responses here: *"If I were going to do something to help other people, what are some abilities I have or things I could do that would be helpful, and who could I help?"*

    _____

    _____

    _____

    _____

    _____

    _____

    _____

5. Please use this space to create a simple plan to start doing one thing for other people during the next two weeks, either based on a suggestion in response to question 4 or to another idea.

    _____

    _____

    _____

    _____

6. What people do you believe, at this moment, really understand and care about your feelings?

    _____

    _____

7. Please think of someone you see in meetings, or in your faith community, or in another setting who seems to have a lot of life experiences like your own and is a wise and gentle person. It's best to choose a person, like a program sponsor, for whom you feel respect but no romantic attraction. Your task during the next week is to approach this person and tell him/her that you would like to talk and get some feedback on issues you're working on. Set a time and place when you can talk for at least an hour without interruptions. When you talk, tell this person about what's

happening in your life and how you feel about it, and ask whether he/she has ever felt the same way. After you do this, please record the other person's responses, and how you felt after the conversation, in this space.

_____

_____

_____

_____

8. The last part of this assignment is to create a plan to reach out for emotional support when you need it, as we all do sometimes. Please list five people you can talk to if you are feeling troubled, confused, or discouraged, and write about how you will approach each of them, in advance, to ask for this support.

Name   **How I Will Ask for Support**

_____   _____

_____   _____

_____   _____

_____   _____

_____   _____

Be sure to bring this handout back to your next therapy session, and be prepared to talk about your thoughts and feelings about the exercise.

HOW FAR HAVE I COME?

GOALS OF THE EXERCISE

1. Cooperate with addiction assessments and accept the diagnosis and treatment plan.
2. Increase awareness of positive changes made in sobriety.
3. Plan for further growth and positive change and reinforce self-confidence.

ADDITIONAL PROBLEMS FOR WHICH THIS EXERCISE MAY BE USEFUL

*   Adult-Child-of-an-Alcoholic (ACOA) Traits
*   Borderline Traits
*   Depression

SUGGESTIONS FOR PROCESSING THIS EXERCISE WITH CLIENT

The "How Far Have I Come?" activity is designed for the client in early- to middle-stage recovery who has difficulty seeing his/her own progress and has problems with confidence in his/her ability to cope with life in recovery. Its approach is to guide the client in a structured assessment of his/her thoughts, feelings, behaviors, and coping skills at the time of entry into treatment and at the present, highlighting progress. This exercise is a good accompaniment to the activities titled "What Do Others See Changing?" and "Personal Recovery Planning." Follow-up can include reviewing the client's findings from this exercise with the therapist, treatment group, and program sponsor.

HOW FAR HAVE I COME?

Sometimes it's hard to see the changes that we're making. Often change comes gradually and is hard to measure. Others may see our progress more easily than we can. This exercise will help you measure how much you've changed in several areas of your life since you began recovery.

1. Please describe how you were thinking, feeling, acting, and coping with difficulties in the following areas of your life _____ months ago (when you first began your recovery work).

Area of Life	Thoughts	Feelings	Actions	Coping Skills
Substance Abuse				
Home/Family				
Work/School				
Friendships				
Romantic Relationships				
Legal Situation				
Finances				

Area of Life	Thoughts	Feelings	Actions	Coping Skills
Communication with Others				
Self-Care				
Leisure Activities				
Spiritual Life				

2. Now describe how you are thinking, feeling, acting, and coping in the same areas today.

Area of Life	Thoughts	Feelings	Actions	Coping Skills
Substance Abuse				
Home/Family				
Work/School				
Friendships				
Romantic Relationships				
Legal Situation				
Finances				

Area of Life	Thoughts	Feelings	Actions	Coping Skills
Communication with Others				
Self-Care				
Leisure Activities				
Spiritual Life				

3. In which areas of life do you see the most change?

    _____

    _____

4. In which areas of life do you see the least change?

    _____

    _____

5. Ask a number of people you trust who would provide constructive feedback about the observable changes they have seen in you. What did they tell you?

    _____

    _____

    _____

    _____

    _____

    _____

    _____

6. Jot down your general thoughts related to the data in questions 3, 4, and 5.

    _____

    _____

    _____

    _____

    Be sure to bring this handout back to your next therapy session, and be prepared to talk about your thoughts and feelings about the exercise.

SETTING AND PURSUING GOALS IN RECOVERY

GOALS OF THE EXERCISE

1. Accept the truth about the problems addiction has caused and enter a program of recovery.
2. Cooperate with addiction assessments and accept the diagnosis and treatment plan.
3. Formulate a set of personalized recovery goals.
4. Learn general goal-achievement life skills to enhance chances of long-term success and quality of life.
5. Increase investment in recovery and practice new skills between sessions and after treatment.

ADDITIONAL PROBLEMS FOR WHICH THIS EXERCISE MAY BE USEFUL

- Eating Disorders
- Living Environment Deficiency
- Nicotine Dependence
- Substance Abuse/Dependence

SUGGESTIONS FOR PROCESSING THIS EXERCISE WITH CLIENT

The "Setting and Pursuing Goals in Recovery" activity is intended for any client who is vague about what he/she wants to see change, or who appears to suffer from learned helplessness or excessive dependence on the therapist or others for direction and assistance. The exercise guides the client in setting concrete goals; identifying reasons, strategies, and resources for each; and making a therapeutic contract to carry out the strategies. Follow-up might include other exercises after some work on the goals set, such as those titled "What Do Others See Changing?" and "How Far Have I Come?"

SETTING AND PURSUING GOALS IN RECOVERY

There is much in our lives over which we have little or no control, and this makes it more important that we change whatever harmful patterns we can. In choosing recovery, we have to change more than just certain habits.

1. Please list three changes you want to make in your life, beyond giving up addictive patterns, to support your recovery and avoid relapse. List behaviors (things you do), not characteristics (things you are). Behavior is changeable. Characteristics may not be. For example, people who are shy may not be able to stop being shy, but they can avoid isolating themselves. Your goals (e.g., avoid isolating):

   a. _____

   b. _____

   c. _____

2. List the reasons you want to make these changes.

   a. _____

   b. _____

   c. _____

3. Now list three methods you will use to achieve each of your goals. Describe what you'll do. (Example: attend three meetings per week; call a friend every day; join a local theater group)

   Goal (a)

   Method (1): _____

   Method (2): _____

   Method (3): _____

   Goal (b)

   Method (1): _____

   Method (2): _____

   Method (3): _____

   Goal (c)

   Method (1): _____

Method (2): _____

Method (3): _____

4. List the obstacles or barriers that could interfere, and the ways you will overcome these barriers.

Obstacles or Barriers   **Methods You Will Use to Overcome**

a. _____   _____

b. _____   _____

c. _____   _____

5. The ways other people can help you, and the ways you will get their help, are:

Ways Others Can Help   **Ways You Will Get Their Help**

a. _____   _____

b. _____   _____

c. _____   _____

6. You will know that your plans are working if you see the following things happen:

a. _____

b. _____

c. _____

7. Others will know your plans are working if they see the following things happen:

a. _____

b. _____

c. _____

8. How often will you check your progress toward your goals and make any necessary changes in your methods?

_____

9. Identify a time line for working on the identified goals. How will you know when you have achieved each of these goals?

a. _____

b. _____

c. _____

10. Please fill out a Commitment Contract for each goal (the form is on the next page). You will sign this contract, as will your therapist and the people who will help you achieve each goal.

Be sure to bring this handout back to your next therapy session, and be prepared to talk about your thoughts and feelings about the exercise.

Commitment Contract:

1. I, _____, will work to accomplish the following goal:
    _____
    and to do so by the following date: _____

2. I will take the following actions as my methods to achieve this goal:
    Method (1): _____
    Method (2): _____
    Method (3): _____

3. My supporters who sign this contract agree to help me with the following suppor-
    tive actions:

    _____

    _____

    _____

    _____

4. My therapist and I will meet to discuss my behavior change progress and to con-
    firm support for my efforts on these dates:

    _____

    _____

5. If my therapist and I don't agree that I'm making satisfactory progress toward this
    goal, I will take corrective action as follows:

    _____

    _____

    _____

    _____

_____ _____ _____ _____
Your signature   Date   Signature of Therapist   Date

_____ _____ _____ _____
Signature of Supporter Date   Signature of Supporter   Date

_____ _____ _____ _____
Signature of Supporter Date   Signature of Supporter   Date

Appendix A

ADDITIONAL ASSIGNMENTS FOR PRESENTING PROBLEMS

Antisocial Behavior

Anxiety

Attention Deficit Disorder, Inattentive Type (ADD)

Attention Deficit/Hyperactivity Disorder (ADHD)

Borderline Traits

Childhood Trauma

Chronic Pain

Dangerousness/Lethality

Dependent Traits

Depression

Eating Disorders

Family Conflicts

Gambling

Grief/Loss Unresolved

Impulsivity

Legal Problems

Living Environment Deficiency

Mania/Hypomania

Medical Issues

Narcissistic Traits

Parent–Child Relational Problem

Partner Relational Conflicts

Peer Group Negativity

Posttraumatic Stress Disorder (PTSD)

Psychosis

Relapse Proneness

Sexual Promiscuity

Self-Care Deficits as a Primary Problem

Self-Care Deficits as a Secondary Problem

Social Anxiety

Spiritual Confusion

Substance Abuse/Dependence

Substance-Induced Disorders

Substance Intoxication/Withdrawal

Suicidal Ideation

Treatment Resistance

Appendix B

STAGES OF CHANGE

Appendix C

ASAM ADULT PATIENT PLACEMENT CRITERIA DIMENSIONS

Criteria Dimensions	Suggested Exercises from the Addiction Treatment Homework Planner		
Dimension 1: Intoxication and/or Withdrawal Potential	Coping with Post-Acute Withdrawal	XL.A	311
	Using Books and Other Media Resources	XL.B	314
Dimension 2: Biomedical Conditions and Complications	Alternative Methods for Managing Pain	IX.A	59
	Coping with Addiction and Chronic Pain	IX.B	63
	Creating a Preliminary Health Plan	XIII.A	89
	Eating Patterns Self-Assessment	XIII.B	93
	Coping with Addictions and Other Medical Problems	XXI.A	150
	Physical and Emotional Self-Care	XXI.B	154
	Planning for Stability	XXXI.B	231
Dimension 3: Emotional, Behavioral, or Cognitive Conditions and Complications	Is My Anger Due to Feeling Threatened?	II.A	8
	Is My Anger Due to Unmet Expectations?	II.B	11
	Coping with Stress	IV.A	22
	My Anxiety Profile	IV.B	26
	Getting Organized	V.A	30
	Negotiating Skills for Success	V.B	34
	Learning to Self-Soothe	VI.B	41
	Corresponding with My Childhood Self	VIII.A	53
	Anger as a Drug	X.A	67
	Correcting Distorted Thinking	XII.A	82
	Am I Having Difficulty Letting Go?	XVI.A	113
	Moving On with My Life	XVI.B	117

Taken from: *ASAM PPC-2R: ASAM Patient Placement Criteria for the Treatment of Substance-Related Disorders,* 2nd edition–Revised. (2001). Chevy Chase, MD: American Society of Addiction Medicine, Inc.

Appendix D

SUGGESTED ADDICTION HOMEWORK TREATMENT PLAN EXERCISES, ASAM DIMENSIONS, AND ASAM LEVELS OF CARE

Criteria Dimensions	Level 0.5 Early Intervention	OMT Opioid Maintenance Therapy	Level I Outpatient Treatment	Level II Intensive Outpatient Treatment/Partial Hospitalization	Level III Residential/Inpatient Treatment	Level IV Medically Managed Inpatient Treatment
1: Intoxication/Withdrawal Potential	XL.A	XL.A	XL.A	XL.A	XL.A	None
2: Biomedical Conditions and Complications	None	IX.A, IX.B, XIII.A, XXI.A, XXI.B, XXXI.B	IX.A, IX.B, XIII.A, XXI.A, XXI.B, XXXI.B	IX.A, IX.B, XIII.A, XXI.A, XXI.B, XXXI.B	IX.A, IX.B, XIII.A, XXI.A, XXI.B, XXXI.B	XIII.A, XXI.A, XXXI.B
3: Emotional, Behavioral, or Cognitive Conditions and Complications	I.A, II.A, II.B, IV.A, IV.B, V.A, V.B, XXVI.A, XXVI.B, XXVIII.A, XXVIII.B, XXX.B, XXXIV.A, XXXIV.B, XXXV.B, XLI.B	I.A, II.A, II.B, IV.A, IV.B, V.A, V.B, VIII.A, X.A, XII.A, XVI.A, XVII.B, XLII.B, XX.A, XX.B, XXVI.B, XXVIII.A, XXVIII.B, XXX.A, XXX.B, XXXI.A, XXXIV.A, XXXIV.B, XXXV.B, XL.B	I.A, II.A, II.B, IV.A, IV.B, V.A, V.B, VI.B, VIII.A, X.A, XII.A, XVI.A, XVI.B, XVII.B, XX.A, XX.B, XXVI.B, XXVIII.A, XXVIII.B, XXX.A, XXX.B, XXXI.A, XXXV.B, XLI.B, XLII.B	I.A, II.A, II.B, IV.A, IV.B, V.A, V.B, VI.B, VIII.A, X.A, XII.A, XVI.A, XVI.B, XVII.B, XX.A, XX.B, XXV.B, XXVII.A, XXVIII.B, XXX.A, XXX.B, XXXI.A, XXXIV.A, XXXIV.B, XXXV.B, XLI.B, XLII.B	I.A, II.A, II.B, III.B, IV.A, IV.B, V.A, V.B, VI.B, X.A, XII.A, XVI.A, XVI.B, XVII.B, XX.A, XX.B, XXVI.A, XXVIII.A, XXVIII.B, XXX.A, XXX.B, XXXI.A, XXXIV.A, XXXIV.B, XLI.B, XLII.B	IV.A, IV.B, V.A, X.A, XII.A, XVI.A, XX.A, XX.B, XXVIII.A, XXX.A, XXX.B, XXXI.A, XXXIV.A, XXXIV.B, XLI.B

(continued)

Criteria Dimensions	Level 0.5 Early Intervention	OMT Opioid Maintenance Therapy	Level I Outpatient Treatment	Level II Intensive Outpatient Treatment/Partial Hospitalization	Level III Residential/Inpatient Treatment	Level IV Medically Managed Inpatient Treatment
4: Readiness to Change	XV.A XXXV.A XV.B XXXVI.A XVII.A XXXVII.B XVIII.B XXXVIII.B XX.B XXXVIII.E XXVII.A XLI.A XXVIII.B XLII.A	XV.A XXXVI.B XV.B XXXVII.B XVII.A XXXVIII.B XVIII.B XXXVIII.D XX.B XXXVIII.E XXVII.A XLI.A XXXV.A XLII.A	XV.A XXXVII.B XV.B XXXVIII.B XVIII.B XLI.A XX.B XLII.A XXXV.A XXVII.A XXXVI.A	XV.A XXXVII.B XV.B XXXVIII.B XVIII.B XLI.A XX.B XLII.A XXXV.A XXVII.A XXXVI.A	XV.B XXXVIII.D XVII.A XXXVIII.E XVIII.B XLI.A XX.B XLII.A XXXIII.B XXXVI.A XXXVII.B XXXVIII.B	None
5: Relapse, Continued Use, or Continued Problem Potential	III.A XXXII.A VI.A XXXII.B VI.B XXXII.C XII.B XXXIII.A XVII.A XXXVIII.A XVII.B XXXVIII.C XXIII.A XXXIX.B XXIII.B	III.A XXV.B III.B XXXII.A VI.A XXXII.B VI.B XXXII.C XII.B XXXIII.A XVI.A XXXVIII.A XVII.A XXXVIII.C XVII.B XIX.B XXIII.A XL.A XXIII.B	III.A XXV.B III.B XXXI.A VI.A XXXII.A VI.B XXXII.B XII.B XXXII.C XVI.A XXXIII.A XVII.A XXXVIII.A XVII.B XXXVIII.C XXIII.A XXXIX.B XXVIII.B XL.B XXIV.B	III.A XXXII.B III.B XXXII.C VI.A XXXVIII.A VI.B XXXVIII.C XVI.A XXXIX.B XVII.A XL.A XVII.B XXIII.B XXV.B XXXI.A XXXII.A	III.A XXXII.A VI.A XXXII.B VI.B XXXII.C VII.B XXXIII.A XVII.A XXXVIII.A XVII.B XXXVIII.C XVIII.A XXXIX.B XXIII.B XL.A XXXIV.B XXXV.B XXXI.A	None

6: Recovery Environment					None
I.B XXIV.A VII.A XXV.A VII.B XXVII.B VIII.A XXVIII.A XI.A XXIX.A XI.B XXIX.B XIV.A XXXVI.B XVIII.A XXXVII.A XIX.A XXXIX.A XXII.B	I.B XXIV.A VII.A XXV.A VII.B XXVII.B VIII.A XXVIII.A XI.A XXIX.A XI.B XXIX.B XIV.A XXXVI.B XVIII.A XXXVII.A XIX.A XXXIX.A XXII.B	I.B XXIV.A VII.A XXV.A VII.B XXVII.B VIII.A XXVIII.A XI.A XXIX.A XI.B XXIX.B XIV.A XXXVI.B XVIII.A XXXVII.A XIX.A XXXIX.A XXII.B	I.B XXIV.A VII.A XXV.A VII.B XXVII.B VIII.A XXVIII.A XI.A XXIX.A XI.B XXIX.B XIV.A XXXVI.B XVIII.A XXXVII.A XIX.A XXXIX.A XXII.B	I.B XXIV.A VII.A XXV.A VII.B XXVII.B VIII.B XXVIII.A XI.A XXIX.A XI.B XXIX.B XIV.A XXXVI.B XVIII.A XXXVII.A XIX.A XXXIX.A XXII.B	VIII.B XXXIX.A XI.A XI.B XIX.A XXIII.B XXV.A XXVIII.A XXIX.A XXXVI.B XXXVII.A

Taken from: *ASAM PPC-2R: ASAM Patient Placement Criteria for the Treatment of Substance-Related Disorders*, 2nd edition-Revised. (2001). Chevy Chase, MD: American Society of Addiction Medicine, Inc.

ABOUT THE CD-ROM

INTRODUCTION

This appendix provides you with information on the contents of the CD that accompanies this book. For the latest and greatest information, please refer to the ReadMe file located at the root of the CD.

SYSTEM REQUIREMENTS

- A computer with a processor running at 120 Mhz or faster
- At least 32 MB of total RAM installed on your computer; for best performance, we recommend at least 64 MB
- A CD-ROM drive

Note: Many popular word processing programs are capable of reading Microsoft Word files. However, users should be aware that a slight amount of formatting might be lost when using a program other than Microsoft Word.

USING THE CD WITH WINDOWS

To install the items from the CD to your hard drive, follow these steps:

1. Insert the CD into your computer's CD-ROM drive.
2. The CD-ROM interface will appear. The interface provides a simple point-and-click way to explore the contents of the CD.

If the opening screen of the CD-ROM does not appear automatically, follow these steps to access the CD:

1. Click the Start button on the left end of the taskbar and then choose Run from the menu that pops up.
2. In the dialog box that appears, type **d:\setup.exe.** (If your CD-ROM drive is not drive d, fill in the appropriate letter in place of *d*.) This brings up the CD interface described in the preceding set of steps.

USING THE CD WITH A MAC

1. Insert the CD into your computer's CD-ROM drive.
2. The CD-ROM icon appears on your desktop, double-click the icon.
3. Double-click the Start icon.
4. The CD-ROM interface will appear. The interface provides a simple point-and-click way to explore the contents of the CD.

WHAT'S ON THE CD

The following sections provide a summary of the software and other materials you'll find on the CD.

Content

Includes all 88 homework assignments from the book in Word format. Homework assignments can be customized, printed out, and distributed to clients in an effort to extend the therapeutic process outside of the office. All documentation is included in the folder named "Content."

Applications

The following applications are on the CD:

Microsoft Word Viewer
Microsoft Word Viewer is a freeware viewer that allows you to view, but not edit, most Microsoft Word files. Certain features of Microsoft Word documents may not display as expected from within Word Viewer.

USER ASSISTANCE

If you have trouble with the CD-ROM, please call the Wiley Product Technical Support phone number at (800) 762-2974. Outside the United States, call 1(317) 572-3994. You can also contact Wiley Product Technical Support at **http://support.wiley.com**. John Wiley & Sons will provide technical support only for installation and other general quality control items. For technical support of the applications themselves, consult the program's vendor or author.

To place additional orders or to request information about other Wiley products, please call (800) 225-5945.